THE LAST BEST PLACE?

THE LAST BEST PLACE?

Gender, Family, and Migration in the New West

LEAH SCHMALZBAUER

STANFORD UNIVERSITY PRESS

Stanford, California

Printed in the United States of America on acid-free, archival-quality paper

Library of Congress Cataloging-in-Publication Data

Schmalzbauer, Leah, author.
  The last best place? : gender, family, and migration in the new west / Leah
Schmalzbauer.
      pages   cm.
   Includes bibliographical references and index.
   ISBN 978-0-8047-9165-6 (cloth : alk. paper) —
   ISBN 978-0-8047-9293-6 (pbk. : alk. paper)
   1. Migrant labor—Montana, Western—Social conditions.   2. Migrant
labor—Montana, Western—Economic conditions.   3. Migrant laborers'
families—Montana, Western—Social conditions.   4. Migrant laborers'
families—Montana, Western—Economic conditions.   5. Foreign workers,
Mexican—Montana, Western—Social conditions.   6. Foreign workers,
Mexican—Montana, Western—Economic conditions.   7. Montana,
Western—Social conditions   8. Montana, Western—Economic
conditions.   I. Title.
HD5856.U5S27 2014
305.868'7207865'—dc23

2014010115

ISBN 978-0-8047-9297-4 (electronic)

Typeset at Stanford University Press in 10.5/13 Bembo

To STEVE,

with love, respect and gratitude

CONTENTS

ACKNOWLEDGMENTS

I want to thank, first and foremost, the women, men and children who participated in this project. Their openness, trust, and friendship made this book possible, and transformed me as a person and a scholar. I hope this book will do justice to their strength, struggles and aspirations.

One of the most meaningful aspects of this project was partnering with community groups and individuals committed to immigrant rights in Montana. I thank the Coalition of Resource Organizations (CORO), under the leadership of Buck Taylor, which provided the spark for this project. I am grateful for the activism of Kim Abbott and Bethany Letiecq of the Montana Human Rights Network, and for that of Shahid Haque-Hausrath, who created the Montana Immigrant Justice Alliance (MIJA) and who provides accessible, social justice–based legal services to Montana's immigrant community. I also thank Shahid for generously answering my queries as I wrote the chapter on illegality. Thank you to Katie Gray for the hundreds of hours she has put into informal social work on behalf of the participants in this study, for reading drafts of my work to make sure participants' identities were adequately concealed and for assisting me with youth interviews. I am grateful to Courtney Wosepka whose outreach work with migrant farmworkers introduced me to the world of H2A workers. Thank you to the Bozeman Children's Museum and Hopa Mountain for their outreach to Latino youth in the Gallatin Valley. Special thanks to my dear friends Bridget Kevane and Hunt McCauley, whose commitment to strengthening the diverse fabric of southwest Montana inspired me to write Chapter 7 on hope and opportunity. Hunt also provided me invaluable research assistance, linking me with agricultural families and talking with me through many aspects of migrant life in Montana. Thank you also to my students Jenna and Jessa Thiel, Lilia Guillen-Sanchez, Frances Moore, Ashley Piper, Yanet and Oneida Eudave and Jessica Cartwright for their steadfast work in bridging Montana State University and the Latino community.

I am fortunate to have received generous institutional support for this project. I thank the Office of the Vice President of Research at Montana

State University (MSU), which granted me funds to support the research, analysis and writing phases of this project. I also thank the office of the dean of the College of Letters and Science, which gave me a semester of pretenure teaching release to pursue my fieldwork. Heartfelt thanks to my MSU colleagues in the Department of Sociology and Anthropology, who nurtured me professionally over the course of this project. Special thanks to David Eitle, whose mentorship was invaluable. Thank you to the American Sociological Association Fund for the Advancement of the Discipline, which supported the early phases of this research, and to the American Sociological Association Community Action Research Initiative-Spivak Program for supporting community-based "know your rights" forums for the participants in this study. I wrote the first draft of this manuscript while a visiting scholar at CIESAS-Pacífico Sur in Oaxaca, Mexico. I thank them, and especially Alejandra Aquino Moreschi, for their support during that critical year. I was half-way through the writing of this manuscript when I received a job offer from Amherst College. I have since been overwhelmed by the kindness and support I have received from my new colleagues in Sociology and American Studies. I owe special thanks to Ron Lembo, Karen Sanchez-Eppler and Jerry Himmelstein, who offered great advice and guidance as I moved my manuscript to publication.

I am very grateful for the support I have received from the fabulous editorial staff at Stanford University Press—Kate Wahl, John Feneron and Frances Malcolm. I owe special thanks to Frances Malcolm. Since our first email exchange, she has been an enthusiastic and inspirational supporter of this project, and I truly appreciate the generous time and thought she has invested in it. My manuscript has benefited significantly from her smarts and poignant insights. Thank you also to the anonymous reviewers, whose thoughtful feedback no doubt made this a stronger book.

I am incredibly lucky to have wonderful friends who share my passion for research and writing. I thank Bridget Kevane, Sara Rushing and Yanna Yannakakis, who, in different combinations, have composed my writing circle and so much more over the past eight years. Their friendship, laughter, honesty, love of food and wine, and solidarity in motherhood energized my writing and kept me balanced and smiling. Thank you to Juliet Schor, whose mentorship and guidance I drew on in each phase of this project, and whose support and friendship I cherish. Thank you also to Linda Young, Frances Lefcort and Adele Pittendrigh for their friendship and mentorship. Thank you to Aiden Downey for his writing support and unique insights into the art of ethnography. Thank you also to Abigail Brooks and Patricia Arend, who offered encouragement at critical points in this project. I am deeply appreciative of the support of Joanna Dreby, who was almost always the first person I turned to for manuscript-related advice, and whose work has influenced my own in a myriad of ways. I also thank Leisy Abrego, Tanya Go-lash-Boza, Hung Cam Thai, and especially Cecilia Menjívar who provided helpful advice as I completed my manuscript and moved it to publication.

I am so appreciative of the support of my family. I thank my in-laws Philip and Ellie Bruner for their genuine interest in my research, and for their love and generosity. I thank my siblings-in-law and my stepfather, Jim Sparks, Rick Bruner, Carolyn and Ben Opps, and Vincent Graziano for making me laugh and for reminding me that there are many ways in which to see the world. I thank my sister, Anna Schmalzbauer, for being a constant source of love, encouragement and friendship. I thank my nieces and nephews, Victor and Olympia Schmalzbauer Sparks and Maizy Opps, for being just plain awesome. I thank my dad, Gary Schmalzbauer, for his humility, generosity and unconditional love, all of which have indelibly shaped me as a person and sociologist. I also thank my dad for his partnership in our unforgettable drive through central Mexico. My mom, Leone Medin, was integral to this project. I thank her for the times she accompanied me in the field, for reading every word of every draft of every chapter of this book, and for giving me invaluable feedback. I thank her for sharing with me her experiences of growing up as the only daughter in a poor Minnesota farm family, which gave me powerful insights into gender, generation and rural life. Most important, I thank my mom for her love, unwavering support and friendship.

This project began soon after the birth of my son, Micah, and followed me through my pregnancy and birth of my daughter, Zola, and into both of their childhoods. I thank them for accompanying me during much of my fieldwork, ensuring me smiles and an enthusiastic welcome wherever I went. I thank them for serving as an ethnographic lens into childhood and family life, for complicating my sociological perspective in fabulous ways, for being great adventurers and for bringing amazing love and joy into my life. Finally, I thank Steve Bruner, my best friend and husband, who is also my moral compass, emotional rock and sounding board for just about everything. I thank him for having the largest comfort zone of anyone I know and for still never being afraid to step out of it. I thank him for reading every chapter draft I sent his way and for his honesty and insightfulness in his feedback. Mostly, I thank him for his integrity, competence and patience, and for his fabulous ways as a father, which inspire me every day. I dedicate this book to him.

THE LAST BEST PLACE?

Chapter 1

Situating Gender and
Migration in the New West

In the summer of 2004 I moved to Bozeman, Montana, to take a faculty position at Montana State University. My partner and I were drawn to southwest Montana's expansive natural beauty and Bozeman's hip college town amenities. Having grown up on the flat plains of the Midwest and having lived for almost a decade in a large East Coast city, Bozeman's mountains, small-town feel and Western vibe were novel and exciting. It did not take long before I had comfortably immersed myself in my new community, exploring local mountain trails, sampling Bozeman's trendy cafes and restaurants and connecting with other thirty-something transplants to the Mountain West. At the same time, I was unsettled by the area's racial, ethnic and linguistic homogeneity.

Several months after my move to Montana, during my weekly Sunday night trips to the grocery store I began to see Latino men shopping together. They were dressed in construction boots and work pants, and their presence surprised me. I was an immigration scholar and activist and had worked closely with Mexicans and Central Americans in Boston and Minneapolis. I associated immigration with cities and corporate agriculture, neither of which were present in southwest Montana. What is more, I never saw Latinos anywhere else or at any other time when I was out and about in Bozeman. When in public, as my trip to the grocery store made clear, their presence was conspicuous, marked by skin color and language in a place that is hegemonically white and English speaking. So if Latinos lived here, they were generally hidden.

For several Sundays I struggled over whether greeting the men in the grocery store would be interpreted by them as a friendly gesture or an invasion of privacy. Finally I decided to say "hola/hello." As I approached two of the men who were stacking tortillas in a shopping cart I was instantly struck by the obvious fear my gesture provoked. Sensing their unease, I quickly explained that I had just returned from Central

1

America and was enthused to hear someone speaking Spanish; that I only wanted to say "hi" and to introduce myself. Warm smiles ensued, and the tension between us dissipated. I learned through our short conversation that, like me, Samuel and Carlos were new to Montana. They had come to work in the booming construction industry, and lived far outside of town. They carpooled into Bozeman on Sunday nights to grocery shop. Otherwise they stayed away. In that moment I became bodily aware of the social ruptures that characterized my new Western home.

Big Sky Country

Southwest Montana is majestic. Awe-inspiring. Here the Rocky Mountains frame a landscape of valleys and rolling foothills that butt up against a very big sky. One can drive for miles without seeing evidence of human settlement. Cattle and, in places, bison dot the land. From late May through mid-August the mountains and valleys are a vibrant green. In the late summer and early fall the green fades to clays, grays and browns. Then the snow comes, often arriving in October and staying into May. Throughout much of the year, the peaks of the Rockies are white. It is beautiful country—wide open, remote, rugged—evoking mythologies of freedom and escape long associated with the West (Kollin 2000).

In "Big Sky Country" nature casts a large shadow over the relatively few people who live in its midst. Montana is the third largest state by geographic size in the Continental United States, yet boasts just a million inhabitants. According to 2010 U.S. Census data, there are only six people per square mile in the state, and Billings, Montana's largest city, has only 105,000 inhabitants, the first and only city in Montana to surpass the hundred thousand mark. Throughout the 2012 presidential campaign, Montana was seldom mentioned in any national political analysis. In many ways Montana is off the political and economic radar screen.

Yet beginning in the 1980s Montana emerged as a powerful presence in literature, film and popular culture. Robert Redford's 1992 film *A River Runs through It* is commonly credited with launching Montana as a fly-fishing and tourist mecca. There are other examples. This book takes its name from William Kittredge's acclaimed anthology (1988) of Montana writings called *The Last Best Place*. Ivan Doig's award-winning novels, especially his 1979 memoir of growing up in Montana, *This House of Sky*, showcases the literary power of the Montana landscape, a landscape that shapes people in its midst and sparks a unique connection to place. Ted Turner's popular chain of bison-themed restaurants, Ted's Montana Grill, has bolstered the cachet of Montana in consumer culture.[1]

Perhaps because of the beauty, nostalgia and growing consumer appeal of Big Sky Country, there has been a large influx of people into the area. Statistics tell the story. Over the past twenty years, the population of Montana has increased from 800,000 to just over one million, and Gallatin County, where I conducted the bulk of the research for this book, has seen its population explode from 50,000 to 92,000 (U.S. Census, 2013). Paralleling this in-migration has been a major transformation of the region's physical, economic and cultural landscapes (Wycoff 2006). In the process, the geographic context of the rural Mountain West has morphed into the conceptual space of the *New West* (Ghose 2004; Hines 2010; Power 1996).

Indeed, over the past two decades, much of southwest Montana has been transformed from cowboy country into a New West playground for the elite and privileged adventuresome. Better said, it has become a place where ranchers, farmers and laborers share the land with wealthy newcomers, often not happily. Bozeman, the regional "urban" hub, with a population of 38,000, is the gateway to Yellowstone National Park and to the ski areas in and around Big Sky, home to multi–million dollar mansions. Bozeman used to be best known for its feed and ranch stores and for Montana State University, which is still affectionately called "Moo U" by aging locals. But things have changed. Bozeman now has a sophisticated local food scene, art galleries, independent cafes, boutiques, bookstores, and wealthy residents. Ted Turner, one of the state's largest private land owners (Wilkinson 2013), and journalist Tom Brokaw, for example, publicly display their love of Montana, calling it home for at least part of the year. There are many others—some famous, some not, but privileged migrants all the same—who now call Montana home.

As one approaches Bozeman, one can see large homes on the mountainsides. From their high perches, wealthy dwellers can see for miles. There are less luxurious housing developments emerging in the pasturelands surrounding Bozeman. A suburban sprawl of sorts stretches from Bozeman's outer limits to Four Corners and Belgrade several miles away. This sprawl includes large trailer courts, one of which was recently eradicated by developers. Moving beyond the sprawl, dairy farms, cattle ranches, and wheat, hay and potato fields produce for the local, national and global economy.

In Bozeman's quaint downtown, students, ski "bums" and young families share the sidewalks with tourists and wealthy retirees, some wearing furs, many wearing cowboy boots. The restaurants and cafes are full. In the latter, faculty members from Montana State University and young professionals work on their laptops. Word on the street and my conversations with baristas suggest that the cafes are the latter's remote offices as they telecommute to

Palo Alto, Seattle, Los Angeles and other cities. One gets a sense that everyone is on a vacation of some sort. Even though Montana has a relatively large American Indian population, and well-known Indian art galleries are located downtown, American Indians themselves are seldom visible in Bozeman. Here, most faces are white.[2]

This is the superficial surface of southwest Montana that has captured the imaginations of the tourist and second home market. This is "The Last Best Place," which is projected in marketing materials and painted on city buses in Minneapolis, Chicago and New York City, enticing the resourced elite to escape to Montana. This, though, is not the real Montana.

The innocent splendor of Montana's natural landscape and pop-culture mythology eclipses a more complex social landscape. Since white settlers violently pushed their way into Montana in the mid-1800s, forcing the Crow, Blackfeet, Cree, Cheyenne, Sioux, Assiniboine, Gros Ventre, Salish and Kootenai onto what are now seven reservations, Montana's economy has been based primarily on resource extraction and agriculture, supported by the labor of poor and working-class men (Malone et al. 1991). For much of Montana's development toward and into statehood, European migrants worked in the mines and later homesteaded the farms and ranches that developed around the mining towns. While men labored outside of their homes, women labored inside their homes. Women's tasks were made all the more challenging by Montana's long and violent winters, during which food was often scarce and amenities nonexistent. In addition to tending their homes, women sometimes assisted their husbands as cowhands and hunters, their roles in ensuring family survival more fluid than popular lore would suggest. Single women had few options, working as ranch cooks or in the infamous brothels that serviced male laborers (ibid.). On the reservations, excluded from economic development opportunities, Native Montanans struggled to subsist in a context of European oppression. For the past 150 years of Montana's history, intersections of race, class and gender have largely determined who can lay claim to which land, which economic opportunities are available, and where one fits in the evolving social hierarchy of the West.

Today, accompanying an influx of wealth and privilege into Montana is a growing inequality most conspicuously articulated along lines of race and class. This inequality can be seen in southwest Montana's growing homeless population.[3] It can be seen as increasing numbers of working and middle-class Montanans line up at food banks.[4] It is symbolized by the many workers who can no longer afford to live where they work, because while their earnings are among the lowest in the country, housing prices are the highest in the state and exceed the national norm.[5] Inequality also finds expression in the region's growing ethnic diversity.

Although the faces in downtown Bozeman are still predominantly white, the official demographics of the region tell a story of change. Montana's new cultural and economic landscapes are intimately linked to an increasing presence of Mexican labor migrants,[6] who perform a critical role in Montana's evolving economy yet live in the shadows of its wealth. Although not mentioned in history books, a segment of Montana's farms and ranches have depended on Mexican agricultural workers for decades. Similarly, many of southwest Montana's new exclusive homes and resorts were built and are now maintained by Mexican laborers. The vast majority of these laborers are men, supported at home by Mexican women who have yet to find a secure footing in Montana's labor force. This is a book about this "other" migration into contemporary Montana.

This is also a book about the ways in which gender intersects with Montana's rurality to shape migrant life. Though race and class are the most visible fault lines in Montana's new social landscape, it is gender that most intensely penetrates migrant life. Gender influences the pragmatic ways that Mexican migrants negotiate daily life, as well as the ways they construct their identities, expectations and aspirations in a context of gentrified inequality. Like the Native and European women of Montana's early history, Mexican women today often live difficult, isolated lives while charged with ensuring their families' survival and well-being. Since the Great Recession a significant number of Mexican women have entered Montana's low-wage service industry, cleaning private homes and hotel rooms and working in fast food kitchens. Still, most migrant women are invisible on Montana's streets and public spaces. Despite their marginalization, it is Mexican women who are leading the effort to create and protect "home" on this new, and in many ways hostile, immigration frontier.

The struggles of Mexican migrant families, both to survive and thrive in what seems such an unlikely place, has inspired me to write the *Last Best Place*. This is an ethnography exploring the complex ways in which the nostalgia symbolic of southwest Montana intersects with the region's structural realities to influence migrant life. What is it like to be a Mexican migrant *here,* in one of the whitest and most geographically dispersed and rugged areas in the country? How do contextual nuances of place intersect with gender, immigration status and generation to influence Mexican migrants' experiences of power and subordination within their families and communities? How does rurality, as it plays out in Montana's physical, economic and social landscapes, influence the autonomy, well-being and aspirations of Mexican migrant women, men and their children? Whereas Montana is just one among many new destinations for Mexican migrants in the United States, it diverges from other destinations in significant ways. In this book I argue the importance of recognizing that places are not objective, that the geographic intricacies of migrant destinations must be taken into account in order to understand the full complexity of migrant life.

New Migrant Destinations

Over the past two decades there has been a surge in Latino migration to *new destinations*, destinations that do not have a recent history of non-European migration. New migrant destinations are concentrated in the U.S. South and Midwest, and as such the vast majority of scholarly studies of this phenomenon are focused there (see Anrig and Wang 2006; Gozdziak and Martin 2005; Marrow 2011; Massey 2008; Naples 2007; Odem and Lacy 2009; Singer 2004; Zuñiga and Hernandez León 2005). Scholars analyze the shift in Latino migration from traditional to new destinations in the contexts of economic restructuring and evolving U.S. border policy (Hirschman and Massey 2008; Leach and Bean 2008; Odem and Lacy 2009; Singer et al. 2008).

When the most commonly traversed U.S. border crossing points were militarized through Operation Hold the Line in El Paso in 1993 and Operation Gatekeeper in San Diego in 1994, migrants began crossing the border in new and more remote places (Massey and Capoferro 2008). In the process they established new migration paths that took them away from traditional destinations (Massey et al. 2002). Networks of family and kin, through a process of *cumulative causation*, maintained migration flows to new destinations, by connecting migrants with jobs, housing and other social supports (Massey and Zenteno 1999).

These new paths followed economic shifts. As processes of deunionization have lowered wages and hampered job security and worker protections, low-wage service jobs have become ever more unattractive to the native born (Parrado and Kandel 2008; Striffler 2007). The majority of new migrant destinations are characterized by growing low-wage service sectors that target foreign workers (Leach and Bean 2008). Ivan Light (2006) suggests that market saturation in traditional destinations has intensified the push of the most recent arrived migrants toward new destinations where labor demand is greater and wages are higher.

New destination migration is concentrated in what Audrey Singer (2008) conceptualizes as *emerging* and *re-emerging* gateways. Emerging gateways are those American cities that have experienced "rapidly growing migrant populations over the past twenty-five years alone" (9). Atlanta is a primary example of an emerging gateway. Re-emerging gateways are those that had a strong influx of migrants in the early twentieth century, then "waned as destinations during the middle of the century, but are now re-emerging" (9). Minneapolis–St. Paul and Seattle are examples. Singer also suggests that there has been a growth in *pre-emerging* gateways. These are places that are just beginning to see migrant settlement and are positioned to see their migrant populations grow in the future. New migrant destinations in the Mountain West—Utah, Wyoming, Montana and Idaho—would most appropriately be labeled as *pre-emerging*. Characterizing all types of new destinations are dynamic, growing economies that have spurred population growth of the native-born as well as of migrants.

New metropolitan destinations are home to a diversity of migrants. In new destinations in the Southwest and Southeast (Odem and Lacy 2009), the majority of migrants are Mexican.[7] In contrast, in new metropolitan destinations in the Midwest and Northeast, which have large refugee settlements, Mexico is not the central sending country (Singer 2008). Another demographic change in immigration patterns can be found in the growing settlement of migrants in suburban areas. Singer (ibid.), for example, finds that the growth of suburban tech industries draws high-skilled Asians to the suburbs, while construction and landscaping work draws Mexicans and Central Americans to the same places (see also Mahler 1996, 1995; Odem 2008). Immigration in turn is revitalizing many areas of the United States that have undergone economic and population decline. Odem (2008) finds that in suburban Atlanta, for example, Latino migrants are reviving struggling areas by opening up stores and restaurants and filling up the housing stock.

Although immigration remains a predominantly urban and suburban phenomenon, new destination migration has also expanded into rural America. As family farms are replaced by corporate farms (Brown and Swanson 2003) and high-wage factory jobs in food processing and meatpacking are deunionized and relocated to rural areas where wages are lower (Hirschman and Massey 2008), the demographics of rural America are changing. Labor migrants are recruited to work in the new rural sectors. Most notably in the South and Midwest, economic restructuring has drawn Latinos, Mexicans in particular, to small towns that do not have a history of Latino migration (Deeb-Sossa and Bickham Mendez 2008; Hernandez León and Zuñiga 2000, 2003, 2005; Marrow 2011).

Yet Mexican migrants are not new to rural America. The Bracero program brought around 4 million Mexicans to rural American outposts to perform agricultural labor from 1942 to 1964. This labor flow was predominantly male, and it was cyclical. Workers migrated in and out of agricultural areas following the agricultural season. When the Bracero program ended, the flow of both authorized and unauthorized migration from Mexico into the United States increased dramatically. As the demand for Mexican agricultural labor persisted, workers kept coming, though as newly labeled unauthorized laborers (Massey et al. 2002). Whereas an itinerant agricultural labor flow still exists, especially between U.S. agricultural states as workers follow the harvest, fewer workers now migrate back and forth between Mexico and the United States. Because the border has become more dangerous and expensive to cross, more Mexican agricultural workers have put down roots in rural America.

The demographics of contemporary labor migration into new rural destinations are different from those to new urban and suburban destinations. According to Jensen (2006), migrants to rural destinations are more likely than those to urban areas to be from rural Mexico, to have low levels of formal education, and to have migrated as families (see also Donato et al. 2008). Ethnographic accounts of migrants in the rural South (Hernandez León and Zuñiga 2000; Marrow 2011; Silver 2012) and Midwest (Diggs 2011; Millard and Chapa 2004; Naples 2007) have put the experience of migrants in rural places on the scholarly map. This book is the first to explore ethnographically the lives of migrants in the rural Mountain West, the newest and least studied of migrant destinations in the United States.

Labor Migration to Montana: The Transformation of the American West

Whereas food processing, commercial agriculture and manufacturing have been the principal draw of migrants to rural destinations in the South and Midwest, medium-scale agriculture and rural gentrification are at the base of Latino migration to the Mountain West. Mexican agricultural workers have been migrating to Montana for decades. Their migration story began in the 1920s as sugar beet workers in the fields of eastern Montana (Kevane 2008). This migration continued for forty years, formalized during World War II as part of the Bracero program. Although the Bracero program officially ended in the 1960s, many Mexican workers continued to cycle between Mexico and Montana, eventually putting down roots in and around Billings, home to Montana's oldest Mexican community (ibid.). In the late 1980s, labor migration in Montana shifted west, as Mexican men began migrating on H2A guest visas to work on cattle and sheep ranches. More recently Mexicans have migrated seasonally from Texas to work on potato farms near Bozeman, and from Washington to work in the cherry orchards near Glacier National Park, while unauthorized Mexicans from Idaho, Washington and California keep southwest Montana's dairy industry afloat.

Agricultural migrants most often live in remote areas near or on the ranches and dairy farms where they work. They tend to be from the poorest and most rural parts of central Mexico, and they now live in the most rural areas of southwest Montana. Agricultural workers and their families are also the least educated of migrants, and the most marginalized, geographically and socially. Although ranch workers on H2A visas migrate to Montana directly from Mexico, living eight months of the year away from their families, most Mexican agricultural workers move to Montana from other U.S. Western states with their wives and children. Mexican agricultural workers in Montana trace their roots to the traditional migrant sending areas of central Mexico, most commonly Jalisco and San Luis Potosi.

Although agriculture remains Montana's largest industry and is the base of the longest-standing migrant stream into Montana, tourism and the second-home market are spurring a new, much larger migrant influx. In southwest Montana, Mexican construction workers and their families, the majority from Aguas Calientes and Zacatecas, come to Montana by way of Colorado, California, Kansas, Minnesota and other states to work primarily as masons, dry-wallers and roofers in the building of exclusive homes and resorts. Like Montana's agricultural workers, most construction workers and their families are from rural areas. Yet unlike agricultural workers, they tend to be from small to medium-size towns. Construction based families have replicated, whether intentionally or not, the semirurality of their childhood years in Mexico, by living on the periphery of southwest Montana's towns.

The migration of Mexican construction families has been generated by the rapidly changing economy of the rural Mountain West. Indeed, the pastoral countryside of southwest Montana is being transformed into a globalized countryside whose economy is shifting away from agricultural production and resource extraction toward consumption (Hines 2010; Keller et al. 2012; McCarthy 2008; Woods 2007). Wealthy urbanites, adventure-seeking service workers and high-tech professionals come to Montana to consume both the natural and urban-transplanted amenities of Montana's countryside—fly-fishing, world-class skiing, the wonders of Yellowstone National Park *and* quaint preserved historic downtowns with great shopping, cafes and restaurants—without needing to depend on the land's productivity for survival.

There are several factors driving this *lifestyle migration* into the New West (Krannich et al. 2011; Nelson et al. 2010; Nelson and Nelson 2011). For one, technology now allows people to visit or live in remote rural areas while telecommuting to jobs in urban hubs (Rasker and Glick 1994). Individuals who have capitalized on financial markets are increasingly investing in second homes in rural areas, where they can enjoy the remoteness of the countryside while still having access to urban pleasures (Cloke 2006; Ghose 2004). Wealthy baby-boomer retirees are a significant segment of this population (Kandel and Cromartie 2004; Nelson and Cromartie 2009). So too are what Nelson et al. (2010) call *footloose service workers*: those who want to enjoy outdoor amenities while supporting themselves via low-end and high-end service work. In terms of the latter, southwest Montana has recently become home to high-tech companies that are strategizing ways to couple business with lifestyle.[8]

Geographers suggest that lifestyle migrants are also attracted to the countryside by a *rural idyll*, which is rooted in nostalgia for a simpler, innocent and more authentic time (Little and Austin 1996; Nelson et al. 2010). Historically, this idyll has drawn those seeking to escape the violence, moral corruption and insecurity of the industrial city for the refuge and simplicity of the countryside (Bunce 1994; 2003). The rural idyll is a social construction of rurality centered on tranquillity and "traditional" values. Family and community lie at its heart, which means that it is implicitly gendered. Women, specifically in their roles as mothers, are charged with reproducing the idyll's values in daily life (Little and Austin 1996).

The surge of wealthy migrants into rural areas has spurred a parallel influx of labor migrants, the vast majority Mexican, to service their lifestyles: a form of *linked migration* (Nelson et al. 2010; Nelson and Hiemstra 2008). Saskia Sassen (1998) theorizes that labor migrants have been pulled into postindustrial global cities to perform the services that support the urban lifestyles of the financial elite. In a similar vein, as members of the financial elite relocate away from the cities to the countryside, labor migrants follow to build and clean their houses and do their landscaping (Nelson et al. 2010). The linked migration of urban capital and Mexican labor distinguishes migrant destinations in the Mountain West from many of those in the South and Midwest.[9]

Gentrification and linked migration have not been without tension. An influx of urban wealth into rural areas has meant a surge in home and property prices and consequent class ruptures within rural communities (Hammer and Winkler 2006). In southwest Montana, it is increasingly only well-resourced residents who can afford to live in town, while former residents have been pushed into the rural outskirts as well as into new suburban-like developments that have sprouted up on former agricultural lands.[10] Tensions ensue between long-time residents and newcomers who tend not to share the same values, politics or cultural preferences (Nelson and Hiemstra 2008; Ghose 2004; Smith and Krannich 2000). Ethnic tensions have developed too, as Latinos move into areas that for the past two centuries have been predominantly white and English-speaking.

Park and Pellow (2011) document another type of social tension connected to linked migration. In Aspen, Colorado, another gentrified area in the Mountain West, lifestyle migrants who identify as progressive environmentalists have built a political power base. In addition to organizing for environmental preservation, they are organizing against the presence of Mexican migrants in Aspen, who they claim are putting undue pressure on the land's resources. Park's and Pellow's research uncovers the racism and classism at the base of some environmental rhetoric, highlighting the hypocrisy of the new rural elite's partial progressivism, in which they simultaneously depend on and reject Mexican labor migration.

It was not until I had lived in Montana for many months that I recognized the parallel flow of Mexican labor migrants to which my lifestyle was connected. I am now critically conscious of the link between the lifestyle migration of which I am in some ways a part and the labor migration that services the many amenities that bring my semirural life urban comfort (see also Nelson et al. 2010).[11] And I am uncomfortably attuned to the coded racial tones of my adopted state's slogan, "The Last Best Place." I often reflect on the likelihood that for some, "The Last Best Place" is "best" because it is predominantly white and European. My reflections about the relationship between race and rural gentrification took even deeper root when, in the midst of the 2006 national immigration debates, a stream of editorials in the local newspaper written by lifestyle migrants from California warned Montanans not to let immigration ruin Montana the way it had ruined California. At the same time, white supremacists targeted migrants. Interestingly and important to this story, I speculate that the most immediate aggravating factor of the white supremacist activity was not Mexican migration specifically, but the migration of wealth into Montana. I have learned from my Montana-born students just how insecure lifestyle migration has made many working-class Montanans. This is an insecurity that some have taken out on the most vulnerable and conspicuous, Mexicans.

A migrant to Montana myself, I now write from an uneasy yet unique vantage point. For nine years, during six of which I was engaged in formal fieldwork, I have been immersed in two very different migrant realities. The first migrant reality is my own. I am a white university professor, a wife and mother, who shops at the local food co-op, drives a Subaru, and frequents

Bozeman's trendy bars and cafes. The other migrant reality is that of my Mexican friends and research participants who are marginalized from the amenities I take for granted, and are rendered invisible to most Montanans. Yet through my research I have learned that despite race, class and cultural differences, people living both realities share a deep appreciation of what Montana represents.

When I first began my field research I thought my future manuscript would tell the story of Mexican migrants' daily life struggles and the multiple barriers to incorporation that are unique to a new rural destination. And clearly, much of my data *does* tell this story. As I detail in future chapters, lack of services amenable to a migrant population, rough mountainous terrain and inhospitable winter weather, high housing costs near town centers and the persistent fear of deportation that results from the impossibility of anonymity in one of the whitest states in the country combine to make migrant life in Montana extraordinarily challenging.

However, my research also highlights a contrasting, seemingly paradoxical theme. Interspersed with migrants' narratives of struggle, isolation and anxiety are narratives espousing their adoration for and connection to Montana, a connection they told me they had not felt in the other places they have lived in the United States. All the migrants I met, whether man or woman, authorized or unauthorized, agricultural or construction worker, told me that if they are to live in the United States, they do not want to live anywhere else. In Montana they feel a sense of security and hope they have not felt elsewhere, and they feel they can be better husbands, wives, fathers and mothers. Men can provide for and protect their families. Women can offer their children a safe, beautiful place in which to grow up. And in Montana, both men and women feel a transnational connection to "home." Through my research I have learned that the rural idyll, despite its superficiality and whitewashing, has meaning, even for those it deems invisible. This book explores that meaning.

Gender and the New West

I did not enter this project with the intent of writing about gender and family. I originally thought this would be a study of race and incorporation in a new migrant destination, one that does not have the white-black binary of the New South (Marrow 2011) or the refugee-migrant mix of the Midwest (Singer 2008). Yet I quickly learned that while race and class delineate inequality *between* migrants and other populations in southwest Montana, gender delineates inequalities *within* Mexican families as well as highlights the most poignant distinctions between the daily life experiences of migrants in different receiving areas. Gender led me into the most intimate spaces of migration and showed me how these spaces are altered by geographic context,[12] a story that has not yet been told.

One of my earliest field observations was that Mexican men are more publicly visible than Mexican women. Men spend their days on construction sites or working the land. They carpooled to their work sites and appeared a part of strong male networks. In contrast, I rarely saw women in public, save for at the food bank and community health clinic, which they visited infrequently, or at Spanish Mass once a month. Most often, if Mexican women were in public, they were with their husbands. In the fall of 2006 when I began my formal fieldwork, there were few jobs available for migrant women. Thus Mexican women spent most of their time at home, working to hold their families together and maintain their own sanity. Women's networks appeared weak and dispersed.

I also learned that while men were at much greater risk of deportation (see Golash-Boza and Hondagneu-Sotelo 2013), and indeed over the course of my fieldwork many men but no women were deported, it was women who had to hold family together following a deportation, a task made uniquely difficult by the vast physical terrain and the economic and social context of Montana. Yet, although isolated and uniquely burdened by their care duties, the migrant women I met asserted agency, choosing to stay in Montana for the well-being of their children, even if this meant fewer opportunities and more stress for themselves personally. I realized early on in my fieldwork that a few of my key observations were missing from, or counter to, research findings from traditional destinations, highlighting the ways the intricacies of place impact migrant life.

Today half of all international migrants are women, and increasingly women are migrating to work instead of for family reunification (Ehrenreich and Hochschild 2002). Growth in the care industry, including demand for nursing assistants, nannies and home health aides, partnered with a spike in domestic and commercial cleaning jobs, draws female migrants to the United States. In many cases women migrate without their children, leaving them behind to be cared for by close family and kin (Carling, Menjívar and Schmalzbauer 2012). This gender transformation in international migration has received increasing attention by scholars interested in transnational families (Abrego 2014; Dreby 2010; Hondagneu-Sotelo 2001; Parreñas 2001; Schmalzbauer 2005; Thai 2008) and the survival strategies migrant women adopt to care for their families in contexts of social and economic marginalization. Scholars place special emphasis on the importance of networks to the well-being of migrant women and their families (Hagan 1994; Hondag-neu-Sotelo 1994; Kibria 1993; Menjívar 2000). Most recently research has introduced discussions of gender and illegality (Abrego 2014; Abrego and Menjívar 2011; Golash-Boza 2012, 2014; Golash-Boza and Hondagneu-Sotelo 2013), investigating the ways men and women are differentially affected by current immigration policy and legal regimes.

The vast majority of the research on gender and migration has focused in traditional migrant cities. There has been scant research on the gender-specific aspects of migration to new settlements,[13] and no ethnographic research to date analyzing gender and migration in a new rural settlement. Although focused on Montana, this book provides theoretical insights into the gender dynamics of migration into rural areas throughout the United States, filling a conspicuous gap in the immigration literature.

This book also contributes a translocal and transnational analysis of how intersections of place and gender shape immigration.[14] Instead of being solely determined by culture, gender expectations and prescriptions are embedded in transnational social structures. Hirsch (2003) advises scholars against over-looking the ways in which the fluidity of gender in migrants' home communities impacts gender formation in their host societies. Heeding Hirsch's advice, I explore gender's iterations in all the critical places, both in Mexico and the United States, where my research participants have lived.

As Mexico's economy has become more globalized and as technological advances have generated changes in domestic labor, gender relations in Mexico have changed. Gutmann's now classic ethnography (1996) on masculinity in Mexico City, for example, shows how "meanings of macho" have evolved with changing economic conditions. Gutmann finds men's roles as husbands and fathers were transformed as more women went to work outside of the home and joined community organizing efforts. Hirsch (2003) expands on Gutmann's analysis, suggesting that as more families in Mexico gain access to electricity, running water, dual incomes and globalized media, women's and men's attitudes about gender are evolving, though not necessarily uniformly. Gender expectations and experiences vary; some men and women are more flexible and open than others, but there is nothing to suggest that gender is ever static. Thus Mexicans do not migrate from "tradition" to "modernity" as they cross from Mexico into the United States. Instead their gendered selves are malleable throughout the process of migration and settlement, and may present themselves differently depending on the specific time and context of their lives.

Still, the regional context of women's and men's lives matters in terms of how they experience and perform gender (Gonzalez-López 2005). In urban areas in Mexico, for example, women tend to have more access to employ-ment, which gives them greater autonomy and power and therefore more options from which to choose how or if they want to create family. On the contrary, in rural Mexico, fewer economic opportunities for women mean they are more likely to find themselves dependent on men and marriage. This is not to say that rural Mexican men and women are intrinsically more conservative than their urban peers, but rather that the context of their lives shapes, in often pragmatic ways, their gender attitudes and practices (ibid.). Social position too can expand or limit the way individuals think about gender. For example, in both Mexican rural and urban contexts, women and men who have greater access to literacy and education, a privilege that tends to be rooted in class position, are more likely to be exposed to and adopt flexible gender norms (ibid.; Hirsch 2003).

In the United States too, urbanity and rurality are critical to the ways migrants experience gender. Hirsch (2003) finds that the anonymity of At-lanta, where she performed her field research, allows for more gender "trans-gressions" among migrant women than were feasible in their rural, home communities, where gossip serves as an important tool of social control. In Atlanta, women do not have to worry about being seen in public with men who are not their husbands because they can easily find places where no one knows or recognizes them. And because the women in Hirsch's study are more likely to engage in wage work and to have access to transportation in Atlanta than in their home communities, they are more autonomous. Thus the urbanity of Atlanta prompts Hirsch's participants to assert "mod-ern" identities.

In Montana rurality and the economic opportunity structures connected to it are the source of rigidly scripted gender roles and expectations. As I detail in Chapter 2, migrant families were pulled to Montana for work in construction and agriculture, both of which are male-dominated. In Mon-tana, female employment niches, such as those of care and cleaning, continue to be dominated by white, native-born women. As such, the economy of Montana is best suited for male labor migrants. Whereas a few women I met worked in Mexico and several worked in other states where they had lived, in Montana, most migrant women find their opportunities are limited. Montana's economy pushes many into "traditional" domestic roles, which some embrace but others resent.

As another example, most Mexican migrants in Montana grew up in rural areas where women rarely learned how to drive. In other U.S. states they had access to public transportation. Yet the rurality of Montana means that migrants are car dependent. As such, migrant women, without easy access to

transportation and without jobs outside of the home, tend to be unduly isolated, which shapes their experience of daily life in powerful ways. Because
migrants in Montana have to cope with economic and rurality-induced
gender divides, social constructions of femininity and motherhood that emphasize sacrifice and care and constructions of masculinity and fatherhood
that center on provision have gained currency in their lives (Dreby 2010).

Social position, as well as geographic context, shape rural women's gender
expectations and practices. Over the past nine years I have observed how
the rural idyll, for example, is gendered in its expectations and prescriptions.
Julie Keller et al. (2012) present a narrative analysis of representations of
rural femininity in two popular magazines, one aimed specifically at agricultural families, *Successful Farmer*, and one aimed at those aspiring to a country
lifestyle, *Country Living*. They found that in the latter, themes of "escape"
and "fantasy" aim to lure urbanites away from the stress of the city to the
tranquillity of the countryside. Images prevail of women leaving their cell
phones behind to make jam and bread and decorate their homes with rustic
furniture salvaged from old farms. They label this phenomenon *transformative
country chic*, suggesting that at the cultural level it symbolizes both the "rural
in the feminine" and the "feminine in the rural." While rugged landscapes
symbolize masculinity, the care and domestic work that permits families to
live in these landscapes are constructed as feminine. Increasingly the latter is
taking on a privileged, consumption-oriented significance.

When I first moved to Montana from Boston I was inspired by these
trendy yet genuine efforts to "downshift" (see Schor 1992). In 2010 my
husband, who has a graduate degree from an elite school, sold his "green"
building business to stay home with our young children, remodel our house,
tend our chickens, make yogurt, bake bread and plant a large organic garden.
While typical gender norms are flipped in our family's case, class privilege
lies at the base of our lifestyle choices and the flexibility with which my
husband experiences his masculinity. It was not until I was years deep into
my fieldwork with local Mexican families that I began to see the gender
and class complexities involved in privileged homesteading. I began to understand in a deeper way why my own mom, who grew up on a small farm
in Minnesota that did not have running water until she was nine, finds no
romance in using an outhouse, while my husband, who lived in a cabin in
the woods for a few years while working for a wilderness adventure organization, embraces the experience for bringing him closer to nature.

I now view the country chic phenomenon with a more critical and skep-
tical eye. I am aware of the striking irony that for Mexican migrant women,
as for women in poor American agricultural families, sewing, outhouses and

domestic agricultural skills are part of survival. They do not represent choice, nor are they chic. For the Mexican women I know, as was true for my own mother, leaving an agrarian lifestyle marked a move toward modernity. And yet, while many Mexican migrant women left behind agricultural duties, they continue to carry the burden of the other domestic responsibilities necessary to maintaining a household. My mom, on the other hand, a white, English-speaking, U.S. citizen, moved on to university and a career as a social worker and then as an entrepreneur. She moved to the city, became a feminist, and never looked back.

In Montana, *country chic* coexists with what I call *survival femininities*, in which Mexican migrant women's social positions as they intersect with the specificities of Montana's economy and physical geography, urge them toward an often isolated role of domestic labor and *intensive mothering* (Hays 1996). Jessica Vasquez (2011) in her study of Mexican migrant families in urban California finds that working-class mothers often enter a *survival mode of parenting* in which they must spend the majority of their time working away from their children, leaving their children in many ways to fend for themselves. Survival femininities are different from a survival mode of parenting, in that although in both cases survival is the families' first priority, in the former survival work is focused mostly if not entirely in the home, because there are few opportunities for employment outside the home. As this comparison suggests, context shapes the ways poor and working-class migrant women perform motherhood.

In Montana, as divergent as are the lived experiences of women aspiring toward country chic and those living a survival femininity, their migrations to Montana both have roots in a globalizing countryside. And while country chic femininity is based on consuming the idyll of the countryside and survival femininity is based first and foremost on family sustainability, both are centered on the expectation that child-focused motherhood is central to womanhood, and the belief that it is easier to meet this expectation in Montana than elsewhere.

Researching and Writing through the Lens of Motherhood

This book is based on six years of ethnographic fieldwork in southwest Montana, where I immersed myself in the Mexican community. My formal fieldwork began in the fall of 2006 when I answered an email recruiting volunteer translators for our local food bank, which had seen an influx of Spanish-speaking clients. This volunteer stint led me deep into the Mexican migrant community. Through my participant observation I got to know many migrant families well. In addition to participant observation, I did eighty-two formal in-depth interviews and three focus groups with migrant mothers, fathers and members of the second generation, both authorized and unauthorized.[15] I followed six families closely over the six-year period, doing repeat interviews as well as spending extensive informal time with them. The majority of quotations in this book are drawn from my formal interviews, but several are drawn from informal conversations I had while in the field. Finally, I did fifteen in-depth interviews with key respondents in the community who interface with Mexican migrants on a regular basis. I use pseudonyms for all the migrants I interviewed. I use the real names of all key respondents who are public personas, except for three who requested a pseudonym.

As I detail in this book, there are unique challenges to being a labor migrant in Montana. Here it is impossible to be anonymous, which intensifies migrants' fears of being targeted. As such there were few reasons that migrants should have given me their trust when I began this research. I am white, middle class, and my native tongue is English. Yet I do speak Spanish, not perfectly, but well, which is unusual in Montana. I also know Mexico and Central America well, which allowed me to spark a cultural connection with Latinos I met. But in the context of earning the trust of my participants, neither my Spanish ability nor experiences abroad were as significant as my identity as a mother, a pregnant mother for a while, with a baby, toddler or small child at my side for much of my fieldwork.[16]

In the summer of 2007 I was invited to attend a Spanish Mass in Bozeman, the first of its kind in southwest Montana. I had become friendly with a few Mexican women who frequented the food bank, and they had invited me. I was both enthused and anxious about the invitation, as I still felt on the periphery of their community. I had intended to leave my son Micah, who was at the time only an infant, with my husband while I went to church. When he was invited to go hiking with friends, I agreed to take Micah with me. Although I was unsure about bringing a small baby, prone to crying, to a formal Mass, I was dedicated to honoring the women's invitation. With butterflies in my stomach, I strapped on my child carrier and headed to Mass.

As I entered the church my nerves quickly settled. Edith, one of the first women I met in my research, saw me and walked toward me smiling. I realized right away that she was smiling not at me but at Micah, who was wide-eyed and cooing. Within minutes I was surrounded by women who wanted to meet Micah.

The church was almost full and I sat down next to Edith and her family. As I looked around the church, I was struck by how many families were in attendance. This was markedly different from church services I had attended in Boston, where I had lived and previously done fieldwork. There many migrants were men and women whose immediate families were in Honduras and El Salvador. Then my eyes caught on a group of single men in the back of the church. In the context of families, they stood out. I later learned that they were H2B workers, in Montana for eight months to work in the booming construction industry in Big Sky. After the Mass, as I was leaving the church, two of the men came over to me and reached their hands out to Micah. We chatted as one of the men took Micah in his arms and bounced him playfully. They told me that they had young children in Mexico.[17] They had not seen them since early spring and were counting down the days, hours, minutes until their reunion in November.

During my fieldwork in Boston, many of my research participants were struck by my single, childless reality. Friendly joking and flirtations accentuated my identity as a straight, single, childless woman. The difference between my own identity and those of my participants was highlighted by my research focus on motherhood and transnational families. In Montana, the migrants I met embraced me initially *not* as a researcher or as a community activist, but as a mother. Micah, and soon after my pregnant belly, and then my daughter Zola, formed a bridge between me and my participants.

My young children ensured me a warm welcome wherever I went. And most important they privileged me with the confidence of the migrants I met. My participants hold family, and especially motherhood, in high esteem. Although I am not Mexican or a labor migrant, I am a mother, which gave me status among them. Gaining trust of the community was surprisingly easy. I just had to be who I was, a mother who cared deeply about the experiences of migrant families. As I have reflected elsewhere (see Schmalzbauer 2013), I am aware of the ways in which I unintentionally capitalized on my identity as a mother. And yet, to give this point too much pause would be to discredit my participants, who choose whom they want and do not want to trust, and whom they want to let into their lives.

Throughout my field research, my family and I were invited to baptisms, dances, children's birthday parties and other gatherings. I was also brought into family crises, in most cases when my language skills or ability to negotiate bureaucracy was helpful. Because of my entree into these intimate spaces, I observed things and heard things to which I likely would not have been privy if I had not had a child in my arms. As such, my position as a mother influenced the themes I highlight in this book. As I wrote earlier, I did not enter this research intending to write about gender, yet soon found gender central to my work. Upon reflection I realize the likelihood that at least part of the reason I found gender to be central in my research is that it was central to my own life at the time. My identity as a new mom impacted the directions that my interviews often took, the private spaces within migrant families in which I found myself, the informal conversations I had in the field and the lens through which I analyzed my findings. Motherhood also influenced my own relationship to Montana and the rural idyll. Security, tranquillity and the natural beauty of the area took on new meaning in my life once I became a mother, while the city lost the strong appeal it had previously had. Here too I bonded with my participants, especially the migrant women I got to know as we were both settling into Montana and motherhood.

Because I lived in my field site before, during and after my fieldwork, my position in this ethnography extends beyond that of researcher to include mother, friend, professor, lifestyle migrant, general community member, activist and informal social worker. I have written myself into this ethnography in all of these capacities. I have done this *not* as an attempt to stand in for others who share these identities, but to make my own interpretive lens clear.

Outline of the book

This book unfolds in six substantive chapters and a conclusion. Chapter 2 describes the gender landscape of Mexican migration to southwest Montana. In this chapter I detail the economic structure that contextualizes migrant family life, the gender division of labor within migrant households and how transnational gender expectations interact with this context. In Chapter 3, I explore the ways in which Mexican migrants to Montana experience illegality, paying special attention to the gender aspects of illegality. I show the importance of rurality in shaping migrants' sense of security and insecurity, and I explore the ways in which illegality penetrates the emotional well-being of migrants, specifically as they try to manage their gendered roles within their families and their gendered positions within rural space. Chapter 4 interrogates the meaning of the rural idyll in the lives of Mexican migrants to Montana. In this chapter I use a transnational lens to investigate why Mexican migrants espouse a special connection to Montana that they have not felt elsewhere. In this chapter I suggest that natural landscapes and cultures of rurality cultivate feelings of belonging for migrants who are otherwise marginalized. I also highlight the ways in which the rural idyll is both gendered and raced, and I investigate the paradoxical relationship between belonging and exclusion. In Chapter 5, I discuss the impact of the Great Recession on migrant families in Montana, paying special attention to the ways in which it altered gender divisions of family labor and challenged gender relations. Chapter 6 centers on the perspectives of the 1.5 and second generation. This chapter exemplifies the ways that childhood both transcends and is bound by geographic context, and how gender shapes the early part of the life course. Chapter 7 touts the importance of safe spaces and individuals, who bridge race and class divides, to migrant well-being. This chapter portrays the hope and opportunity that exist for migrant incorporation and community building in the New West. In Chapter 8, I conclude by returning to the book's title, paying special attention to the question mark at its end. Is Montana the last best place for Mexican migrants? I answer this question by theoretically interrogating my key findings and suggesting how the findings from Montana can inform immigration research more broadly. Overall, the goal of this book is to give readers an intimate look into the gendered lives of Mexican migrants to a new rural destination in the Mountain West, and in the process to show the importance of place in experiences of migration and incorporation.

Chapter 2

Economic Opportunities and Gender Divisions of Labor

Roberta and Ernesto have been together since they were young teenagers. They grew up and will likely grow old together. When I met them in 2007, Roberta was a vivacious twenty-year-old. Already the mother of three, she appeared unfazed by the demands of caring for two rambunctious toddlers and a baby. During my first visit to her home, I watched in awe as she changed a diaper while calming her two-year-old, who had tripped and fallen on her trailer's uneven linoleum floor, all the while continuing to chat with me without distraction. While Roberta is overtly maternal, she is also tough. Her gentle spirit, warm smile and feminine dress contrast strikingly with her *campesino* tongue.[1] No matter with whom she is talking, she installs no verbal filter, cussing regularly and without hesitation.

Ernesto is a few years Roberta's senior. He radiates kindness through his bright smile and warm demeanor. But despite his smile, and unlike Roberta, Ernesto has a soberness about him. He has been engaged in hard, agricultural labor since he was nine years old, first in Mexico and now in Montana. Roberta, his young children, and his parents and siblings in Jalisco rely on him for provision and protection, a heavy weight for Ernesto to carry in a climate of relentless legal and economic insecurity.

For their first few years in Montana, Roberta and Ernesto lived about fifteen miles outside of Bozeman in a dilapidated trailer. They lived then, as they do today, removed from the New West mansions that dot the local landscape, in an area of large working family farms. The view from their home includes majestic peaks and rolling hills, but no glitz. I often wonder how long it will be before this agricultural area too is transformed into nonproductive homesteads. The beauty of the area, coupled with its proximity to Bozeman, Yellowstone National Park and Big Sky ski area makes it ideal for development. For now, it is a segment of southwest Montana that maintains its agricultural roots.

When I first met Ernesto and Roberta I was struck by their isolation, living far from any neighbors and with few social outlets. Roberta seemed especially isolated. Whereas Ernesto went to work six to seven days a week managing 750 dairy cows on a neighboring farm, Roberta spent her days at home caring for their children, leaving only to go to Wal-Mart with Ernesto on Saturday nights. Roberta does not have a driver's license, nor does she know how to drive.

Roberta and Ernesto try to stay out of the public eye. They are among the many Mexicans I have met who are leery of the growing migrant population in southwest Montana. In their estimation, "Mexicans bring trouble with *la migra* (Immigration and Customs Enforcement—ICE) and the police . . . and they lower wages." Unauthorized and struggling to get by in a low-wage economy in which they have no legal protections, for Roberta and Ernesto social isolation has become a goal and source of happiness. What they appreciate most about Montana is that they can keep to themselves. As such, I have come to realize that what at first appeared to me a dismally isolated life is a life of refuge of sorts for them, especially for Roberta. "I have no friends," Roberta told me matter-of-factly during our first interview in 2007. "But it's OK. I don't mind . . . I like it at home." On each of the half-dozen or so times I visited their trailer the blinds were closed. The darkness contrasted starkly with Roberta's bright spirit.

Roberta's and Ernesto's situation changed quite a bit over the course of my fieldwork. In 2009 Ernesto's cousin, Juan Carlos, his wife, Julisa, and their three children moved to Montana from Washington. For two years the families lived together, ten people in a trailer with two small bedrooms and bathrooms, one of the bathrooms lacking a functioning door. Privacy was nonexistent. Juan Carlos worked with Ernesto. Julisa stayed home with Roberta. For the first time since arriving in the United States, both Roberta and Julisa enjoyed female friendship. "We help each other a lot," Julisa told me during one of our visits. "We are family and life is good here together." Do you ever argue? I pushed, in disbelief that two families could coexist so peacefully in such a small space. "No, no. It is fine. We get along well and there are no problems." Julisa seemed surprised by my question.

Soon after Julisa's and Juan Carlos's arrival, I began to notice a change in Roberta. She became more adventurous in her daily life activities. Most notably, she began to leave the house more often. Julisa is unique among migrant women in Montana in that, although she does not have a license, she knows how to drive. Access to regular transportation expanded Roberta's geographical world. Together Roberta and Julisa went to the grocery store, to the food bank, and to the community clinic if one of their children was ill. Then, through Ernesto's boss, Roberta and Julisa found part-time work sorting potatoes at a nearby farm. Their wages were meager but they assured me they enjoyed the work. While they still lacked a network of female support, in each other Roberta and Julisa found companionship and their autonomy increased.

In 2011, Ernesto's boss offered to let him live in a small house on the edge of his dairy farm. Roberta and Ernesto jumped at the opportunity. Their "new" house, although neglected and characterized by the persistent stench of cow manure, is a dream come true. For the first time in their lives they have their own bedroom, and their children have a large inside play space, which is especially appreciated during Montana's long winters. What is more, Ernesto no longer has to commute to work, lessening his fear of a traffic stop and deportation. Although moving to their new house meant that Roberta and Ernesto had to separate from Juan Carlos and Julisa, they still spend a lot of time together.

With the move to the new house came an even bigger change in Roberta's life. Ernesto's boss asked Roberta if she wanted to milk cows two days a week. Their children now in school and her days therefore free, Roberta agreed. She was eager to contribute more to the family income, and Ernesto supported her enthusiasm. Roberta was intimately familiar with agricultural life and comfortable with dairy cows. On the *ranchito* (small, subsistence ranch) where she grew up, cows and corn constituted the livelihood of all the families she knew. She was confident she could manage whatever work her new boss sent her way.

Roberta's and Ernesto's rural Mexican roots inform their migrant lives. They both hail from southwest Jalisco, where they lived in a small, impoverished area of subsistence agriculture located far from a commercial center. Roberta attended school for six years, Ernesto for only three. As is the case for most men from his hometown, Ernesto is highly skilled in agriculture yet he cannot read or write. Roberta can sign her name and read at a basic level, but her literacy extends only slightly beyond this. Whereas women in Roberta's and Ernesto's hometown are typically better educated than men, they lack autonomy. There are few opportunities for women outside of their domestic duties, and rarely do women learn to drive, further limiting their scope of exploration. Both men and women work hard, but their work is divided. While women often help in the fields and with the cows, their work is first and foremost focused in the home and in the care of family. Men are expected to provide, and it was Ernesto's commitment to provide for his ailing mother that ultimately motivated him, with Roberta at his side, to leave his ranchito and cross "to the other side" in search of wages.

In many ways Ernesto and Roberta have bucked patriarchal gender norms. Ernesto is supportive of Roberta's work outside of the home, and he lauds her strength and competence. He draws a clear distinction between being *macho*, which he describes as being tough and hard-working, and *machista*, which he associates with disrespecting women. He characterizes himself as macho, but not machista. His respect for Roberta is genuine and deep. In addition, he loves to spend time with his children.

Yet in other important ways, Roberta's and Ernesto's lives continue to adhere to the gender script of the rural Jalisco of their childhoods. Taking care of her home and children remains Roberta's top priority. While Ernesto loves to play with the children, he does not cook, wash dishes or do laundry. And when money is tight at the end of the month, it is Roberta's responsibility to figure out how to make ends meet, a job made all the more challenging without regular access to transportation, basic social services or a network of support on which she can draw. While Ernesto depends on Roberta's basic literacy and domesticity, Roberta depends on Ernesto for transportation and income. They are a team, yet gender rigidly stratifies their opportunities, family roles and daily life experiences. Their gendered lives were first scripted during their childhoods in Jalisco and continue to be shaped by the intersections of their social positions and the geography and economy of southwest Montana.

As is true for migrants throughout the United States, gender shapes Roberta's and Ernesto's individual roles, responsibilities and expectations. It also influences their relationship with their children and with each other. Whereas in many ways Roberta's and Ernesto's story is typical, in other ways it breaks the mold, exemplifying the fluidity and complexity of gender in migrants' lives. Roberta works outside of the home with Ernesto's full support, and she exerts an assertiveness that I have observed in few migrant women in Montana. Also notable, the spatial and social isolation of Roberta's life has thus far not manifested itself in depression or anxiety as has been the case for many women, a few of whom I introduce below. As these exceptions indicate, gender can be dynamic in how it is practiced and experienced, even among men and women from similar backgrounds. Still, I observe striking patterns in terms of gender roles, relations and expectations within migrant families in southwest Montana. In this chapter I explore these patterns and the nuances within them, analyzing how economic opportunities influence gender divisions within migrant families.

Searching for Wages

> We came because there was a lot of work and there were not so many people that worked in construction in comparison, for example, to Colorado. There, there were so many people looking for work. And here, when there is work, there aren't enough people to do it. There are fewer people searching for work, and this in one way is beneficial . . . . Here we can work more hours and they pay us better. (Pedro)

As I outline in this book's introduction, the initial draw for Mexican families to Montana was the abundance of work and high wages in the state relative to others. Small numbers of Mexican agricultural workers have been coming to Montana for decades to work temporarily on H2A visas on cattle and sheep ranches, seasonally on potato farms and long term, and typically without papers, in the dairy industry. Mexican construction workers, on the other hand, followed new wealth into Montana, their migration linked to that of the lifestyle migrants and tourists who started to arrive in the 1990s. With new Montana wealth there was demand for workers to service it. Migrants responded to this demand. As boutiques replaced seed stores, hobby ranches replaced working ranches, and the faces of the Spanish Peaks were transformed into ski slopes, relatively large numbers of Mexicans began to settle in southwest Montana.

Migrant men arrived with skills, ambition and the willingness to do the arduous jobs that the local population left unfilled. Migrant women arrived at their partners' sides.[2] In Colorado and California, where the majority of Mexicans lived previously, wages were stagnant, as both states have large surpluses of migrant labor.[3] In Montana, as development boomed, demand for male migrant labor was high and as a result so were migrant wages. Mexican families put aside their anxieties about moving away from family and friends to a place with few services for a Mexican population and winters that can last from October through May, and relocated to Montana in search of opportunity.

Upon arrival labor migrants alerted family members and friends that prospects in Montana were good. Networks kicked in, and a steady migration stream began to flow. Before the recession took full hold in Montana in 2009, the men in my sample worked an average of six days a week for a culmination of fifty-plus hours of hard manual labor. While migrant men worked long hours for good pay, most migrant women were in charge of the home front: a team effort to support their families' socioeconomic mobility.

Pedro is originally from Calvillo, Aguas Calientes. He migrated from Colorado to Montana with his wife, Angela, in 2003. In Colorado he first worked in the peach fields, doing what he described "as hard, hard work." His salary was $4.25/hour. When his brother Abraham told him that in Montana there were high-wage construction jobs available, he was immediately intrigued. In 1999, Pedro began migrating between Colorado and Montana to do masonry work, a skill that he had honed in Mexico. Four years later, as the economic boom in Montana neared its climax, Pedro and Angela made the decision to move their family to Montana. Whereas in Colorado they could barely pay their bills, in Montana Pedro was making $15/hour, they were saving money and their dream of buying a house, which had been buried for years, resurfaced. Whereas Angela missed the network of support she had had in Colorado, she embraced the opportunity and financial security Montana promised.

After much hesitation, Victoria and Candido, both of whom are from Zacatecas, also moved from Colorado to Montana. Victoria loved life in Colorado. "On every corner in Colorado you can buy tacos, Mexican food, enchiladas, and the stores are full of Mexican products, Mexican drinks, meat, everything. It felt like we were in Mexico . . . . And in the schools and clinics, everyone speaks Spanish." Yet the cultural comforts of Colorado were overshadowed by the static economic situation that contextualized their lives. Victoria explained what finally prompted their move:

> We couldn't save anything. I had a savings account with $1,000 in it and for five years no matter how much we worked it stayed at $1,000. And every winter the work in Colorado was less and less. And so Candido told me, "I'm going to Montana." But he didn't go for a while because I was unsure. Then finally life just became too tough . . . . I had started watching two kids in our house but I was making very little money. We couldn't take it anymore. So we left for Montana. And wow . . . there is such a big difference between what they pay here and what they pay in Colorado. Here they pay twice and sometimes three times as much.

Pedro's and Victoria's accounts of why they moved are representative of the construction and agricultural families I met in my fieldwork. Many hesitantly left other states where they had lived, in most cases leaving behind strong networks of family and friends. They moved for the work and for the wages that Montana yielded. For migrant families who had been struggling to achieve upward mobility, Montana represented a new shot at the American Dream. Dorotea, for example, told me that her husband began working in Montana for $16/hour, then moved to a job making $18/hour and then moved to another job that increased his salary even more. In California he had earned only minimum wage. But accompanying this new-found opportunity was a profoundly different life. Moving to Montana was a trade-off between work and wages, and kin support and cultural resonance, a trade-off felt most intensely by migrant women who were blocked from joining the economic boom and found themselves removed from social networks that in other places gave them critical support.

Place-Based Barriers to Women's Autonomy

Migrant families in Montana strategically organize their labor in order to secure survival and to strive for economic mobility. Social structures shape household gender roles as well as the rituals of daily life. Before the Great Recession hit southwest Montana, ample opportunities in construction and high-skill agriculture meant that, almost without exception, men worked for wages while women managed the home front. When migrant men moved to Montana their lives changed very little. They worked long hours with other Mexican men. If anything their lives improved as their egos were boosted by the higher incomes they were bringing home, and they got more attention from their wives. As Pedro said, "Because Angela was always home, dinner was waiting for me every night." Women's lives, on the other hand, changed drastically when they moved to Montana and were confined to the domestic sphere. Thus, although many migrant women spoke to me with optimism about the centrality of family in their lives, I sensed that for some women embracing domesticity was their means of coping with the limited opportunity that Montana offered them.

For Malía, Montana was the first place she lived where she was not able to work. "I have a college degree. In Mexico I worked. I worked in Florida . . . . I love to work! But here I am in the house day after day." Moving to Montana meant Malía was forced into a dependent female role. She was frustrated and discouraged. Similarly, Rebeca, originally from Nayarit, moved to Montana after having lived in Texas for eight years, where she always had a job. Like Malía, she grieved the loss of independence that life in Montana entailed:

> I like to work. In Texas I always worked. Even when I had my children
> I worked and continued working. It was only when I arrived here that I
> stopped working. I miss having my own money, money that I can send to
> my mom, money that I know is mine so I don't have to depend completely
> on others . . . . I know not everyone feels this way. I know women who like
> just being in the house. But for me, I miss my independence.

Agosta too worked, as a teacher in Guanajuato, before migrating to the United States to join her husband. She has the legal authorization to work, but she is discouraged that despite her experience and education, the only job she can find in Montana is one cleaning houses. Before ultimately leaving Montana, Agosta spent two days a week, while her children were at school, volunteering at the food bank. Although her work there did not help with the family income, it was meaningful and allowed her to escape the doldrums of being at home.

Migrant employment niches in Montana are narrow for both men and women, but whereas for men the niches are narrow but deep, containing opportunity for economic mobility, the niches for migrant women are narrow and shallow. While there exist a few opportunities for migrant women to work in restaurant kitchens and to clean private homes and hotel rooms, Montana lags far behind other migrant destinations where Latina migrants dominate the domestic and care industries (Ehrenreich and Hochschild 2002; Hondagneu-Sotelo 2001).[4] Natalia, who moved to Montana from California, theorized in her interview with me that "Montanans still do not trust Latinas with their homes or their children." Before the recession, only four of the migrant women I knew were working outside of the home, and only two were working full time.[5]

Legal documentation presents another gender barrier. Whereas migrant men have developed sophisticated networks that have facilitated the ability of those who are unauthorized to acquire false papers, this has not been the case for migrant women. I know only two unauthorized women in Montana who have false social security cards. In other states where women worked in the informal care industry, cleaning or caring for children in private homes, they did not need papers. Although in Florida Malía found many opportunities to work, in Montana she was limited by her unauthorized legal status:

> Well, yes there are [Mexican] women who work here but the truth is that there is not much work for women. I have seen women most often find work cleaning houses, but there aren't many women doing this. Just a little while ago a friend invited me to work with her cleaning houses in Big Sky, but the owner of the cleaning company asked me for my papers. So I told her the truth that I didn't have any. She let me work for three days because she really needed someone but not any more after that.

Susana, who is from Aguas Calientes, moved with her husband to Montana from Colorado in 2006. Like Malía she has been frustrated by the lack of employment opportunities for Mexican women in Montana. "All of the bosses know that most Mexican women here do not have papers. So there might be work cleaning houses but they are going to ask to see your papers.

Even in McDonalds, in the kitchen, they ask to see your papers." I asked her if it was easier for women to find work in Colorado. She replied, "Yes, of course, because there are many more Hispanics there, even the *gueros* speak Spanish, and it is just a lot easier for women to find a job."

Notably, few women who have legal authorization to work have actually sought work outside of the home, suggesting that illegality and job availability are not the only factors limiting migrant women's labor participation. Low female wages further dissuade women. Before the recession, migrant men could earn upward of $25/hour in construction or in the dairies, but the female options of kitchen work and hotel cleaning tend to pay minimum wage. Victoria explained:

> Here I know women who have their papers and I ask them, "Why don't you work?" They tell me that their husbands earn enough so that they don't have to work. If they went to work they would not make much and just have to pay taxes to the government, so it wouldn't be worth it. So, they say, "My husband is not short of funds so I will just stay here and make my enchiladas."

Early in my fieldwork, when the construction industry was booming, the only women I met who worked outside of the home did so because they had no other choice. Gaby originally migrated to Montana from Monterrey on a tourist visa that her husband at the time arranged for her and her two sons. Months after they arrived, Gaby's husband left her for another woman. Gaby had just had a baby, Raul. She was alone and broke. She found an employer who accepted her expired tourist visa as work authorization when she promised him that her other papers were in process. A short while later, Gaby was the first migrant woman I knew in Montana to secure a false social security card. With this she found work in a hotel, followed by a string of stints in restaurant kitchens. But even today, working forty-plus hours a week, Gaby barely makes ends meet.

Child care challenges also make wage work difficult for women. For the first two years of her son Raul's life, Gaby shuffled him between Rebeca, whom she had gotten to know at church, and her teenage sons, Bruno and Mateo, while she went to work. When her oldest son, Bruno, dropped out of high school he cared for Raul full time. Gaby never felt completely comfortable with the setup, as she suspected Bruno was experimenting with drugs, but she had no choice. As a single mom, Gaby has few options when it comes to negotiating work and child care. She must work, and, as such, she often must rely on less than ideal child care.

Dual parent families also struggle with child care issues. Ernestina became a U.S. citizen in 2010. She speaks English quite fluently and works in a community health clinic where she helps translate for migrant families.[6] Ernestina explained the barriers she sees to combining mothering with wage work in Montana:

> The deal is that almost all the Mexican women here have children. So there are two choices. You can work and give the money you make to a daycare. Or you can stay in the house and take care of your own children.

Ángel, a construction worker, said a version of the same:

> My boy is still little, and the work that my wife could do wouldn't be well paid and it wouldn't be conducive for taking care of him. It just wouldn't be worth it. So we decided that she wouldn't work and we wouldn't leave our boy.

Victoria concurred during our first interview in 2007. She worked in Colorado before having children, but when her children were still very young she felt that working did not make financial or practical sense. "For women it makes it difficult because, well, we have to care for our children, and if we worked we would have to pay someone else to watch our children, or what?"

In Mexico and in the other places in the United States where migrants lived, extended kin networks provided supplementary child care support (see Boehm 2012; Dreby 2010; Hagan 1994). Yet the large distances between households in Montana and women's relatively small numbers of acquaintances hinder the development of child care networks. Jose, whose wife, Judith, stays home to care for their child, represented the sentiments of many migrants I met when he told me:

> Well, here there is no one to help women care for their children. It's difficult to pay a daycare, and anyway we don't have that culture in Mexico. In Mexico it is always the mother or the mother-in-law who cares for the children.

The women who have access to child care support either live close to other Mexican families or have extended family close by. They are the exceptions. Victoria and Dorotea, for example, often watched each other's children when they were neighbors in a trailer park. As another example, Nora, until her return to Mexico in 2007, relied on her sister Edith to help her with her new baby. Edith in turn could rely on Nora for help with her young daughter. As sisters living near each other they benefited from both access and trust. While I observed other temporary child care swaps, most women told me that they did not have someone whom they would feel comfortable calling for help with their children even if it were an emergency.

Montana's physical rurality presents yet another barrier. Specifically, the vast terrain of southwest Montana reinforces and reproduces the constraints women face in terms of network creation, which further limits their employment opportunities. Whereas I observed, over the course of my fieldwork, a few small networks develop within the Catholic Church, and later among the wives of dairy workers, for the most part migrant women do not have access to strong networks. In urban areas, social networks help migrant women find work and access services and resources essential to their families' well-being (Cerutti and Massey 2001; Hagan 1994; Menjívar 2000). While the social and structural aspects of urban settlements facilitate women's network formation (Hondagneu-Sotelo 1994), the marginalization that characterizes rural settlements like Montana limits it (Dreby and Schmalzbauer 2013). And where women's networks are weak, women tend to increase their dependence on men, undermining their position in the household (Parrado and Flippen 2005). Gender relations within migrant households in Montana bear this out. Most women feel they have become more dependent on their male partners since moving to this rural state and less connected to other women.

Geographer Doreen Massey (1993) theorizes that places are gendered, and that gender is shaped through local economies as well as through the organization of public space. And so it is in southwest Montana. Here migrant men's lives are centered on wage work that takes them out of the house, onto the roads and into the community. Most women's lives, on the other hand, are characterized by an isolated, resource-strapped version of what Hays (1996) terms *intensive mothering*.

On the Homefront

Although most Mexican women in Montana are excluded from wage labor, it is their responsibility to care for their families with limited resources. They embrace what I term *survival femininity*, a version of femininity centered on family survival in which women's work is focused in the home. They cook, feed, nurture, clean, do laundry and tend to family members when they are ill. They tell me that their husbands rarely help with these domestic chores. Many assert that because their husbands work so many hours on their jobs,[7] they would not think of asking them for help in the home or with the children. Most women speak of their domestic responsibilities with a placid acceptance, and they celebrate their prominent place in their children's lives. Yet several women also admit that being alone with their children day after day is stressful.

Migrant women I met in Montana present themselves not as victims of gender inequality but as women who are doing what they have to do for the well-being of their families. Sacrifice is a central part of their survival femininity (see also Dreby 2010). And yet family carework is extraordinarily challenging for them, which makes their strength and resourcefulness all the more notable. Unlike in other migrant destinations, in Montana women confront long distances between their homes and the town centers where services are located, a generally weak social service base and social and geographic marginalization.

Hirsch (2003) finds that in Atlanta having a driver's license is "a hallmark of independence among migrant women" (33). In many ways, the same is true in Montana. Although migrant men and women report that driving in Montana is treacherous and frightening, being able to drive means being able to manage daily life alone. And yet, very few migrant women in Montana possess this privilege. Alternative transportation options are limited. While Bozeman has a free public bus, most migrants cannot access it because they live outside of town. Although women are excluded from driving and public transportation, they have domestic responsibilities that often demand they find a way of getting to their children's schools, the health clinic or the grocery store. Most often they must rely on their husbands. Thus their carework mandates dependence.

In November 2007, before Roberta and Ernesto were joined in their home by Juan Carlos and Julisa, Roberta called me to ask for transportation help. Her young son was experiencing a reoccurrence of an intestinal infection and she wanted to take him to the hospital. Ernesto was at work, unreachable by phone, and Roberta did not know what to do. She was afraid to call an ambulance because she does not speak English and she was worried they would ask to see her papers. She called me because at the time I was one of only two people she knew, aside from her husband, who spoke Spanish and had a car. I brought Roberta and her three children to the hospital.[8] While Roberta was bold and resourceful in calling me, whom she did not know well at the time, she was rendered dependent.

Whereas Montana's economy and rurality are at the crux of rigid divisions of family labor, cultural ideologies of masculinity and femininity, which are formed via a dynamic interaction with social structure, further entrench them. The context in which migrants came of age is a central component of their gender formation. The *habitus* (Bourdieu 1984)—the context, norms and practices that feel most comfortable and familiar to them—of migrants from rural Mexico continues to shape their gender performativity and expectations in the United States (Falicou 2002).[9] In general, research has found that the fewer opportunities women have for wage work in Mexico, the greater their subordination (Aysa and Massey 2004; Gonzalez-López 2005). Although there are exceptions (see Mummert 1994), opportunities for women in Mexico are most limited in rural areas, where the majority of my participants originate (Aysa and Massey 2004). Accordingly, cultural expressions of rural patriarchies tend to be more "hard core" than urban patriarchies, where women have more opportunities to challenge gender inequality (Gonzalez-López 2005). Similarly, where women have fewer opportunities, femininity tends to be constructed around stricter moral regulation, strengthening patriarchy's hold (Dreby 2010; Gonzalez-López 2005). The similar economic and geographic contexts of central Mexico and southwest Montana nurture the replication of migrants' gender habitus transnationally.

In the area of rural Jalisco that Roberta and Ernesto call home, the only income-earning activities available are in agriculture, a sector traditionally gendered as male. Women there, as is true in much of rural Mexico (see Dreby 2010), are expected to play the role of devout wife and mother, caring and sacrificing for their families while submitting to their husbands. This patriarchal expression resonates in many rural outposts of the United States, including places in Montana, where women's domesticity is held in high esteem. In U.S. agricultural families too, men have historically been charged with providing for their families while women have been charged with managing the homefront. Even today, with the decline in the number and productivity of U.S. family farms and families' consequent growing dependence on female wages, long-standing gender divisions of household labor remain firmly rooted (Tickamyer and Henderson 2003).

For Mexican migrant families in Montana, employment opportunities and cultural expectations map onto each other. Roberta and Ernesto are illustrative. Relatively high wage agricultural work pulled them to Montana, which in turn reproduced a rigid gender division of labor within their family *and* reinforced the constructions of rural Mexican femininity and masculinity with which they had come of age. Even though Roberta now works outside of the home, Ernesto's job pays more and is valued more, and the home is Roberta's domain. To them, the way they divide their labor makes pragmatic and cultural sense. Their story is common.

Martín and Lia are originally from rural Guerrero on Mexico's central Pacific Coast. While in Mexico, Lia managed their humble home, which they shared with Martín's sister. She made tortillas, washed and mended clothes, cooked, cleaned and did all the other tasks necessary to care for her family. Lia knew no women who worked outside of the home. She analyzed this to be a function of "traditional Mexican values," while also noting that there were no jobs available for women. Lia's aspirations are shaped by her values as well as the limited opportunities that have contextualized her life. She asserts that her destiny in life is to be a good wife and mother and to provide a refuge for Martín and their children.

Martín and Lia spent their first few years in the United States in southern Utah. Martín worked in construction. Lia stayed home, taking care of their first child, who was born soon after their arrival. Lia was pregnant with her second child when they left Utah for Montana. As was the case in Guerrero and Utah, in Montana Martín went to work and Lia stayed home. Their decision about how to divide their family labor continued to be in part a practical one; Martín can command a much higher wage than can Lia. But more important, they tell me, theirs is a values-based decision. They both believe that a woman's place is at home with her children. Martín told me:

> Well, I work a lot, and the truth is that I don't want her [Lia] to work, because particularly I do not want another person to watch my children . . . . When someone else watches your children . . . they don't care for your children like the mother does . . . . When I am at work I want to know that my children are in their mother's hands.

Lia supports Martín's sentiments. She has never had a job outside of the home and she never wants to have one. A devout Mormon, having converted while living in Utah, she believes now more strongly than ever that motherhood is her calling.

Pedro and Angela too claim a values-based division of family labor that they trace to Pedro's upbringing in Aguas Calientes and hers in Jalisco. They both consider that having Angela at home with their children is worth sacrificing whatever additional income she could bring in. Pedro is not shy about touting his beliefs: "Maybe I'm wrong, but my idea is that it is best for women to stay home. It doesn't matter if the child is very small or if they have 12, 13, 15 or 18 years. Always, I think it is best that she is with them." Pedro believes it is Angela's responsibility as a mother to pass down religion and culture to their children. "Mothers have the important job of teaching their children values. No one else can do this like the mother. So for us we follow the tradition that the mother should be at home." Pedro believes that his beliefs are representative of most Mexicans, who always "care most about the family." It is in the family's best interest, according to Pedro, that "men work to help the family get ahead and women stay home teaching the children the importance of family" and taking care of their needs.

I found staunch differences in gender attitudes and practices between migrants in my sample who are from rural and urban Mexico. Evelín, for example, grew up in Mexico City, in what she describes as a working-class family. She started working at a young age while focusing intensely on her studies. With help from a scholarship, she worked her way through university beginning in Mexico City and finishing in Ciudad Juarez. Along the way she developed strong career ambitions and began working as an accountant. Through her job she met a white, native-born Montanan named Mark who was studying across the border in El Paso. They eventually married, she received her U.S. residency and they moved to Montana where they now operate a thriving restaurant.

Evelín never wanted children because she felt that they would hinder her independence. She also wanted a marriage based on equality and respect. She made her desires known early in her relationship with Mark, and he agreed. Both Evelín and Mark work long hours outside of the home, and they share chores within the home. As a childless, middle-aged business woman with a progressive husband, Evelín feels little connection to the majority of Mexican women in Montana, even though they share a similar class and ethnic background: "We are so different that we don't have anything to talk about."

Gaby and Lourdes also hail from urban Mexico, Gaby from Monterrey and Lourdes from Mexico City. While they are similar to their migrant peers in some ways—namely, in their devotion to the Catholic Church and their outward expressions of femininity—in other ways they break the gender mold. Perhaps most notably, they are the only single mothers in my study. Their femininity, while encompassing motherhood, does not encompass marriage, and as such they both have had to find ways to be financially independent. Both Gaby and Lourdes long to find male partners, but they are also not ashamed or afraid to be on their own. They view marriage as a choice, not a moral or economic necessity. Lourdes made clear in our interview that she will settle for nothing less than a good man "who is responsible." Before coming to the United States she was partnered with a man who was verbally abusive and ambivalent about his children. She left him and crossed the border with her children to escape the dysfunction of their lives. She swears she will never go back to an abusive man and that while it is not her ideal, she is all right if she remains alone.

Finally, social position, as it intersects with place, plays a critical role in shaping gender norms and expectations within migrant families. Rigid gender divisions of family labor and gender expectations present special challenges to young Mexican women who have been educated in the United States, and whose social positions are shifting. I interviewed four young adult women, Vera, Sandra, Juliana and Olga, who came of age in the United States, living at least part of their youth in Montana. Over the course of my fieldwork they all graduated from the local university, the first in their families to do so, and Vera and Juliana went on to graduate school. All four told me that since they were children their mothers stressed the importance of education and embracing life's opportunities. At the same time, their mothers touted the value of marriage, motherhood and domesticity. While they appreciate their mothers' enthusiasm for education, and while all espouse tremendous respect for their parents, they do not want to emulate their lives. And yet they feel conflicted about the "modern" values they have come to embrace through their educations.

Vera remembers her mom working at home, always at home. She also re-members that her mother had different expectations for her than she had for her brothers. When Vera told her mother that she wanted to go to college in a neighboring state, as her older brother had done, and not attend the small state satellite campus near their home, her mother was adamantly opposed. "You can't do that [go to school away from home], she told me. You are a girl." Vera went anyway, eventually gaining her mother's support, but it was a rough path toward acceptance. Now done with college and graduate school, and recently married, Vera works hard to selectively retain the domestic skills and cultural values she learned from her mother. She makes tamales, is a devout Catholic, and maintains close ties to her family. Yet she has career ambitions and a marriage based on equality and shared domestic duties.

Sandra was born in Mexico, spent her early childhood in California, and has since lived in Montana. When I interviewed her she was finishing her second degree at the state university. Sandra, who identifies as a feminist, finds it a constant struggle to resist her family's expectations of domesticity while maintaining strong ties to them and to Mexican culture. Her words summarize the gendered challenges that persist within migrant families across the generations:

> We are trying to step into something new . . . like our parents migrated from Mexico, to a different culture, and we are trying to an extent keep our culture, but better ourselves, when it comes to education. And people don't understand that so it's kinda hard . . . because more or less, we are trying to make a choice, do we wanna keep this chain going or do we wanna break the chain because . . . like, I said, in our culture, men are dominant, and there is a lot of machismo. I guess they just don't want to take the time to show their wives how to be independent. Because independence is not something positive in the family, because independence means not being at home, not cooking, not taking care of the kids.

The gender-based generational tensions with which these young women struggle are triggered in large part by their own upward social mobility. They have been exposed to more opportunities than their mothers, most notably formal education. While mothers support their daughters and encourage them to be ambitious, their daughters' social climb has also been unsettling for them. It is likely that gender and generational tension are not the product of culture solely, but of the divergent social and economic opportunities available to mothers and their daughters.

When Home Is a Prison

Many women I interviewed celebrate their domesticity, highlighting the privilege of living in a safe place where they can care well for their families. Yet although many migrant men and women espouse the belief that a woman's place is in the home, home is not always a woman's refuge. Throughout my interviews and field notes I have "home" coded both as "refuge" and as "prison." Indeed, intersections of social position and context shape the way migrant women experience home (Silvey 2006). For some women, home, especially when one does not have an easy option of leaving it, can be a place of loneliness and boredom, which can culminate in stress and anxiety.

Susana, who was two months pregnant when I interviewed her, described her life at home as one of confinement. "I think that there is a lot of stress that comes with so much time closed in at home. I almost never leave. And as a result I often feel really bad, depressed." Many women uttered similar sentiments. Agosta, for example, told me, "For us, home is like a jail." Even though she has legal residence, she has no social support system and no job. She leaves home twice a week to volunteer at the food bank, but other than that she stays put. Even women who said they themselves did not feel cut off and alone could detail the situation of a woman they knew who did. For example, Ernestina told me she knows many women who are beaten down by the seclusion of daily life:

> Women here are very isolated. For one thing they don't work. And they don't speak English and they don't drive. There is no transportation if they wanted to leave and they are afraid to get in a car anyway. So this means they stay very isolated.

Rosalia, Miguel and their children have been in Bozeman for more than ten years. They live in an immaculate home in a development that was built in the 1990s on former ranch land outside of Bozeman. They are proud to be one of the first Mexican construction families in southwest Montana. In many respects, their immigration story encapsulates the American Dream. Miguel crossed the border in 1985 without authorization. After working for several years first in agriculture and later in construction, and crossing the border every few months to see Rosalia, he received his U.S. residency. For the next ten years he continued to migrate between California and Mexico. During this time he and Rosalia had two children who remained with Rosalia in Mexico. Miguel continued to work in the United States while going through the long process of securing visas for Rosalia and their children. When the paperwork was finally complete he brought his family to the United States. By that time Miguel had moved from California to Colorado, and finally to Montana to become a partner in a budding masonry company. The timing of his last move was perfect, as his masonry company was able to take full advantage of the development boom that swept across Montana in the 1990s. By the time Rosalia and his children joined him, he owned a new home.

Whereas Miguel is the family's main bread winner, he has always supported Rosalia's desire to work outside the home. When Rosalia and her children migrated from Aguas Calientes to Montana, Rosalia spoke not a word of English and knew no one. Despite having U.S. residency, owning a house and having a supportive husband, she struggled to find meaningful work that would ease her isolation. She finally found a part-time job cleaning the homes of two families that Miguel had met through his masonry work. Rosalia has been cleaning the same houses for several years, yet she still feels isolated. She spends the majority of her time at home, alone. When I interviewed Rosalia and Miguel in 2008, Miguel told me that he worries about Rosalia and about other Mexican women who are in the same situation:

> For women it is very difficult because she is always in the house, which
> is like being in prison, no? There is nothing for them. They don't have
> anywhere to go .... For us, for men, we leave to go to work, so there is no
> problem. But for women, no. They are imprisoned, and they don't know
> anyone.

Rosalia nodded in agreement, adding that because of the isolation "depression happens to many women." No matter the support she receives from Miguel, and despite her legal residence, the structural context of her life limits Rosalia's autonomy and is detrimental to her emotional well-being.

Sara and her husband, Reinaldo, are from rural Zacatecas. Like Rosalia, Sara is unusual among migrant women in my sample in that she is a U.S. resident and she and Reinaldo own a house. Yet when I first met Sara she was among the most socially marginalized of all the women in this book. Although she has a driver's license, for years Reinaldo forbade her to drive. He also forbade her to work. So Sara stayed home, leaving only to go to

Mass or to Wal-Mart. Sara's relationship with Reinaldo, what Joanna Dreby and I (2013) term her *relational context*, was characterized by inequality and oppression. As Hirsch (2003) concurs, marriage and husbands' expectations are important factors shaping women's autonomy. In Sara's case, the inequality in her marriage, centered on Reinaldo's expectation that she remain in a strictly domestic role, for a long time overpowered her legal privilege.

Sara, Reinaldo and their youngest son, Brian, live in a working-class development on the outskirts of Bozeman. I have been there several times over the past few years, and it is always immaculate. Typically there is something cooking on the stove and there are fresh indentations on the carpet indicative of a recent vacuuming. In September 2010, as Sara and I sat down for an interview, I asked her how it was that she managed to keep the house so neat. Sara is shy, very shy, and with her head down and a slight giggle, she answered, "Ah . . . I haven't even cleaned yet today, and you think it looks clean?" She then became more serious. "I clean every day while the kids are at school. It's what I do. I have nothing else to do. Reinaldo doesn't want me to work. So, I clean."

By then I knew Sara quite well, but until that moment I had never fully sensed her boredom and stress. Sara and Reinaldo have the most rigidly defined marriage of all the families in my sample. When Sara was a teenage girl, Reinaldo kidnapped her into marriage, a practice that was common in rural central Mexico in the 1960s (ibid.). Sara is not an outwardly strong woman. She is admittedly submissive to Reinaldo, and she offered no resistance when he literally "took" her to be his wife. A strong Catholic, she still believes she did the right thing. Marriage is her cross to bear. I do not know if Sara loves, or even likes, Reinaldo. Still, she puts his needs above her own as well as above those of her children. She would never leave him. She accepts Reinaldo's machismo for what she sees it to be, "part of his Mexican roots." "Well, it's a form of thinking that comes from his ancestors and he does not want to change. He cannot change," she told me.

While at home Sara creates beautiful Mexican culinary dishes and baked goods in her kitchen. On a few occasions I have purchased her cakes, which are ornately decorated and delicious. Sara would like to have a catering business or a restaurant. When she speaks about her dream of being a professional cook she lights up. This is especially noticeable because most of the time Sara's face is pale, painted over with the gray of depression.

"What would happen if you asked Reinaldo if you can work?" I asked Sara during a conversation in 2010. Her response was immediate:

> I could never do that. I have thought many times about this and I have decided that I would rather keep my marriage together. If I tried to work, he would leave. That's it. I will not risk that. My family has to come first.

And so, until very recently, Sara stayed put. She took pills for depression. She continued to dream about getting a job, but she was hesitant to act She went to Mass. She mothered Brian, a delightful young man with good grades and a passion for classical music and American football. And she kept a perfect house, the one area of her life over which she could exert control

Reinaldo is serious, stoic and quiet, yet always publicly pleasant. I would not have sensed his "hard core" (see Gonzalez-López 2005) patriarchal ways if it were not for Sara's powerful testimony and other women's validation of it. Yet when I formally interviewed Reinaldo, his position in the household hierarchy was obvious. While he sat in his recliner, Sara served us bottled water, chocolate and popcorn. Reinaldo never looked her in the eye. Actually, I have seldom seen Reinaldo and Sara talk to each other. During the majority of our interview Reinaldo referred to Sara as *mi señora* (my woman) instead of by name.

And yet I sense that Reinaldo has only his family and Sara's best interests at heart. He makes the household rules, one of which is that Sara must stay at home, because he believes his rules are best for everyone. When I asked him to detail how he and Sara divide their family labor and responsibilities, he told me that she is in charge of the house and he is in charge of providing an income. When I asked him how they decided on this division of labor his response surprised me. He asserted status through Sara's position in the home, proud that they do not have to utilize a "survival mode of parenting" (see Vasquez 2011), in which mothers are not present for their children:

> It is a privilege for the woman to be in the house .... If I was working and she was working, who would the kids find when they returned from school? They would just leave with whoever and do whatever. But we would not know who they left with and what they were doing .... Having the woman in the house is best for everyone .... If not, the children grow up and move in bad circles and they do not respect their parents.

Reinaldo presents Sara's domesticity as a gift he has bestowed on her. Because Sara is at home, Reinaldo is confident that the values he brought from Mexico will be reproduced in the lives of his children. In our interview he did not acknowledge Sara's unhappiness or loneliness, although at one point he said he could imagine that she is at times "bored." I pushed Reinaldo to tell me about his relationship with Sara, but he skirted the topic, bringing the discussion back to the model he feels best for his family—father working and mother at home. And so it is that despite a relationship steeped in inequality, in which Sara openly speaks of her seclusion and depression, this marriage is solid. They may not have found happiness, but they have found a way to survive and they feel righteous in their commitment to each other.

Place-based Meanings of Macho and
Transnational Divisions of Labor

While I found isolation to predominantly be a part of women's experiences in Montana, motherhood to be scripted around care and sacrifice, and fatherhood around provision, there is a significant exception in my data. Fathers on H2A visas, who work in ranching jobs away from their families for eight months of the year, transcend typical gender norms in important ways, exemplifying gender's fluidity. As Gutmann (1996) explains, meanings of macho are formed in specific socioeconomic and historical contexts. In my research I found that temporal and geographic contexts of masculinity and fatherhood also influence the way gender is experienced in daily life.

In 2010, as I followed a few unemployed construction workers onto the ranches and dairies of southwest Montana, I encountered a population that had until that point been hidden from my view. H2A workers have been coming to Montana since the program was expanded in 1986 (Hahamovitch 2003). The H2A program provides guest visas to agricultural workers from other countries to come to the United States seasonally.[10] When their stint ends, they are under legal obligation to return to their home country. The program does not provide for family reunification, and so most H2A workers live a temporary and transnational existence, cycling in and out of their families' lives (see Schmalzbauer forthcoming). As most H2A workers are men, the program encourages a transnational gender division of labor in which productive wage labor is done by men in the United States, while carework to support family well-being is done by women in the home country.

All seventeen of the H2A workers I interviewed reported working ten- to twelve-hour days, six days a week, with a half day's work on Sundays. They seldom call in sick and would report an injury only if it were debilitating. Although ranch work is excruciating, none of the workers complained about it. "The work is not the problem," said Max, who has been coming to Montana from Jalisco on a visa since 1990. "We are used to working hard and here we have machines instead of machetes. What is hard is being away from our families. This is the greatest sacrifice we make. But we do what we have to do."

Men's pain of missing family is made worse by the lonely drudgery of daily life. Ignacio, who has been coming to Montana seasonally from Guanajuato since 1998, told me that he would better be able to cope with his rigorous work and schedule if his family were with him. As it is, he finds it hard not to be "apathetic." He focuses constantly on the countdown clock, indicating when he will finally get to be reunited with his loved ones. "Are you depressed?" I asked. His response was immediate. "No, I have never been depressed. I may be sad, but not depressed . . . . I am consoled knowing that I am here fighting for my family. This lifts me up." For Ignacio as well as for the other H2A workers I interviewed, their own struggles are central to the sacrifices they make for their families. Through sacrifice, they find strength. Yet other workers did admit to depression. Timoteo told me that he feels a heavy weight all the time. "Yes, it's like a depression." Jesús detailed how when he has to say good-bye to his little boy at the end of his stay in Mexico he is overwhelmed with sadness. "I suppose some would call me a coward. There are nights when I cry and cry."

The emotional challenges that H2A fathers endure while away from their families are compounded by the isolating contexts of their lives. Unlike H2A workers in other agricultural states, H2A workers in Montana do not work on corporate farms with many other workers. Instead they tend to work on medium-size family-run operations, a few that employ only one H2A worker. Those who are the only guestworker in an operation, and who therefore work with no other Spanish-speakers, may go weeks without having a face-to-face conversation. Geography further limits sociability. Miles of rugged terrain separate Montana ranches, and because H2A workers have only one day off a month, they have little time or opportunity to commune with other workers. "It's an isolated life," Abel explained solemnly. "Once in a great while we might have a bbq with other workers, but mostly we just work."

Fathers cope by calling home often, focusing their energies on staying involved in their families from afar. Their connection to home more closely resembles the characterization of transnational mothers highlighted in the sociological literature, who call home regularly, than the prototypical trans-national father whose parenting centers on discipline and remittances (Dreby 2010; Parreñas 2001). I found that workers' isolation has bolstered their commitment to family, nurturing their empathy for the struggles of their wives and children whom they leave behind. Although the H2A fathers I met are still motivated by the responsibilities they feel to be good providers they are also in charge of all domestic tasks during their time in the United States, and they exhibit parenting sensibilities that are most commonly associated with femininity. The rural, transnational context of their lives, as it intersects with their employment position, has shaped them as geographically distant and isolated fathers who are emotionally present in their families' lives.

Conclusion

Intersections of gender, place and economy exert a tremendous influence over how migrant men and women experience daily life. The rural context of Montana confirms public space as male and the domestic sphere as female. The transnational context of migrants' lives further nurtures constructions of femininity and masculinity that celebrate women's roles as mothers and caretakers, and men's roles as breadwinners and family heads (Guendelman et al. 2001). In Montana, most migrant women embrace their roles within the household. Their femininity is based first and foremost on family survival. Men too embrace their prescribed gender roles. In Montana their lives are centered, as they always have been, on hard physical labor. Indeed, most migrant men's lives changed little when they moved to Montana.

Migrant women in Montana, like Mexican migrant women everywhere, face barriers to well-being based on their ethnicity/race, class, gender and legal status. But in Montana, there are additional challenges. Here, large geographic expanses and limited employment opportunities combine to isolate women and in many cases imbue their lives with emotional struggle. Furthermore, Mexican women in Montana lack the large, extended kin networks that are such an important part of daily life, and specifically child care, in Mexico and other migrant destinations. They compensate by mothering more intensely, which can further their isolation.

Yet the experiences of guestworker fathers remind us that it is too simplistic to map certain gender experiences onto men and others onto women in an either-or fashion. Guestworker fathers are similar to other fathers in this study in that they work in grueling physical jobs with long hours and are the main breadwinners in their families. Yet aside from their labor and responsibility for provision, the gender lives of H2A workers diverge in important ways from the lives of geographically proximate fathers. Working eight months of the year on remote ranches away from their wives and children and also separated from other Spanish-speaking workers, transnational fathers in Montana struggle with loneliness and isolation in ways similar to migrant women. Also similar to migrant women, H2A fathers find strength through self-sacrifice on behalf of their families, narratives typically constructed around motherhood.

My data also suggests that migrants' relational contexts are critical to understanding the expectations and well-being of migrant men and women. In a rural destination like Montana, in which few opportunities exist for women and geography limits network development and mobility, women's relational contexts take on more importance. The level of gender equality within migrant marriages has a great impact on how women in particular navigate daily life. In households where "hard core" (Gonzalez-López 2005) patriarchy reigns, women, even those like Sara who have residency, are more likely to be isolated and to lack autonomy.

No matter the level of inequality in migrant households, I find that ultimately family solidarity supersedes gender divisions. Even though Sara is depressed because Reinaldo forbids her to work, she swears allegiance to him. In part because of the challenges of living in a new rural destination, family members look to each other, because they have few others in their lives on whom they can rely. For migrant men and women, family solidarity is a means of coping with persistent marginalization and vulnerability. One of the greatest indicators of vulnerability is illegality. In the next chapter I explore how intersections of illegality, gender and rurality impact migrant life.

Chapter 3

Illegality, Rurality and Daily Life

Gaby's voice was shaking as she told me that both of her teenage sons, Bruno and Mateo, had been arrested at work. I tried to calm her as she frantically relayed the story. She did not know where they had been taken. She did not know how to contact them. Worst of all, she had been told by her sons' boss that Immigration and Customs Enforcement (ICE) now had her home address. As we spoke she was in the process of moving out of her trailer. Her friend Dorotea had offered to shelter her and her young son, Raul, for a while. "Leah, I am scared. What if they find me? What will happen to Raul?"

Every migrant I met in my fieldwork fears arrest more than just about anything. Gaby's fear and desperation were obvious. Gaby's son Raul is almost the same age as my son, Micah. When they were both babies Gaby and I had conversations about the intensity of motherhood and the emotional vulnerability that accompanies it. I often reflect on how much more vulnerable motherhood makes Gaby than it makes me. Gaby's vulnerability is not rooted in emotional fragility or insecurity. She is neither. She is more vulnerable simply because of her position in the world: an unauthorized migrant, who is poor and single, and who lives in a place with weak networks and few social supports.

I had gotten to know Gaby well in the three years leading up to her sons' deportations, baby-sitting Raul on Saturday mornings when she had to work, and engaging in long chats with her at her home when I went there to buy the tamales that she sells informally to boost her income. I often heard her bemoan how difficult it is to be a single mother and how she wants to find a good man to join her in raising Raul.

I understood and continue to understand Gaby's yearning for a partner. She is one of only two single migrant mothers I know in Montana. She is also one of the few migrant women I have met in Montana who have consistently worked outside of the home. Gaby is a clear exception to the migrant demographics of the region. Whereas many unauthorized women in Montana try to stay out of the public eye, Gaby has had no choice but to traverse public spaces daily. She must drive, even though she does not have a license, and she must go to work, take Raul to school, and do the myriad of other tasks involved in family survival. Gender, geography and illegality color her every move. Having a husband, ideally a U.S. citizen, would make life so much easier, it would seem. I have gleaned from my research that the context of southwest Montana is most conducive to living in nuclear, heterosexual migrant families with traditional gender divisions of labor.

I met Gaby's boyfriend, Rob, a white, native-born American, on a Saturday morning in 2009 when I went to her trailer to pick up Raul. It was 9:00 a.m. and Gaby had been at work since 5:30. The trailer was a mess. A television blared in the background. Rob, who was barefoot and disheveled in ripped jeans and a dirty t-shirt, did not look me in the eyes when he answered the door. He proceeded to hand over Raul without a smile or an attempt at conversation. Raul remained stone-faced. I could tell that his diaper was full. Gaby had told me that Rob does not speak Spanish. At the time, Raul understood no English. I sensed the situation was tenuous and I found Rob to be conspicuously creepy. Yet when I subtly inquired to Gaby about their relationship later that afternoon she assured me that it was fine, that Rob was "a good man." A few months later they separated. As an explanation, Gaby told me that while Rob was good at his core, he had a bad temper. She did not go into details, and I did not pry.

About a month after her sons' deportation Gaby called to see if I would accompany her to the local high school. She was trying to enroll Bruno and Mateo in school in her home city of Monterrey where they were both now living, and she needed their U.S. transcripts to do so. She asked if I would help her translate her request to the guidance counselor. Bruno's and Mateo's deportations had been traumatic, but they were starting to feel more settled in Mexico. They had no plans of attempting a return to the United States, knowing how difficult and dangerous an unauthorized border crossing would be. I could sense that Gaby was both relieved about their decision to stay put and sad that her separation from her eldest sons would be indefinite.

As we walked under the hot mountain sun, she told me that despite the horror that had befallen her family, her luck seemed to be turning around. Rob had called two weeks earlier and told her that he missed her. "It was like fate, because Dorotea had just told me that I couldn't stay with her much

longer . . . . So Rob and I are together again, and this time we are going to get
married. Raul will have a dad, finally." I did not try to conceal my concern.
"What about his temper? Are you sure this is a good thing?" I could tell by
her face that despite her words she shared my unease. "I know. But you have
to trust me. I need to find a more secure situation. Rob could be my answer.
Really, we'll be ok."

They were not ok. Two months later Gaby called again in tears. "It's awful.
I think that Rob is doing things to Raul. I can't even talk about it . . . . It's
really bad. We're leaving tomorrow morning. I am going back to Dorotea's
for now . . . . I'm scared for Raul. I don't know if he's going to get over this."
Ironically, Gaby wanted to stay in Montana because she believed it to be
a safe and beautiful place to raise Raul. The ugliness and insecurity of her
situation painted a striking contrast to Montana's idyll.

Gaby's experience of illegality has been shaped by multiple factors, both
social and place-based. She is poor, single, unauthorized and brown-skinned.
She is the mother of two unauthorized young adult children, now deported,
and a young U.S. citizen child. These factors are critical indicators of the
opportunities, responsibilities and expectations that characterize her life. Yet
they are not the only influential factors. The geographic context of her life
also matters. Gaby lives in a rural area with a predominantly white population, a relatively weak social service base, few Spanish speakers and even
fewer trained translators, limited public transportation and long distances
between the places where she can afford to live and the places where she
works, shops for groceries and attends to her family's basic needs. This context bears heavily on how Gaby experiences daily life. The entanglement of
Gaby's social position *and* the geographic characteristics of southwest Montana make her uniquely vulnerable.[1] Indeed the intersection of Gaby's social
and geographic positions has intensified her illegality, and it has brought
violence, both physical and emotional, into the most intimate and mundane
areas of her life.

Illegality in Context

Changes in U.S. immigration policies over the past two decades have
made life for migrants, especially those who are unauthorized, more difficult.
While historically immigration control was focused on the physical border
between the United States and Mexico, in the past ten years enforcement has
expanded into the U.S. interior. Local police departments and Immigration
and Customs Enforcement increasingly collaborate, focusing on worksite

deportations and deportations based on minor criminal infractions (Go-lash-Boza 2012). Kanstroom (2007) suggests that two 1996 laws, the Antiter-rorism and Effective Death Penalty Act, and the Illegal Immigration Reform and Migrant Responsibility Act, laid the groundwork for a post–September 11 "extended border enforcement regime." Immigration policy in turn has come to serve as a tool of social control, regulating the lives of certain groups in the name of "homeland security." The expansion of immigration control has turned the United States into what Kanstroom terms a "Deportation Nation."

Between 2009 and 2012, a record high of 1.06 million migrants were deported, 400,000 each year. This is more than twice the 189,000 who were deported in 2001 (U.S. Department of Homeland Security 2011; 2010). In the first six months of 2011, the Department of Homeland Security de-ported more than 46,000 parents of U.S. citizen children (Wessler 2011). To be sure, Gaby's fear of being forcefully separated from Raul is not unfounded. It should be no surprise that feeling the constant "threat of deportability" (De Genova and Peutz 2010; De Genova 2005) has come to characterize the migrant experience for many in the United States (Dreby 2012; Gon-zalez 2011; Menjívar and Abrego 2012). According to a 2010 Pew Research Center report, more than 50 percent of migrants surveyed feared their own deportation or a deportation of a loved one. While fear of deportation most directly impacts migrants who are unauthorized, it also impacts migrants or the children of migrants who have legal authorization to be in the United States, especially those who fear separation from unauthorized family and kin (Dreby 2012; Gonzalez and Chavez 2012; Menjívar and Abrego 2012).

Physical deportations have increased alongside a swell of denigrating so-cial constructions of migrant illegality. The association between immigration and criminality that is presented in policy and media discourses has fueled the convergence of immigration and dangerous deviance in the public imag-ination (Chavez 2008; De Genova 2005). Consequently, antimigrant senti-ment, and in extreme cases vigilantism (Kil, Menjívar and Doty 2009), has intensified in both traditional and new migrant destinations throughout the United States.[2]

Fear and anxiety, coupled with the actual exploitation and oppression that current immigration policies foster are not benign. On the contrary, they can do grave harm to the physical and psychological well-being of migrants and their families. Menjívar and Abrego (2012) maintain that the damag-ing manifestations of the current immigration climate in the United States amounts to *legal violence,* the social and structural violence that emanates from living with a tenuous legal status. Legal violence includes the overt physical harm that can come to migrants as they attempt to cross a highly militarized border (Abrego 2014; Boehm 2012), and the bodily injuries that have been reported in the places where unauthorized migrants work (Striffler 2007). But more important, legal violence encompasses the psychological and emotional damage that is rampant among those trying to survive in what Menjívar (2011) terms *geographies of marginalization*.

For unauthorized migrants, legal violence involves enduring the constant fear or actual realization of deportation and of being separated from loved ones. It includes the unrelenting anxiety that results from not being able to provide for your family because of insecure employment and low wages, and consequently never knowing what your future holds. Legal violence has been normalized in the institutions, attitudes and actions that structure everyday life. As such it is violence that is typically not analyzed critically. Its insidious normalization means that even those who endure it often do not question its presence (ibid.).

Intersections of race, class and gender influence how migrants experience illegality and their relationship to legal violence. In the United States, migrants who are poor and unauthorized are disproportionately vulnerable to abuse and exploitation (Salcido and Adelman 2004). Gender compounds this vulnerability. Many migrant women bear the physical and emotional scars of sexual violence that they endured while crossing the U.S.-Mexican border (Abrego 2014; Boehm 2012). In the United States, migrant women often occupy jobs with the lowest pay, and find themselves at an increased risk of physical violence in the public sphere (Abrego 2014). Home is not always a refuge. Unauthorized women, especially those in mixed status partnerships in which power is implicitly skewed, find themselves at a heightened danger of domestic violence because their migration status discourages them from reporting it or seeking support services (Boehm 2012; Menjívar and Salcido 2002; Salcido and Adelman 2004; Villalón 2010).

Whereas the threat of deportability is a common burden borne by migrants, it perhaps weighs heaviest for unauthorized mothers who care for their children in a context of physical and economic insecurity, and who fear mother-child separation (Abrego and Menjívar 2011; Golash-Boza 2012). While unauthorized men are more likely to be deported than unauthorized women (Golash-Boza and Hondagneu-Sotelo 2013), it is women who must hold things together when the men go (Dreby and Schmalzbauer 2013; Dreby 2012). This is an especially daunting task in places with limited economic opportunities and social supports.

The ways in which migrants experience illegality are also place-specific (Nelson and Hiemstra 2008). Local geography, economy, demographics and political climate combine to impact migrant life. In Montana, the threat of deportability has roots in all of these factors. In the fall of 2012, Montana residents voted overwhelmingly in support of LR121, a bill that would eliminate social services for migrants.[3] Hostile letters to the editors in Montana's newspapers symbolize the passionate antimigrant sentiment that is brewing in many communities. This social-political context is critical to migrants' experience of illegality. Southwest Montana's social and geographic contexts also matter. The threat of deportability has roots in the institutions and landscapes that migrants must navigate to accomplish quotidian tasks. In Montana, limited or no translation services in public schools, hospitals, jails and social service agencies, racial profiling by police, the *impossibility of anonymity* in one of the "whitest" states in the country (U.S. Census 2010) and icy, mountainous terrain that is difficult to traverse all contribute to the construction of migrant illegality. It is here, in the mundane, place-based experiences of gendered illegality, that I focus the rest of this chapter.

Fear and Daily Life

> Here one can leave their windows and doors open, and their houses open, and nothing will happen. There is not the crime and insecurity that there is in other places. This is what I like most about Montana. But what we fear are the police. They are very bad here and much worse with the Hispanics."
> (Jaime)

Aside from work and wages, migrants tell me that what they appreciate most about Montana is its low level of crime and general sense of tranquillity. For the vast majority who have lived in other places, most notably Los Angeles, California's Central Valley, Colorado and the urban Midwest, Montana feels very safe. As exemplified in Jaime's quotation above, and as I detail at length in Chapter 4, migrants commonly paint the idyll of their safe rural community throughout their complex narratives of migrant life. Yet often accompanying their idyllic narratives is a story portraying the other, not so idyllic parts of migrant life. For Jaime, for example, security from crime coexists with his fear of the police. Reports of overt racism, discrimination and profiling abound in my interviews. Montana is a place where migrants regrettably find that it is impossible to be anonymous,[4] where it is easy to be targeted, and where it can be uncomfortable just going about life's most basic activities.

"It's not like in California," Jose told me, when comparing his life there with his life in Montana. "There no one notices you on the streets. But here people notice you everywhere." This sentiment resonated in many of my interviews, as migrants described the stares and glares that they commonly receive at the grocery story, the gas station, picking their children up from school or simply walking down the street. The stares intensify when they speak Spanish. "One time I just couldn't take it anymore," said Juliana, a university student who is fluent in English and Spanish. "We were at a basketball game and I finally turned around and said to the boy who was staring, 'Haven't you ever heard another language before!?' He just looked away."

The impossibility of anonymity is most obtrusive on the roads of rural Montana, where there is little traffic and the police can easily spot a car or truck whose inhabitants do not fit the typical Montanan ethnic profile. Of all the fears and anxieties that surfaced in my field research, fear of driving and, more specifically, the dread of being pulled over by the police while driving, emerged with the most prominence. Montana is large and sprawling. For the majority of people who live here, managing daily life mandates driving relatively long distances. For many migrants, especially men, getting into a pickup truck is at the center of one's daily routine.

There are several place-specific factors that intensify the vulnerability that migrants feel on the roads. The first is that in order to get a driver's license in Montana one must show proof of legal residence. As such, the only unauthorized migrants who have licenses are those who came to Montana from other states with more liberal licensing laws. The vast majority of migrants I met in my fieldwork drive without licenses. For most migrant men a license is a formality, albeit a critical one. They have been driving for as long as they can remember, having been taught on the roads of rural Mexico as young boys. As such, they are capable and confident behind the wheel. But the story is starkly different for Mexican women, most of whom never learned how to drive. Not only do most women not have licenses, they could not pass a driving test if they had the opportunity. And yet, at some point a situation arises that mandates driving.

Ana laughed as she described how her husband, Rogelio, taught her to drive on the back roads of the ranch where they live. Learning how to drive was part of their safety plan. If something were ever to happen to Rogelio, Ana would have to know how to drive. Rogelio had sharp instincts. A few months after Ana first took the wheel, Rogelio was deported, the result of a traffic stop.

At the time of Rogelio's deportation, Ana and three of her children lived in a trailer far from town. After Rogelio was gone, Ana had to drive to the grocery store and into town to a house cleaning job she had managed to secure to make up for Rogelio's lost income. Her blood pressure rose every time she opened the car door. "I make sure to drive slowly, but not too slowly," Ana told me, "and I obey every rule." Of course, part of the challenge Ana faces is that she, like many, does not know the rules specific to Montana. A driving manual that lays them out does not exist in Spanish. Of course, even if it did, it would do Ana little good, as she does not know how to read. The intersection of Ana's social and geographic locations intensifies her vulnerability at the wheel.

Even though the migrant community in Montana is dispersed, rumors and gossip travel quickly through key transmittal points where migrants congregate—Wal-Mart, the food bank, and the monthly Spanish Mass. Rumors about racial profiling by the police are rampant. Common too are rumors that the police work closely with ICE.[5] In an interview that took place in 2008 while several states were in the midst of heated debate over antimigrant legislation, Esteban informed me that "what's happened is that there is now a law in the United States that the police have to help Immigration, so now the police can stop whatever Latino they think is illegal." Although this was *not* the case in Montana, media coverage of state-level anti-immigration movements, which was then distorted through the local rumor mill, ignited the belief among many migrants that the police could legally target them. I heard this misinformation repeatedly throughout my fieldwork that summer. And yet my data from Montana and evidence from other migrant destinations (see Rios 2011) suggest that police profiling is common. Thus rumors about immigration enforcement often serve as valid warnings.

The circulation of stories about deportations and traffic stops heighten the anxiety migrants feel about driving. Several migrants whom I interviewed recalled the same story of an unjust traffic stop that they had heard through the rumor mill. The story goes like this: Cecilia's son, a U.S. citizen teenager, was stopped by the police in the Wal-Mart parking lot, seemingly for no reason. The police did not give him a ticket, they just asked for his papers. Defiantly he told them that he was a U.S. citizen and that he would not show them his papers because as police they had no jurisdiction over immigration. According to the story, the police proceeded to call ICE, who arrived in minutes. Eventually, after verbally harassing him, the joint team of police and ICE let him go without an apology. Participants told me this story to make the critical point that in Montana it does not matter what your legal status is or what the "real" law says. If you appear Mexican, the police will target you, and if they do target you and you do not have papers, you will be deported because ICE and the police are working hand in hand.

Jaime was awaiting his voluntary departure when I interviewed him in 2008.[6] He was one of five male construction workers who were stopped by the police on the way back from a job in the Paradise Valley. I am still struck by the irony that Jaime's deportation journey began in a place called Paradise. "When they see anyone brown, anyone hispano, they stop them," he told me shaking his head with a slight smile, as if he still could not believe his misfortune and what the police were able to get away with:

> The thing is that when police stop you in Colorado or in Chicago, they never ask for your papers. They just give you a ticket or a warning and that's it. They never ask you if you're legal or illegal. But here they don't even bother with the ticket. They just want to know if you're legal. This just isn't right. Here if the police stop you, you are going to be deported.

Jose, who moved to Montana from California, similarly pointed out the discrepancy between police stops in Montana and other places:

> It's more difficult here because all of the police want to investigate you. In Los Angeles if they stop you and you don't have a license or you don't have insurance, they say ok, I have to tow your car and you have to walk home, because you are not supposed to be driving. Then in 30 days you get your car. But nothing else happens. But here, they arrest you because you don't have papers. This is the problem.

Most migrants I met agreed with Jaime's and Jose's assessments that the police are out to get them. As a result they told me that they would never ask the police for help even if they had been victimized by a crime or felt that they were in danger. In our first formal interview, long before her sons were deported, Gaby aptly analyzed migrants' situation with the police:

> Ok, so it's funny, for example, because the police are supposed to be there to help us, but the same people who are supposed to be there to help us want to deport us. We can only hope that with the grace of God if we run into trouble we will be lucky enough to meet up with one of the good police. But, really, I just try to stay away from them.

While most migrants agree that not all police are bad, and indeed there have been a few good-will gestures that have come from the police and most notably from the local sheriff's department, stories of traffic stops, harassment and deportations outweigh stories of kindness and support. This coincides with Marrow's (2009) findings in rural North Carolina that law enforcement are the least open and forgiving of all the public services dealing with migrants. Instead of making migrants feel safer, law enforcement in Montana heightens fear and anxiety, intensifying migrants' embodiment of the threat of deportability. Because the geographic and demographic contexts of southwest Montana make it more difficult to "blend in" than elsewhere, and because the police in Montana are seemingly less preoccupied with serious crimes than are the police in other places, migrants seem more in danger of profiling and subsequent arrest.

Gendered Burdens and the Threat of Deportability

Gender influences the way migrants experience the threat of deportability, indicating both *where* they feel most under threat and *how* they experience the threat. Specifically, place-based experiences of fear and anxiety are directly connected to women's roles as caretakers and men's roles as financial providers and family protectorates.

MEN GET DEPORTED AND WOMEN PICK UP THE PIECES

Men most fear arrest while they are driving to work, as many have long mountainous commutes between their homes and the exclusive resort developments where they work. Pedro got choked up when he told me, "Every morning when I leave for work, Angela and I say a little prayer together, praying to God that I won't get stopped, and that I will return to her and the kids." Pedro takes pride in being *macho*. His manhood centers on being able to provide for his family. His greatest trepidation is losing this capacity. In his words, "A deportation means you lose everything, and you return to Mexico, with nothing. And your family has nothing and you have to start from zero."

Deportation emasculates men, stripping them of their socially constructed value as husbands and fathers and stigmatizing them (see also Dreby 2012; Golash-Boza 2014). Ernesto, who was commuting several miles to his job on a dairy farm when I first met him, told me, "Yes, there is always fear, because every day you do not know when or if you will come home. The fear is leaving your family, leaving them without income." And Ángel shared:

> I'm always worried that I will have bad luck, leaving my house, going to the store, and running into the immigration patrol. If I have this bad luck, what will I do? What would happen to my kids and my wife? They totally depend on me . . . . To be illegal is to never have security. Nothing is secure.

Men's sense of masculinity is also eroded when they are disrespected by authorities, when they feel as though they have been treated as criminals even when they have done nothing wrong. Jaime's spirit and self-esteem were scarred by his arrest. His descriptive language symbolizes the intimate attack that his arrest launched on his manhood:

> Yes, because they treat you as if you were a delinquent. When they detained me they put me through the process as if I were a criminal and one feels impotent because they have not done anything wrong. It is ridiculous that

they stop us for doing nothing wrong, that we have to go to jail just for going to work. Then they detain us like we are criminals, like those that sell drugs . . . . One feels completely impotent. It's like they take your courage away.

In Montana, where few jobs exist for women, and those that do pay little, most families depend on male income. The commute to work is where men are most aware of this dependence and of how devastating a deportation would be for their families' economic survival. This fear has become normalized, an emotional weight that one carries to and from work every day along with their lunch and masonry equipment. Marco is now a U.S. citizen, but he was unauthorized for his first ten years in the United States and he has known many friends and coworkers who have been deported. He insists that to stay sane you have to try to ignore the fear:

> Every day it is the same, so you have to try to put the fear aside and make a normal life. But still one knows that they can stop you and deport you. So even though you push the fear aside, and sometimes they forget the fear for a while, it comes back.

Pedro's sentiments concur:

> One has to try to live normally despite the insecurity. I'm always afraid of la migra (ICE), but I say to Angela that even with this fear we have to try to be good people to work hard and do things that will help us improve our situation, that will open doors with people in our community, with the church, with work and with our friends.

Pedro told me that he has to stay strong for his family. Angela bowed her head when, a year later in a separate interview, we talked about Pedro's creed. She applauded Pedro for his bravery, then confessed that fear structures her life. Angela is not weak. She crossed the border alone twice, once while pregnant, and endured immigration jail. Yet in Montana, Angela looks to Pedro to provide for and protect her and their children. Her fear emanates from knowing that his ability to guard them from danger is uncertain at best.

As is the case for men, fear and anxiety are at the core of migrant women's daily lives. Like Angela, who prays with Pedro before he leaves for work every morning, women are hyperaware of the danger confronting their husbands and partners during their commutes and in their workplaces. They also know that if their husbands are arrested, they will be the ones left to pick up the pieces. When Nora's husband, Alejandro, was arrested she had to figure out where he was being held,[7] how to raise money for a lawyer, when he would be tried, when he would leave the country and where he would be sent upon deportation. Would they deport him to Ciudad Juarez, or would they transport him all the way to Aguas Calientes? But most important, Nora had to figure out what she and her baby, a U.S. citizen, would do. Should they stay in Montana? What would be best for her baby and family?

Whereas Nora thought that if she stayed in Montana she could find a job in the kitchen of a Mexican restaurant where she had worked previously, she also realized the difficulty of working when she did not have steady daycare options, and she knew she could not earn enough to support them. A return to Mexico had its own challenges. As a citizen her son had access to all the opportunities the United States had to offer. In Mexico it would be difficult for him to learn English, and he would attend schools that are mediocre at best. There were also pragmatic challenges associated with return. She and her son did not have Mexican passports. She was advised by her mother that she should go to a Mexican consulate to obtain them. Yet there is no consulate in Montana. To get her papers to leave the country and enter Mexico, she would have to travel to Boise or Seattle, an eight- to twelve-hour trip that was daunting considering the circumstances.

Nora's challenges were intensified by the language barriers that exist between families undergoing deportation proceedings in Montana and the legal options available to support them. In 2007 when Alejandro was arrested, there were only two full-time practicing immigration lawyers in Montana. Although both were passionately committed to advocating for the new migrant community, neither spoke Spanish proficiently and neither was located nearby. Utilizing their services entailed finding a translator and driving to the state capital, Helena, an hour and a half away. That hour-and-a-half drive was a terrifying prospect for Nora at the time, foremost because she did not have a driver's license. Ultimately Nora was able to get passports when the Boise Mexican consulate visited Bozeman, and she returned to Mexico to join Alejandro. The process was traumatic and the family was separated for several months.

When Rogelio was deported, Ana went through a similar struggle. Although she knew she wanted to stay in the United States, she worried about how it would be possible. Three of her four children are U.S. citizens, and although her only son was born in Mexico she held out hope that he would be able to regularize his status at some point through his citizen sisters. Her oldest daughter, Elena, was at the time a straight-A high school student with high hopes of attending university. I first interviewed Ana soon after Rogelio's arrest. Ana was clearly distraught. "I want to stay and we know that Rogelio will try to return, but I don't know how we will manage. Maybe I will have to go. How am I going to pay the rent? How am I going to maintain my children?" Ana was emotional throughout the interview as she detailed her persistent struggles with depression and anxiety.

Ana did not like to leave her isolated trailer. Yet because of Rogelio's deportation she had no choice but to do so. Her family's survival literally depended on it, as Elena, her oldest daughter, still had not obtained her driver's license. Leaving home made Ana anxious. So did other things. Ana worried about paying the bills. She worried about Rogelio's safety in Mexico and how he would manage to cross the border again. They did not have money to pay a *coyote* (smuggler), and Ana was well aware of the lawlessness and danger Rogelio would most certainly meet in the desert crossing. And she was exhausted by the difficult emotional labor she had to undertake to make her children feel safe: to assure them, especially the youngest, who was two at the time, that everything would be all right, that their dad would return and things would go back to "normal." "Where is Papi?" her youngest daughter would ask. "It's toughest for her, because they have a special bond. He has a special love for his little girl. She doesn't understand why he didn't come home."

Enduring the mental anguish of a deportation and family rupture is to suffer a form of legal violence. In this difficult context, women's responsibility as caretakers mandates that they hold the family together as best they can. Women must do the physical, emotional and wage labor necessary to ensure family survival, an extraordinarily exhausting and exigent feat. It is no surprise that women's own mental health and well-being, as signified by Ana's anxiety and depression, suffer as a result.

Whereas the lingering fear of having to maintain one's family in the aftermath of a husband's deportation is distressing,[8] the dread that bores most deeply into the psyches of migrant women in Montana is the fear of their own deportation and their unthinkable separation from their children. Deportations emasculate men by stripping them of their capacity to provide financially and protect. They also revoke women's femininity, which is rooted in sacrifice for and the direct care of one's family (Dreby 2010; Parreñas 2001).

FEAR OF FAMILY SEPARATION

Natalia came to the United States when she was only fifteen years old. She was raped during her crossing and imprisoned by her smugglers for a month en route to Los Angeles. She was later beaten so badly by a boyfriend that she ended up in the hospital for two months, in a coma for part of it. "He had just thrown me on the street to die. Luckily someone found me and called an ambulance or I would have died." The physical violence she experienced in her past is difficult to comprehend, and difficult for her to talk about. And yet Natalia told me that being separated from her son would be much worse than all of the physical violence she had endured. She told me that motherhood is what she lives for. It is what has redeemed her from her ugly past. It is why she believes there is a god. Motherhood is her duty. Natalia is unauthorized, and her son is a U.S. citizen. Her greatest fear is losing him:

> Well, like many Mexicans here I'm afraid. I'm afraid that one day they're gonna come and take me back to Mexico or, you know, separate me from my son . . . . And I don't want that . . . because I know about a lot of cases that when women were deported they separate them from their kids, and I don't want that. That's the worst thing that they could do to me. Every day I live with that in my head. You know, sometimes I don't sleep, sometimes I'm restless because I'm just thinking about that.

To protect themselves and their children, many women stay home, isolated and often lonely, but safe from the police, and from being recognized as a migrant. Until Rogelio's deportation this was Ana's strategy. "Home is the only place I really feel safe," is a response I heard repeated constantly in different variations throughout my fieldwork, especially in the early years. Whereas leaving home and escaping the loneliness prompted by persistent isolation can be empowering, I found that, more often than not, leaving home breeds stress and insecurity.

Victoria dyed her hair a shade of red and practiced saying local phrases with a Montanan accent in the hope that she would blend in when in public. "I watch the women at Wal-Mart and I study them," she told me in a mix of Spanish and English. "Then I practice acting and talking just like them. What else can I do? I have to go to the store. I can't just stay home and hide." Victoria is strong, independent and ambitious. She dreams about being a teacher, an occupation for which she seems organically suited. I was able to see her in action when I hired her to teach Spanish to my son Micah for a few months before he began kindergarten. I was awed by her creativity, patience and energy, and also by her tough negotiating skills. "I may not have papers, but I will charge what the best Spanish teacher in Montana would charge," she warned me with a smile when I asked her if she had an interest in working with Micah.

Victoria has a sophisticated understanding of the legal violence at play in her life and in the lives of other unauthorized migrants. My first glimpse of Victoria's politicization will forever be etched in my memory. It was one of the first Spanish Masses I attended. On this hot July Sunday in 2007, after offering a traditional confessionary prayer Victoria stood in the front of the congregation and asked God to stand with all of the exploited workers who deserve social justice. Victoria is strong willed and she speaks her mind, "a lion" as one of her friends described her.

Yet despite Victoria's *coraje* (courage) and *fuerza* (strength), she is unable to shake the fear of being separated from her children. It is a possibility that fills her with dread and anger. She feels powerless to protect her family from separation. The feeling of powerlessness is one of the most damaging aspects of illegality. Unauthorized women realize that there is little they can do to lessen the risk of their own deportation. They can try to isolate themselves at home and to live noble and law-abiding lives. They can pray and go to Mass. But the nightmare of deportation always looms. A significant challenge of migrant motherhood is to make one's children feel safe and to try to mother "normally" no matter the perpetual threat that confronts them. Although Victoria told me on many occasions how much she worries about her own deportation, she promises her young daughters, the oldest of whom understand the potential implications of her unauthorized status, that she will never abandon them:

> They don't care if they separate families. They don't care about the psychological damage that happens to children [of migrants] in a country that claims to care so much about the rights of women and children. But where are the rights of children when they take away their father or their mother and send them to Mexico only because they don't have papers? . . . My children are American citizens. We came here to have a better life and here we had our children. Here we do everything for our children . . . . I will tell you that I grew up always without my parents. They were never there and I don't want this for my children. I never want them to say that "my mom was not with me." I want them to say that "my mom was with me always, always." My oldest daughter sometimes doesn't like to go to school, and I tell her, "My love, when I returned from school as a little girl, my mother wasn't there, only my sisters. You know that when you return from school your mama will be there to give you soup or a cheesecake. Your mama will always be there."

When Victoria and I had coffee in the spring of 2012 toward the end of my fieldwork, she told me that her anxiety and frustration were getting to be too much. She had recently re-engaged with an immigration lawyer in an attempt to regularize her status. She had been hopeful that it would happen. But she had just heard that to follow through on legalization she would have to return to Mexico. At first the thought of return terrified her. Victoria is from rural Zacatecas, where narco-violence is on the rise. She would never knowingly expose her children to any danger. That is indeed one of the reasons her family has stayed in Montana, because they believe it is safe. But then Victoria's attitude about return began to change. One of her sisters, a teacher near their town, assured her of the safety of raising children there. Return gained more appeal when Victoria learned that her father's health had worsened. Victoria is a caretaker. She had not only her children's well-being to consider but also that of her father. "It's so awful," she once told me, "that being a good mom by staying in the United States to give my kids opportunities, means being a bad daughter. My parents need me and I am not there." For the first time in the six years that I had known Victoria, I heard her speak with conviction about returning to Mexico:

> I think we will go back. If there is no change in immigration policy by the election, that's it. In Mexico life would not be so uncertain . . . I could help my father and I could go to university. Here it is just too hard. It's too hard to live all the time with uncertainty.

There were a few important reasons Victoria had for contemplating a return to Mexico. They included: a weakened construction market, her diabetic father's declining health, and her own frustrated ambitions. But I realized by the end of our long conversation that Victoria's strongest push toward Mexico was the exhaustion she felt living with the constant fear of a family rupture, of being pulled over by the police and arrested, and of her children coming home from school and her not being there.

Although most unauthorized women in this study believe that having papers would lift the fear of deportability and family separation from their shoulders, legal authorization does not ease all anxiety. Lisa, now a U.S. resident, hails from Mexico City. She is one of only a few women in this study whose Mexican roots are urban, and she is one of only two of the mothers I interviewed who have a university degree. Lisa explained to me the depth of insecurity that the demographic context of Montana generates for migrants:

> Yeah, it's scary because most people here in Montana, they are white . . . .
> And I had, I had the potential, and I was still afraid, and I had the visa, and I was still afraid. It is weird. I can understand them [women without papers] because I was married and legal, I had my papers and I was going crazy. I can imagine for those people, to be in the same situation without papers, you know?

For a few years, Lisa took on a role of informal social worker for unauthorized women in the community. Before she left Bozeman in 2008, she helped two women who were seeking an escape from their abusive husbands to find a shelter, and she was often called on to help with medical emergencies or problems that children of her unauthorized friends were having at school. As her English improved and she got to know more people in Montana, much of her own fear subsided. She even wrote two letters to the editor in 2006 during the battles over immigration reform, advocating for migrant rights. Yet Lisa never got to the point of feeling completely at ease. Right before she left town she told me that "there are many people here, especially the rich ones from California, who do not want Mexicans in Montana." As our conversation ended I realized that the demographics of Montana make life uneasy for all migrants, including those who are authorized.

Gloria is a U.S. citizen. She was born in the United States, and raised in rural Chihuahua. She speaks English well, though with an accent that signals her formative years were spent in Mexico. At the time of our interview, she had lived in the United States for ten years, the majority of that time in Minnesota and Utah. Until moving to Montana, she had never been afraid of being in public. This changed in 2007 following a confrontation at a public park.

It was a beautiful summer day, as Gloria described it, the perfect day to spend outside. Gloria's children were playing as usual. Realizing her youngest needed a diaper change, Gloria left her ten-year-old daughter in charge of her two toddlers while she ran to her car for her diaper bag. When Gloria returned, a woman whom Gloria did not recognize approached her angrily, berating her for leaving her children alone and accusing her of being "a bad mom." The woman went on to accuse Gloria's three-year-old son of hitting her own son. By this point in the story Gloria was in tears. "I know my son can be rough," she acknowledged, "but he's only three. He doesn't know." The woman pointed her finger at Gloria and scolded, "That's what's wrong with you people. You come here and you have too many children. If I see your children at the park causing problems again I will call social services."

By this time Gloria was sobbing. I asked her if she wanted to stop the interview. Her three-year-old son was with her at my house for the interview and had caused not a stir. I had a hard time believing he was the bully the woman at the park had portrayed. Gloria insisted that we finish the interview. "I will never go back to the park. The thing is, I do not feel safe." But you are a U.S. citizen, I reminded her. "That woman cannot hurt you." Gloria quickly corrected me. "Oh, but she can. If she calls social services, who are they going to believe? Me, a poor Mexican, or a white woman?" I did not have a response. It seemed possible that depending on who was called, Gloria could be at risk of losing her children.

FEAR THAT DISRUPTS CARE

The fear that unauthorized women have of being deported and separated from their children influences the way they manage their roles as family caretakers. It discourages some migrant mothers from attending parent-teacher conferences and school activities, and dissuades others from entering into relationship with the social service sector. In 2006 when I began my formal fieldwork, the burgeoning Mexican population had caught service workers by surprise. In a 2007 survey I gave to twenty-six local service providers, only two reported that their organization had a fluent Spanish speaker on staff, and none were confident in their knowledge of eligibility rules for migrants. Marrow (2009) suggests that service workers have influence as *street level bureaucrats* in the immigration system in that they are able to decide whether to abide by or bend the rules, either in favor of or to the detriment of their migrant clients. In Montana, migrants recognize this power. They fear, often because of experience, that service workers will not know the rules, or that they will interpret the rules in a way that causes harm. Women report that in other places where they have lived it was much easier to access social services to meet their families' basic needs, and they had more faith in social service workers.

Dorotea, an unauthorized mother of three, contrasted Montana's social service sector to that of California's, where she had lived previously:

> They gave me Medical Assistance in California. They give it to all pregnant women . . . . There it doesn't matter if you have documents, or if you earn a lot or a little. None of that matters to them. So they gave me medical help and they attended to me like they would to any other woman. No one asks questions. But it's not like that here.

Similarly, a young pregnant woman whom I met at the food bank early in 2007 told me that she was going to return to Colorado to have her baby because there they did not ask for your papers and they have doctors and nurses who speak Spanish. Her plan was to come back to Montana once her baby was born, since she believed Montana, service access aside, was the best place to raise children.

Feeling the threat of deportability can also discourage migrants from accessing emergency care. Buck Taylor, chief operating officer of Community Health Partners in Gallatin County and a leading advocate for the migrant community, shared with me a story of a call one of his community clinics received in 2006 from a frantic mother whose toddler had fallen from a table. The little boy had been unconscious for a short period of time, and although he had regained consciousness he was not acting normally. The Bozeman Community Clinic, under Buck Taylor's direction, was one of the first places in southwest Montana to reach out to the migrant community and establish itself as a safe place. They were the first social service entity to hire bilingual staff and to disseminate public health materials in Spanish. As such, a Spanish-speaking staff member was able to take this mother's call. Having heard a description of what had happened to the child, the clinic staff member, on the advice of the clinic nurse, urged the mother to call 911 immediately. The mother was hesitant. "Was there no other way to help their child besides calling 911?" Someone in the house was unauthorized, and the family feared that the police would accompany the ambulance and fire department. "It was an intense moment of realization for me," Buck Taylor noted in our interview:

> I'm not only a clinic director, but I am a trained emergency responder and volunteer fire fighter. I was shocked that a parent would hesitate to seek emergency care for their child. And yet, upon reflection I realize how deeply rooted the fear is that migrants live with. Of course the mother wanted to help her child, but she was intensely afraid of the authorities.

The community clinic staff member finally persuaded the family that emergency responders should not be feared, that they were there to help. Ultimately the mother called 911 and the child was treated at the hospital without issue. Unfortunately Buck Taylor's story is not an isolated one. Woven throughout my field notes and interviews are stories of families who have forgone medical care or advice, or who have not applied for the Food Stamps or scholarships to which they or their children were entitled because they did not want to interact with the public sector.

Before he was deported, Gaby's son Bruno struggled through a period of deep depression. On one of the darkest nights of his depression, Bruno told Gaby that he did not want to live anymore. Bruno had dropped out of high school and he did not have a job. He had struggled with drugs and alcohol, and he had recently been hanging out with a "bad crowd." Bruno was desperate and hopeless, his life at a seeming dead end. Gaby called me the night of his suicide threat. She too was desperate and exasperated, not knowing how to protect her son. I called an acquaintance that works for an emergency mental health hotline and learned that the safest place for Bruno was the hospital emergency room. There a hospital social worker would be able to establish a plan for him while he was being supervised closely. I relayed what I had learned to Gaby, promising her, as I had been promised, that Bruno would not have to provide immigration papers to the folks admitting him to the emergency room.

Despite my assurances, Gaby was adamant that she would not take Bruno to the hospital. "I just can't do it," she said. "I don't trust them and I don't want the situation to be made worse by Bruno or me or both of us being arrested." I was not able to change Gaby's mind. Instead, she stood watch over Bruno throughout the night, and the next morning she took him to the community clinic where she felt safe and where someone could refer Bruno to a counselor. Bruno went through counseling for several months and, according to Gaby, he eventually rebounded at least somewhat from his depression. A year later, as I detail in this chapter's introduction, he was arrested at work and deported. This story has an ironic end. Whereas Gaby was able to get mental health help for Bruno without incident, ultimately he was deported. The threat of deportability that migrants experience is not rooted in neuroses, but in the reality in which they are immersed. Security and danger are often intertwined in the lives of migrants in Montana.

Ambiguous Laws and Unchecked Authority

Sociologists Kil, Menjívar and Doty (2009) assert that heightened border security policies mixed with a societal focus on patriotism have fueled a climate of vigilantism in the United States. Well-known vigilante groups like the Minutemen patrol the U.S.-Mexico border in large part unchallenged by local officials, garnering celebratory media attention on some television programs as well as on right-wing talk radio (see also Chavez 2008). This type of vigilantism has had what Kil et al. term a *spillover effect*, as antimigrant intimidation tactics are increasingly used beyond the U.S.-Mexican border, at work sites and schools, and to put pressure on public officials. Vigilante activities contribute to an atmosphere conducive to legal violence under the guise of patriotic resistance. The harassment that Gloria encountered at the park could be characterized as part of vigilantism's spillover: a regular citizen taking it upon herself to regulate immigration in a public space.

The "border," which has inspired the spread of vigilantism, is a nebulous concept. While the physical border between the United States and Mexico continues to be the most significant political border in the debate over immigration, social borders have been drawn in new migrant destinations signifying the arenas and institutions where migrants do and do not belong (Deeb-Sossa and Bickham-Mendez 2008). As such, the spillover effect of heightened border security and vigilantism can now be seen in Nebraska, Alabama, Virginia and Montana, to name just a few states, as well as in Arizona, Texas and California. It can be seen in the antimigrant stances taken by individuals and groups who claim that they are doing their patriotic duty by cracking down on immigration even if the law does not give them its blessing.

The defiance demonstrated by Sheriff Joe Arpaio in Arizona, who continues to claim he will arrest migrants even if the law forbids it, is the most infamous example of vigilantism's spillover.[9] But it is not the only example. In Montana I have found that a similar inflated sense of patriotism has empowered some public officials and social service workers to act punitively toward migrants even when they lack the legal mandate to do so. In some situations, public officials and service workers misinterpret laws and policies out of ignorance. In others, they misinterpret laws or policies out of anger. When there is nothing in place to check people in power, laws and policies are open for reinterpretation and reconstruction. In Montana, where, as Buck Taylor described, "Latinos literally seemed to arrive in the clinics and social service offices overnight," it took a while before those with the knowledge to challenge abuses of power were organized in their resistance. In the mean time, powers were assumed and abused, intensifying a climate of legal violence.

The ways migrants experience extralegal actions are gendered. As detailed above, migrant men have experienced vigilantism's spillover in their interactions with the police. Specifically, migrant narratives suggest that the police have at times reinterpreted laws and violated migrant rights by soliciting immigration papers from those they pulled over for questionable traffic violations and by calling ICE for backup on the mere suspicion that they have unauthorized migrants in their midst. I have been advised by an immigration lawyer in Montana that both actions are unconstitutional. For women, the rewriting of eligibility rules in the social and public service sectors has been most damaging.

In the fall of 2007 I drove to Roberta's trailer to pick her up for an appointment at the social security office. In her family's move from Idaho to Montana, Roberta had misplaced her oldest daughter's social security card. She asked me to accompany her to get a new one. I was a bit uneasy when, upon my arrival, Roberta let me know that her three young children would be coming with us. I looked at the worn out booster chairs Roberta had in her hands and the small back seat of my Subaru. As the mother of a one-year-old, and pregnant with my second, I was hyperaware of car seat rules. I knew that her children were too young to be in boosters, and that two boosters plus my son's car seat would be a tight, probably unsafe, squeeze. Roberta is unauthorized, and the last thing I wanted was to be responsible for a traffic stop and the questions about her immigration status that might ensue. Roberta ultimately convinced me that her youngest could ride in Micah's car seat and the other two were big enough to ride in the boosters. I stepped back and let Roberta work magic as she managed to squeeze all of the seats into the back of the car.

President Bush's photo and the American flag were the first things I noticed as we entered the Social Security office. A bold sign posted on the back wall reminded us that we were in a U.S. government building. Roberta and her children took seats in the waiting area as I approached the counter. Except for the staff, the office was empty. Still, the woman who greeted me told me that we would have to wait. Before I could explain why we were there, she disappeared into the back of the office. I went to join Roberta and her children. It was several minutes before another employee emerged, this time a thirty-something-year-old white man. I returned to the counter and explained that I was there as a translator for Roberta, who needed to apply for a new social security card for her daughter. I immediately sensed that the man was perturbed by our presence.

"I will have to see everyone's immigration papers," he asserted. My heart started racing.

"Um, sir, the only person here who needs assistance is the little girl. She has her birth certificate and her passport. She was born here. All she needs is to apply for a new social security card."

"I will have to see her mother's papers," he responded curtly.

I took a deep breath, trying to stay calm. "Sir, we only brought the papers for the little girl who is in need of a new card." I could see Roberta through my peripheral vision bouncing her little boy nervously on her lap.

"Mam, I suggest you find a way to prove that this woman is legal or I will have to call ICE."

A heated exchange ensued during which he claimed that I was a mandated reporter and could be arrested if I was knowingly helping an "illegal alien." I assured him that I was not a mandated reporter. I turned to Roberta, indicating with my eyes that I was worried. She pointed to the door. I did not question her urge to flee. I grabbed Roberta's hand and we literally ran out of the building and over the icy sidewalks to my car, pulling her oblivious toddlers along behind us.

This was the most frightening experience I had in my field research. Whereas I knew that authority had been abused, I felt powerless to do anything to right the wrong. While we were in the office I realized that no matter the laws that were in place to protect Roberta, she was at risk of being reported to ICE. Roberta swore to me she would never return to that office again, and she made me promise not to report the incident. If I had been in Boston, where I lived previous to my move to Montana, I would have gone directly to one of three migrant rights organizations that I knew well. I would have told them what happened without revealing anything about who Roberta was. With thousands of Latinos in the city, Roberta would easily remain anonymous. The organization would know how to respond, and I imagine that the racist worker ultimately would have been fired. At the time, in Montana, I had nowhere to turn.[10] Most important, I feared outing Roberta if I reported the incident to anyone, which would have broken my promise to her. To this day, Roberta has not replaced her daughter's social security card, and I am still dumbfounded that the extralegal powers assumed at the social security office went unchecked, a case of vigilantism's spillover.

Deeb-Sossa and Bickham-Mendez (2008) assert that social service workers can act as agents of social exclusion by treating migrant clients with hostility (see also Marrow 2009). Whereas I have been struck by the goodwill and openness with which the majority of social service workers I have come to know in Montana have welcomed the new migrant community, I have also been frustrated by occurrences of blatant abuses of power. Whereas I cannot be sure whether all the abuses I heard about or witnessed were the result of malicious intent or ignorance, the implications were the same. Families were caused stress and in some cases denied basic services to which they were entitled.

In the fall of 2009, Lourdes, an unauthorized mother of two unauthorized children, was told by a new office worker at her children's school that in order to continue to be eligible for the free lunches they had been receiving she needed to show proof of their citizenship. Lourdes was scared and perplexed by the abrupt policy change. Her daughters had been receiving free lunches for more than a year, and she had only had to supply her pay stubs as proof of eligibility. Unsure of what to do, Lourdes called Jennie, a community organizer who is widely known, trusted and respected among the Mexican community.[11] After several phone calls Jennie learned that the school should not be requesting proof of migration status from anyone. The woman working in the office had taken it upon herself to make sure that no one who was "illegal" was taking resources from U.S. citizen children. She claimed that she did not want to cause harm, she was just doing what she thought was right. At long last the lunch tickets were reinstated, but not without an anxiety-filled period during which Lourdes was certain the school was going to report her to ICE. Without an intervention, the reinterpretation of public school policy would have denied Lourdes's children their most stable meal of the day. Lourdes would have been helpless to do anything to stop it.

When social services are denied to migrants, children are often the victims. In many cases the children who are victimized are U.S. citizens. Child development expert Hiro Yoshikawa (2011) finds that citizen children of unauthorized parents are typically at a development disadvantage. Their parents' low socioeconomic levels negatively impact the resources they are able to impart on their children. A parent's unauthorized status also means they are less likely to enroll their children in the entitlement programs for which they are eligible. My research confirms that a parent's unauthorized status can erase their children's *authorized status*. This is what happened to Gaby when the nonprofit organization that provided Raul with a child care stipend learned that she was unauthorized.

Gaby's misfortune has roots in her sons' deportations. When ICE learned of Gaby's identity and residential address she chose to quit her job and find a false name under which to work. Luckily, she was able to maintain her child care stipend throughout the entire ordeal. Then, in the spring of 2011, just when Gaby thought everything had settled, she received a formal letter from the organization that had been subsidizing Raul's child care. The letter stated that a change in organizational policy mandated all clients submit a new round of paperwork to renew their child care stipends. The revised application requested pay stubs and a letter of verification from the parent's current employer. Gaby was faced with a dilemma. Gaby was a great worker and she was on good terms with her current boss. But Gaby's boss thought her name was Maria. She was stuck, absolutely in need of the child care stipend, yet unable to provide pay stubs that matched the name with which she had originally applied for child care support. She asked me for advice. Should she try to manufacture fake pay stubs? Or should she tell the providers of the child care stipend the complicated truth, that she is an unauthorized migrant who chose to work under a false name after her sons were deported? After talking to several people I encouraged Gaby to tell the child care organization the truth. They were known for being advocates for the migrant community.

I accompanied Gaby to the offices of the child care organization. We were both nervous as we entered the office, still not completely sure that coming forward with the truth was the smartest thing to do. I relaxed a little when I recognized the receptionist as one of my former students. "Hi Leah!" she said warmly. A good omen, I thought. My student led us back to the office of the caseworker who would help us. As we entered the office, Gaby whispered to me that the caseworker was not the one she had worked with in the past. When I inquired about where Gaby's regular caseworker was, I was informed she was on maternity leave. The woman introduced herself as a temporary replacement. A bad omen. I looked at Gaby and she nodded to signal that we should proceed with our plan anyway.

After some small-talk, I explained Gaby's situation. I made clear that every choice Gaby had made, from coming to the U.S. to assuming a false name to avoid detection by ICE, was for her children's well-being. She was a good mom. Yet instead of responding with empathy as we had hoped, the caseworker curtly responded in the negative. "I'm sorry. It is our policy that the parents of the children in our program be U.S. citizens." I pleaded with her, reminding her that Raul was a U.S. citizen, and that their policy was unfairly punishing him. She would not budge. "I'm sorry," was all she said. I asked if Gaby could maintain her stipend until the end of the month. Again, she responded in the negative. The stipend would be cut off the next day. Gaby grabbed my arm, beckoning for us to leave.

Once back in the car, Gaby started to sob. She had no other options for child care. We went to Head Start. Raul was too young. We went to another relief organization. They did not offer child care stipends but could give us free shampoo. No help. When Gaby dropped me off at my house, we still had not come up with a solution. Gaby called in sick for the next week until she was able to find an acquaintance from her church, Liliana, who agreed to watch Raul. Liliana continued to watch Raul until he qualified for Head Start. Raul had loved his preschool and his teachers. He never got to stay good-bye. Another rupture.

Danger at Home

A discussion of gender and illegality in rural Montana mandates an exploration of domestic violence. Whereas many women in this study maintain that home is where they feel safest, this is not always the case. For some women in this study, home is where they are most in danger. The immediate danger they confront in their domiciles is not from the police or ICE, but from their male partners.

Domestic violence is an issue of power. In most cases, when power in a partnership is skewed, women find themselves at a greater risk of violence than if power between them and their partners is on an equal footing. When women are unauthorized, and especially when their partners are authorized, their risk of violence is thus heightened. Boehm (2012) theorizes that immigration can further exacerbate the threat of domestic violence for women, because men may use violence as a means of recouping their masculinity and power that were eroded by immigration. According to Boehm, violence can stem from *threatened masculinity*.

The context of reception in which migrant women live may buffer this threat. For example, Hirsch (2003) suggests that whereas illegality and isolation can put migrant women at an increased risk of domestic violence, immigration may also make women better able to protect themselves against abuse than when they were in Mexico. This is because in the United States migrant women can call on a *gendered code of behavior* that mandates respect, and they can seek support from the church, community organizaticns or local authorities. Hirsch conducted her research in an urban context with a large migrant community, and urbanity is central to her analysis. The situation in rural Montana is strikingly different. Menjívar and Salcido (2002) find that isolation can bolster the risk of domestic violence in migrant families. This suggests that women in rural areas, such as Montana, are uniquely vulnerable.

In my research I found structural inequalities, geography and cultural expectations to contribute to domestic violence. Inequalities in migrant couples are often rooted in gender relations and gender scripts that migrants bring with them from rural Mexico where, as Gonzalez-López (2005) asserts, limited opportunities for women mean that an overt and rigid patriarchy contextualizes daily life. In traditional sending areas in rural Mexico, there is a history of entrenched gender inequality in which sexual and domestic violence has had a role. Gender inequalities within the families in this study are also rooted in and compounded by the context of rural Montana, where the protections and power equalizers that migrant women may have access to in urban destinations (Pessar 1999; Hirsch 2003) do not exist. The context of rural Montana thus increases women's vulnerability to abuse and lessens their ability to protect themselves from it once it is happening.

I have encountered several dramatic stories of domestic violence in my fieldwork. A few of the stories have come to me firsthand. I have heard the others indirectly from friends or family of women struggling with abuse. For all of the cases I pledged to maintain absolute confidentiality. As I will reiterate and detail further in this section, the context of Montana makes anonymity difficult to achieve and, even if it is achieved, difficult to protect. As such, I have decided that although the story of domestic abuse is too important not to tell, I will tell it in generalities minus the ethnographic detail that I use throughout the rest of the book.

Many of the migrant families in this study are mixed status families. In most of these mixed status families it is the woman who does not have papers. Being in the unauthorized position within a mixed status couple puts women most at risk, as an authorized husband of an unauthorized wife can use the threat of deportability as a weapon. On several occasions in my field research I heard stories of husbands telling their wives that if they told anyone of their abuse they would call the authorities, setting their wives up for deportation. This threat alone is enough to keep most abused women quiet and under the control of their husbands. Whereas threats within a mixed status couple are controlling in all contexts, they have more force in Montana, where local geographic and social structures are hostile to women seeking an escape.

As I detail in Chapter 2, the migrant economies of southwest Montana make it difficult for women to achieve independence. The majority of living wage jobs available to migrants are in construction and agriculture. They are typically filled by men. The jobs that women have secured, most notably following the crash of the construction industry in 2009 (see Chapter 5), are in the low-wage service sector, where pay is not conducive to supporting a family in most cases. Just as Ana and Nora had a difficult time imagining how they would support themselves after the deportations of their husbands, women suffering abuse wonder how they would be able to financially support themselves and their children if on their own.

That many women in this study do not drive further skews power in their households. It is hard for women to imagine leaving an abusive relationship when they do not have the ability to get around on their own. For women who live in the most isolated rural areas, their escape is harder still. Unlike in a large city, they are unable to leave their home and walk or hop a bus to the nearest shelter, or to the home of a friend or kin who would protect them. Living miles outside of town, many migrant women are literally trapped.

A plethora of research shows the importance of networks to migrant women's survival strategies and well-being (Hagan 1994, 1998; Hondagneu-Sotelo 1994, 2001; Menjívar 2000; Pessar 1999). In Montana, women's networks are relatively weak and dispersed. Whereas women report that their networks of friends and kin are growing, geography ultimately limits network formation as well as the usefulness of networks. Unlike in cities where migrants are apt to live in ethnic enclaves (Kibria 1993; Menjívar 2000; Portes and Rumbaut 2001), in Montana, migrants most often live in isolated trailers or in town homes without any Mexican neighbors nearby. The lack of strong and accessible women's networks increases migrant women's vulnerability and isolation, further discouraging them from leaving abusive situations.

There is only one domestic violence shelter in the region, and it is small and difficult to find. This shelter has been amazingly supportive of the migrant women who have, against most odds, made their way through its doors. Yet it lacks the resources and outreach capacity to support all of the women who need its services. As my fieldwork wound down, the shelter was prioritizing the recruitment of Spanish-speaking volunteers, and it was building its connections with lawyers who are familiar with immigration law. I thus left the field hopeful that more migrant women would be served by the shelter in the future. And yet a plea-for-funding-email I recently received from the shelter was a sobering reminder that a small gender-based nonprofit in a poor state will likely always struggle for resources and support.

It is critical to highlight the importance that the impossibility of anonymity has in the lives of abused migrant women in Montana. Towns and cities in Montana are small. Women fear that if they do leave their abusers they will be unable to hide their whereabouts. Leaving town might seem an option, but custody battles, especially the messy ones that occur in mixed status families, typically prevent women from relocating out of state. They may have the legal option of leaving, but not with their children. As I hope earlier sections of this chapter make clear, no woman that I met over six years of field research would ever voluntarily leave her children.

Conclusion

Migrants' experiences of illegality are shaped by multiple factors. In this chapter, I show how geographic context intersects with gender and illegality to influence daily life. Several of the themes I highlight transgress geographic context. Both migrant men's and women's fears of deportation have been reported in traditional and new, and urban and rural destinations alike. Mothers' anxieties about being separated from their children are also common across context. Yet my data suggests that specifically *where* and *how* these fears and anxieties are manifested and embodied may vary by geographic context. For example, in Montana, both men and women struggle with the impossibility of anonymity. They equally feel most vulnerable in their cars, where they sense they are most at risk of being noticed by the police. And, indeed, in my fieldwork traffic stops are the most common roots of deportations. In California, where many of my participants lived previously, they could manage daily life without depending on a car. Public transportation was available, and they did not fear the police in the same way. More research is needed to compare experiences of illegality across context of reception.

Gender impacts migrants' legal vulnerability. Because the vast majority of migrant jobs in Montana are in agriculture and construction, both sectors that are socially constructed as male, more men than women work outside of the home. Most migrants live long distances from their work sites. Thus men cannot avoid long commutes through public space, and commutes are where arrest is most likely. Women, on the other hand, many of whom do not know how to drive, feel most at risk when engaged in the carework that takes them outside of their homes, such as going to the grocery store, the health clinic, a public park or picking up their children from school. Whenever they can, most women stay at home, isolated, but safe from deportation. The anxiety and depression associated with their isolation is place-specific. Women's networks are weak in Montana, limited by geographic distance and a lack of enclaves and gathering places. And whereas women are seemingly not as likely to be deported as men, they are faced with the burden of holding things together if their partners are arrested. This is made all the more challenging because there are few jobs available for migrant women that pay a living wage, and the social service sector is weak at best and hostile at its worst. The lack of access to immigration lawyers, and the fact that there is not an immigration lawyer in the state who speaks fluent Spanish, intensifies women's challenge to hold it together when legal trouble arises.

Although migrants told me repeatedly throughout my fieldwork that they would rather live in Montana than anywhere else in the United States because of the area's beauty, tranquillity and opportunity, they also said that their love of Montana endures *despite* the unique vulnerability they feel to deportation. This suggests that as all-encompassing as the threat of deportability and the experience of legal violence appear, they do not solely define migrant life, nor do they erase migrants' connection to place. Even after the deportation of her eldest sons, Gaby does not want to leave Montana. The next chapter grapples with the paradoxical relationship between vulnerability, marginalization and belonging, a grappling that inspires the question mark I have placed at the end of the book's title, *The Last Best Place?*

Chapter 4

Transnationalism, Belonging and the Rural Idyll

> I am in love with Montana. For other states I have admiration,
> respect, recognition, even some affection, but with Montana
> it is love, and it's difficult to analyze love when you're in it .
> . . . It seems to me that Montana is a great splash of grandeur.
> The scale is huge but not overwhelming. The land is rich with
> grass and color, and the mountains are the kind I would create
> if mountains were ever put on my agenda . . . . It seemed to
> me that the frantic bustle of America was not in Montana . . . .
> The calm of the mountains and the rolling grasslands had got
> into the inhabitants . . . . Again, my attitude may be informed
> by love, but it seemed to me that the towns were places to live
> in rather than nervous hives. People had time to pause in their
> occupations to undertake the passing art of neighborliness.
> —John Steinbeck (1962). *Travels with Charlie, In Search of America*

In 2004 I moved to Bozeman with trepidation, from Boston, where I had
been a graduate student, via Minneapolis, my home city. I had long considered myself an urban creature, energized by the opportunity, chaos and
diversity of the big city. The entire state of Montana contains fewer people
than each of the urban areas I had lived in previously. Yet upon arriving in
Montana, I immediately felt a strong sense of belonging and, like Steinbeck,
a love of place—its landscapes, skies, energy and people. I felt at home.

Montana's gentrification enables the nurturing of my urban sensibilities in
the midst of a majestic wilderness.[1] Immediately upon moving to Montana,
I was seduced by Montana's idyll of authenticity, simplicity and freedom.
Nine years later, I still celebrate the lack of entitlement of my working-class,
first-generation university students. I embrace the security I feel walking
alone through downtown Bozeman, even at night, and letting my young
children ride their bikes freely up and down the sidewalk outside our house.
I am warmed by the community festivals and parades that symbolize, in a
mythical sense, an Americana of times past when things were simpler. Here

I have a sense of escape from the turmoil and stress that characterize the rest of the world, which literally and figuratively is so far away. Most important, I am drawn in by the adoration for Montana that everyone around me seems to share, including the Mexican migrants I got to know in this study.

This chapter explores the translocal and transnational contexts in which Mexican migrants' sense of belonging in Montana is positioned, as well as their complex relationship to the rural idyll. When my research participants speak of their affection for Montana, their narratives reflect my own. While they do not speak of gentrified amenities like wine bars, running trails and local organic food, they do speak of tranquillity, security, beauty, family and community. Despite the many challenges of living in a new rural migrant destination, my participants tell me they want to stay. Aspects of the rural idyll, whether real or imagined, and paradoxical in their entanglement with fear and struggle, are central to their lives.

Nurturing a Connection to Home

Bourdieu (1977) conceptualizes *habitus* as the relationship between individuals' cultural dispositions and the context of their daily lives. Habitus is intimately connected to social class and is conditioned by one's history of socialization and daily life practices. Whereas one's habitus can be transformed through social mobility, or in this case migration, Bourdieu maintains that habitus is more obstinate than fluid. When individuals experience upward social economic mobility, for example, they may experience emotional challenges as they negotiate between the tastes and preferences they developed in their childhoods and the different expectations of their new class position and cultural context (Lee and Kramer 2013). More often than being transformed, one's habitus is reinforced by the context of his/her life.

In my fieldwork I found that in addition to having a sociocultural habitus that has roots in social class and ethnicity, the Mexican migrants in my sample exhibit what I term a *geographic habitus*. By geographic habitus, I mean a disposition they have developed through their relationships with the natural landscapes and built environments that have contextualized their lives. Building from Bourdieu, I propose that one's geographic habitus is greatly influenced by the context of one's childhood and coming of age. In this section I argue that when migrants move to a place that geographically approximates home, their geographic habitus is reinforced. They are able to escape potential feelings of alienation, tension and unease that can be associated with a drastic change in geographic context, such as when an individual from rural Mexico migrates to East Los Angeles or another large urban area.

I wrote the first draft of this manuscript from Oaxaca, Mexico, during a year-long sabbatical. My time in Mexico gave me deep insights into the geo-

graphic habitus that my research participants embody and have thus carried
with them from Mexico to the United States and ultimately to Montana. In
August 2012, I drove with my dad from the state of Colima, on Mexico's central Pacific coast, to Oaxaca, a fifteen-hour drive through the heart of central
Mexico. As we left Colima and entered Jalisco, I was struck by the similarities
between the landscapes of southwest Jalisco and those of Montana.[2] Jalisco is
rural, much more rural than I had realized before my cross-country trek. As
is the case in Montana, in Jalisco we drove for miles without seeing a town.
For long stretches we saw only a few humble dwellings dotting the hillsides.
Majestic mountains and rich agricultural land envelop the interstate toll-road.
Central Mexico's landscape is beautiful. The mountains are rugged, but richly
green. As in Montana, the sky is big. As we made our way through Jalisco, I
could picture Ernesto, who grew up on a *ranchito* in Villa de la Purficación, as
a young boy leading his cows and burrows on rocky trails to the river. After six
years of fieldwork in Montana, while in Mexico, I began to grasp the power
of migrants' connection to the rural landscapes they left behind.

Pablo has been coming to Montana from Nayarit as an H2A worker since
1991. Every year, from March to November, he lays irrigation pipe and tends
cattle on a large family-owned ranch. He has been working with cattle since
he was a young boy. With only six years of formal education, he has never
dreamed of doing anything else. The *campo* is in his blood, so to speak. In
Montana, Pablo feels a strong connection to the land and an emotional tie
to his ranchito in Mexico. The rurality of Montana makes the transnational
context of his life more seamless than a life in the city:

> Do you know what I like? What I like is agriculture. I am a person of the
> campo. Here I feel free. I feel like I am in Mexico. For me, my work in the
> campo is liberty .... I have worked in cities, but I do not like the city. I am
> not accustomed to live like they do. I am happy here. There is nothing so
> beautiful as to live in the company of animals and nature.

Jesús also works in Montana eight months of the year as part of the H2A
program. He first came to the United States in 1995 to work as an unauthorized laborer in the fields of central California. In 1998 after returning to
Mexico, he was able to secure the H2A visa that brought him to Montana.
He has been migrating seasonally to Montana ever since. Like Pablo, Jesús
feels a strong connection to the Montana countryside. Rural Montana re-
verberates with the core of his identity:

> Well I am accustomed to it here, in the campo, to the lifestyle of the campo.
> I really like it here in Montana. Like I told you, I believe in the work of the
> campo .... I prefer living in the peace of the campo, where I spend more
> time with animals than with people. The campo is part of who I am.

The pueblo where Ángel was raised in Zacatecas is small and isolated. On the one hand the isolation signifies poverty. Ángel migrated because he could not earn enough there to support his family. But on the other, the isolation of Ángel's pueblo symbolizes tranquillity. It is the latter that he missed most when he first migrated to the United States, to work in California. After several years in California, Ángel came to Montana to work as a mason on the construction of expensive homes in the ski area of Big Sky. In Montana he works mostly outside, removed from the busy-ness of urban life. "It's better here (than in California). Here it is more or less like Mexico. It is peaceful and beautiful. I am from a small, peaceful town. And I feel like here it is more or less the same." Life is by no means perfect in Montana. Ángel is aware that many native-born Montanans do not want to work beside Mexicans, and he grieves the fact that it is hard to find good Mexican food or a doctor who speaks Spanish. He struggles with cold and snow. He dreams of the day when he will have saved enough money to return to Mexico. But until that day arrives, Ángel would like to stay in Montana.

Elena was born in the United States and returned to Mexico with her family while she was still an infant. She spent her early childhood on a ranchito in the mountains of Jalisco. When she was a young teenager, her family migrated to California, and shortly thereafter to Montana. Elena told me that she is homesick for Jalisco. Whereas Montana has not completely alleviated her yearning for home, it has eased it. "It was very boring in California," she told me during a formal interview in the spring of 2011. "I had to stay in the apartment all day watching TV. In Mexico I was outside and running everywhere. In California I missed the campo a lot . . . . Montana reminds me of home. It's like I'm back in the mountains of Jalisco."

Many of the migrants I interviewed expressed similar sentiments about Montana's rurality. The connection they feel to Montana is generated in a transnational context. Although in Mexico rurality typically equates with poverty and struggle,[3] migrants' nostalgia for home often glosses over this endemic struggle, centering instead on the beauty and serenity of their homeland. Montana's landscape and low-population density triggers this nostalgia and brings migrants a semblance of comfort and happiness, despite the insecurity of their lives. In my many conversations with migrants, I sensed that the physical, geographic aspect of the rural idyll provides a buffer against feelings of displacement that ensue because of living far away from family, friends and the familiarities of home. Rurality also has cultural resonance for many of the migrants I met.

It was a Saturday night, Valentine's Day, 2009. Not one for Hallmark holidays, my husband encouraged me to leave him home with our baby and toddler so

I could attend the area's first-ever Mexican Valentine's Day dance. The dance had a dual purpose. The first was to celebrate Valentine's Day. The second, and more important purpose, was to raise money to buy new songbooks for the monthly Spanish Mass. A small group of Mexican women from the Catholic Church had worked for weeks to organize the *fiesta*. There would be food, music and games for the children. Two colleagues and I set off together, winding our way through the dark roads outside of Bozeman in search of the warehouse where the dance was being held. At several points I was certain we would never find it. Finally we came upon a cluster of warehouses that were set back from the highway. Pickup trucks lined the dirt road and *ranchera* music blared from inside one of the buildings, confirming we had found the right place.

Inside the warehouse men in cowboy boots, cowboy hats, pressed jeans and big belt buckles danced with women in tight, brightly colored dresses. Balloons and streamers covered the dank walls, giving the otherwise cold space a feeling of warmth. In the back of the warehouse a small group of women sold tamales, *posole* and gelatin deserts. Young children ran around happily and energetically, the girls wearing puffy dresses with ruffles and the boys pressed jeans.

As I chatted with friends and tried my hand at dancing ranchera, I was struck by the transnational resonance between the cultural practices of central Mexico that were on display and those of pregentrified Montana. In the pregentrification context of southwest Montana, most Montanans worked the land and dressed the part. Despite gentrification, this agricultural culture persists in myth and reality. Despite an economy that is shifting away from agriculture and extraction to services, agriculture remains Montana's largest industry (mt.gov). Many native ranchers and farmers from the area balk at the commodification of their lifestyle by wealthy urban newcomers.[4]

Mexicans, although considered outsiders to the native-born, have not contributed to this commodification. To the contrary, agriculture is at the core of many Mexican migrants' identities. As is the case for second-, third- and fourth-generation Montana ranchers, globalization, trade and commercialization have disrupted Mexican agricultural life (Patel 2008). In my fieldwork I have been struck by the surface similarities between those from rural Mexico and native-born farmers and ranchers from Montana. They drive the same vehicles—big pickup trucks—and the men dress in the same attire: pressed jeans, cowboy boots and buttoned shirts. What is more, they speak of similar values—those of family, God and community, and the importance of hard work.

In Search of Tranquillity

> Here no one takes anything if you leave it outside your house. The people
> are just more honest here. And it is peaceful. Where I lived before in
> Colorado there were people in the streets at one in the morning . . . . For
> me we had great luck coming here because it is better than Colorado and
> all the other places we have been. (Nora)

> If you are in the city you have to be careful of who is around you . . . . For
> example, that is the way it is in California. Here we don't have to worry if
> we leave our car open or if we leave our keys in the car. And we don't have
> to worry if our kids go outside alone to play. In California, you have to be
> careful about everything, absolutely everything. You can never relax. (Pedro)

Security and tranquillity, whether real or imagined, are at the heart of the
rural idyll. Ironically, narratives espousing both abound in Montana at the
same time that Montana is infamous for having the country's highest suicide
rate (Uken 2012) and a well-publicized problem with methamphetamine
(National Public Radio 2007). Yet, in Montana, overall rates of crime and
violence remain relatively low. I believe that Montana's *relative* security and
tranquillity are a key aspect of migrants' consumption of the rural idyll. The
vast majority of migrants I interviewed and met in my fieldwork migrated to
Montana from other states. As such, they have developed their relationship to
Montana translocally, comparing their feelings of connection and tranquillity
with the emotional experience of living elsewhere. Just as migrants' love of
Montana's rural landscape and countryside has a transnational footing, their
appreciation for Montana's sense of tranquillity and security has a translocal
base. This comparative aspect helps explain why migrants characterize Montana as tranquil and secure even though they live within a context of social
and geographic marginalization.

Martín and Lia left Guerrero for the United States after narco-violence
killed one of Martín's colleagues on the rural police force of which he was
a part. Martín told me that he literally feared for his life during the months
before emigrating. Clearly, not everything in Mexico was idyllic. Martín and
Lia were poor, and violence was encroaching on their lives.

After a tumultuous border-crossing Martín and Lia migrated to Utah,
where Martín's cousin had assured him there was good work in construction.
Life was good in Utah, for a while, until a tragedy occurred. Martín's sister,
who migrated soon after him, was raped, an incident that caused grave emotional injury to his family. The rape combined with a drop in wages spurred
their second migration, this time to Montana. In Montana, Martín and Lia
told me they finally feel safe. "For me, what I like most is the security,"

Martín asserted after relaying his entire migration story in detail. "And I like the lifestyle here because it is more tranquil, it does not have the stress that comes with living in the city." I then sensed an idyllic nostalgia come into play. Martín has never lived in a city. He just imagines the city to be stressful. And whereas Martín had only minutes before told me that he literally fled Mexico in fear for his life, he said the following:

> I think I am accustomed to life here because where we are from in Mexico is also a small town, and it is very peaceful, where we all know each other. I think it's because of this that after two years in Montana we still maintain our customs.

Despite the violence that racked much of central Mexico during the bulk of my field research (Seeley et al. 2013), most migrants spoke with longing about the tranquillity of the Mexico of their childhoods. Unlike other migrant destinations in the United States, to them, Montana mirrors the peace of their homeland. "What is most important here is the security," Agosta asserted. "You can be out at all hours of the night and not be afraid. I have been at Wal-Mart at 11 and 12 at night and I've never felt afraid." Jose echoed her sentiments. "For example, I go to the mall and I leave my car open and nothing ever happens. Everything here is *tranquilo*." In the majority of my interviews, I heard migrants espouse their appreciation for "being able to leave their doors open." This was especially poignant for me, because my husband often says the same thing. When we first moved to Montana he chided me for locking the door when we left the house. Having been a single woman in Boston, living alone for a couple of my years there, locking the door is second nature. But it goes against the idyll of Montana's security.

Not all of migrants' feelings of security in Montana are rooted in nostalgia. Some are generated comparatively from real incidents of crime and violence that they have experienced elsewhere. For example, Miguel and Rosalia told me the story of the murder of four Mexicans in the trailer court where they lived in Colorado. Rosalia emotionally asserted that she never felt safe in her home following the incident. No one in the community did. The fear that inundated her senses in Colorado subsided soon after she moved to Montana, nurturing her connection to her new home.

I heard other stories of crime and violence, all told in vivid detail. My participants remember them as if they occurred yesterday. For example, Sandra came to Montana from California as a preteenager. She is now in her mid-twenties. Her memory of her early childhood in California is sharp. When I asked her to describe it, she described crime and insecurity:

> It was a horrible area where we lived. We had this little fenced in area outside our house and there were drug dealers and prostitutes all around

us. We did not know at the time that they were prostitutes. I remember wondering why the women kept leaving with different men and then returning with others. Now I know!

Vera, who also moved to Montana as a preteenager from California, told me a similar account of her childhood:

> It was a city where we lived in California. And yeah, that was one of the reasons you can't, you know, you can't really be outside, I guess, or my parents were afraid that you know, something would have happened to us. There was like an incident where, well, I think we had a baby-sitter at the house, and there was some activities going on next door with guns and stuff, and the police showed up. So I just remember, you know, like, our baby-sitter saying, stay down, stay down. You know, so that's there and there's another incident, it happened to my older brother. He was coming back from school . . . a few gang members started chasing him . . . . We went to the store, I remember, and came back and he was just hiding in the truck, you know. So I don't know what that was like for him, but I do remember that incident. And when we walked to school we always had to, we either walked together, or, you know, my mom would take us, or something. But we always tried to avoid a house that was like on the way there, you know, cause it was, it belonged to *cholos*, you know, gang members.

Angela also centered her critique and memories of life in California on the gangs that she believed threatened her children's safety and well-being. Although she did everything she could to protect her children, such as walking with them to and from school, and not leaving until she was certain they had safely entered the building, she felt as though she still could not protect them. She was constantly angry and frustrated that none of the local officials, including teachers, administrators and the police, seemed to care about the gang activity that had over-run her children's school:

> Well, my son, Chaba, in his high school, well he had to face gang members. They tried to hit him, and they threatened him with knives and guns. He was afraid all the time . . . . In the school they allow the kids to have guns and knives, and the police do not say anything. And the teachers don't say anything either. No one seems to care.

The crime and violence that my participants describe has left an indelible mark on their lives. It has also generated their appreciation for Montana, where there has yet to develop a conspicuous gang scene and the murder rate is relatively low.[5] But murder, theft and gang activity *do* exist in Montana, just not to the extent that they do in other places. The rural idyll is intensified because Montana is *not* California, not because Montana is crime free and without problems. When participants moved away from crime-ridden areas to Montana, they describe having felt the liberating rush of having escaped a situation in which they were certain they would have ultimately fallen victim to violence. Most important, my participants believe they have rescued their children from a future of gangs and guns. I find the latter to be quite ironic, as Montana has one of the largest gun-toting populations/capita in the nation, with 57.7 percent of Montanan households owning at least one gun (Boodman 2006). But there is a difference between Montana's gun culture and those that my participants describe. Hunting and sport are at the base of Montana's love of guns, which migrants interpret as distinct from the handguns and assault weapons they feared in other places.

Motherhood and Family Well-being

The centrality of family within the narrative of the rural idyll reinforces traditional gender relations within migrant households. Whereas both the Mexican migrant men and women I interviewed praised the security and tranquillity they feel in Montana, women typically extended the analysis, making connections between Montana's security and tranquillity, and motherhood. Specifically, despite having experienced place-specific fear, anxiety and discrimination, migrant women say they can care for their families more effectively in Montana than they could in other places they have lived.

The construction of the rural idyll implies gender roles in which mothers are charged with caring for their children and managing the domestic front, and fathers are expected to provide (Little and Austin 1996). Because in Montana migrant enclaves and sophisticated networks have yet to develop, family has special significance. Migrant women find themselves in a precarious situation, in which their position in the family is one of both privilege and subordination.

Southwest Montana's agriculture- and construction-based economy has fortified long-established gender relations within Mexican migrant households, confining women to the domestic sphere. As I detailed in Chapter 2, narratives of isolation are dominant in migrant women's interviews, as are those of fear of deportation, loneliness and barriers to service provision. Yet the lives of migrant women are nuanced, and to say that their lives are defined first and foremost by struggle is too simplistic. Women also express optimism, specifically regarding their ability to be good mothers. While migrant women face unique hardships in Montana, they also report finding comfort in the opportunities and safety Montana represents for their families and especially for their children.

As such, some of the same elements that operate to the detriment of Mexican migrants as individual women empower them as mothers. Living on a vast, sparsely populated landscape far from an urban center means it is difficult to get around, access services and remain anonymous. On the other hand, these geographic characteristics signify clean air, beauty and serenity. Limited employment opportunities mean women are confined to their homes. Yet most say that although they struggle with isolation, they appreciate that they can be with their children while they are not in school and that they have a simple life. Indeed, there is a trade-off between the anonymity, large ethnic enclaves and migrant networks that traditional urban destinations offer and the physical security and relative calm of a rural settlement. Migrants in this study prefer the latter.

In their narratives, migrant women hold up the rural as morally superior to the urban, characterizing the latter as violent, drug-infested and devoid of values. In addition to crime and violence, mothers told me that in the city they worried that their sons would be recruited into gangs, and they feared their daughters would be in danger of an early initiation into sex and romance with boys who were "no good." Because many women worked while living in other places, they were not able to be as present in their children's lives and thus to pass down the values they deem most important. In Montana, women view their omnipresence in their children's lives as a means of protecting them and raising them to be good citizens. Most say they are willing to give up the autonomy they had in the other places they have lived in order to enhance the lives of their children and shield them from danger.

Lia echoed the feelings of many of my participants when she said, "It is the security . . . . I love that here my children can play outside and I don't worry that someone is going to take them." Similarly, Victoria expressed that even though at first she missed the Hispanic culture that surrounded her in Colorado, she immediately appreciated the security she felt in Montana:

> It is so peaceful here and I like this for my children. We never hear about robberies and murders, or gangs and drugs like you do in the cities. In Colorado, if you left your bicycle outside someone would take it. Or if you left your car door open, someone would steal your stereo and your cd's. Here no one steals. It is *tranquilo*.

Sara moved to Montana from Wichita, Kansas, in 2000. As I detailed in Chapter 2, although she has permanent residency and has been in Montana longer than most participants, she is socially isolated, perpetually anxious, and often depressed. She constructs her identity as a mother around sacrifice. Living in Montana is the sacrifice she has made for her children. "I sometimes feel really sad here, mostly because I do not know many Hispanic people and things like that. But I accept my sadness for my kids. Because here it is a better life for them." Even though it was her husband, Reinaldo, who directed their move from Kansas to Montana, Sara firmly believes that she is a better mother in Montana and Reinaldo is a better provider than in Kansas. This makes her personal suffering worthwhile.

Children have agency in their families. They influence the way their mothers in particular feel about living in Montana and their decisions to stay in Montana (see also Dreby 2007). Natalia, for example, told me that her son has made it clear that he never wants to return to California, which he perceives to be violent and dangerous. In fact, at one point when Natalia contemplated moving back to California to be near family, her son resisted. "Marco likes it here and he doesn't want to go back . . . he was crying. He said, please don't take me back to California . . . . I like it here. It's more comfortable. We don't have shootings and people fighting." Natalia told me that after her son expressed his resentment toward California, she made up her mind that she would find a way to stay in Montana. Although she misses the help she received from extended family in California, her son's feelings of security take first priority.

Not all children loved Montana when they first arrived. Yet with time, many developed a fondness. Young adults I interviewed told me that as they grew up their appreciation for Montana grew. Sandra, for example, resisted coming to Montana at first. She still grieves the ties to Mexican culture that she believes were severed when her family left Mexico and then California. But in the big picture, she is now certain that culture is secondary to the security and opportunity that Montana has provided her:

> Montana kinda made me the person I am now. . . . I always tell my parents, as much as we hated coming here, and as much as we have lost our culture, we are grateful for the fact that they brought us up here, because if they didn't, who knows what we would be like . . . . Like in California, my sister was in a gang . . . . I mean, I think that in the end, you have to think about the future. And, I think that's what my parents were doing, thinking about the future, yes they understood that we were gonna go through many, many things here, and yes it was gonna be hard, but in the end, when it comes to a future, we had a better chance here.

Vera also grew to love Montana. She recognizes that her mother made a huge sacrifice in moving here from California, where she had a job, family and many friends:

> I think it was tough, just because, her saying you know, that she didn't really want to move up here and, just that you know, we lived out in like, a ranch, so it was kinda, isolating too, you know. I just remember her saying she did

miss her friends and you know, she says that, but she says she did it for us, for her kids. Because of the whole gangs. It was too dangerous and, they just didn't wanna see us going in that direction. With drugs or whatever it was, you know.

Migrant women believe that Montana is good not only for their children but also for their marriages. This further validates their sacrifice. In several interviews women mentioned that their husbands are at home more than they were before migrating to Montana. They do not have to work as much and, more important, they spend their time off with the family instead of drinking with their friends. Olivia, for example, told me, "I wanted to come to Montana because my husband was an alcoholic. Therefore he was always out drinking with his cousins and his friends. I wanted this to stop, and it did when we came to Montana." Similarly Olivia is happier now because her family life is much calmer than it was in Colorado. There, she almost never saw her husband:

It's better here because there aren't so many men that go to the bars and parties with their friends. It is a more peaceful life here in the family. I don't think this is just for me, but for all the women who have moved here with their husbands. I have heard other women who have moved from Denver say that in Denver their husbands disappeared every weekend, drinking, always drinking. There is more opportunity there to do that, more bars and everything. Here it is more peaceful. Men go to work and they come home.

I am reminded of the idyll's reverberation in the lives of migrant families at small Mexican gatherings for birthdays and baptisms. The typical scene sparks feelings of nostalgia, simplicity and tradition, a throwback to a different time that exists more in fantasy than in reality. Children run around playing games, while women lay out an abundance of food, and men stand around an old truck drinking beer and taking turns fiddling with an engine. An outside observer would not intuit the many barriers and emotional struggles facing the families in attendance. During these snippets of time, life's struggles are temporarily suspended and positive emotions about place are created. Thus, although almost all migrants in my sample can tell of at least one personal experience in Montana of overt hostility, and women especially talk about their newfound isolation, their narratives of peace and family unity are more pronounced, narratives that they link directly to Montana's rurality. As Victoria told me in one of our many conversations, "Montana is good for our family. It is more like home. Here we know our kids are safe, we go to church, we have picnics, and we can stay together." Despite the many unique challenges of life in Montana, I have yet to meet a Mexican migrant here who wants to be anywhere else.

This section is not meant to gloss over the multiplicity of difficulties inherent in women's lives. For sure, the security that migrant women celebrate in Montana is precarious. They are marginalized on a macro level by economic and political forces and on a micro level via daily interactions with racist authorities and community members. Although there are relatively few violent crimes in Montana, a persistent focus of those I interviewed, daily life for migrant women requires constant negotiation of racism and sexism. Still, physical safety seems to trump emotional struggle and discrimination for the women in this study.

A Paradox of Migrant Exclusion

Montana's slogan "The Last Best Place" is marketed through images of simplicity, beauty and tranquillity, set in contrast to the stress of urban America. A popular Bozeman bumper sticker touting, "Slow down: Did you move here to be in a hurry?" serves to remind people of the laid-back aura that drew them to the New West. "The Last Best Place" is supposed to be a happy place. Yet the idyll of "The Last Best Place" has another side to it that is seldom interrogated. Montana is also a relatively "white" place, with the lowest number of black Americans (U.S. Census 2010) and the third lowest number of international migrants (Migration Policy Institute 2012) in the United States.

As has been true in other new migrant destinations (see Bohon 2006; Fennelly 2008; Jiménez 2010), there has been resistance to Montana's Mexican influx by native-born, white Americans. As I mentioned earlier, letters to the editor and recent incursions by white supremacists symbolize this most overtly. Racist incidents that migrants have experienced at school, work and in public are also testament to existing tensions. Yet to my surprise, white, native-born Americans are not the only ones resisting the migration of Mexicans to Montana. I also found that many of my Mexican research participants are unhappy about Mexican migration to Montana. For them, one of the critical reasons they deem "The Last Best Place" to be "best" is that, in their words, "There are not many Mexicans here."

Bourdieu (1984) theorizes that when individuals unconsciously internalize cultural domination, they experience a form of symbolic violence (see also Menjívar 2011). Symbolic violence is a means of controlling and disciplining individuals so as to maintain the social hierarchy. When migrants divert blame for the poverty and violence confronting many labor migrants to the United States away from a system of inequality and exploitation and toward other migrants, symbolic violence is at play. My data suggests that symbolic violence is embedded in the experience of many Mexican migrants to Montana who internalize social constructions of illegality, conflating immigration and criminality. By distinguishing themselves as "good" Mexicans and others as "bad" Mexicans, migrants erode the potential for ethnic solidarity in the face of larger structural threats (see also Jiménez 2010). This is a part of legal violence.

Many of the migrants I interviewed associate Mexican migrants with crime, increased incidents of racism, racial profiling by the police, lack of good housing and low wages. They told me that if they had their way they would keep "bad" Mexicans out of Montana. In some ways they have consumed the *Latino threat narrative* that criminalizes immigration in the public imagination by perpetuating myths and stereotypes that conflate Latino immigration with crime, violence and weak values (Chavez 2008), a form of symbolic violence. In their consumption of this narrative, Mexican migrants to Montana construct themselves as different, as noncriminal and more like the native born. If the community stays small and the "bad" Mexicans stay away, they told me, tranquillity and opportunity will endure. Whereas if the demographic makeup of Montana continues to shift and the Mexican population increases, some fear that Montana will become more like California, Florida, Texas, Arizona and Colorado, which they deem to be increasingly hostile places for "good" Mexicans. The irony is that recent research (Sampson 2008; Rumbaut and Ewing 2007) finds that when Latinos migrate into new areas, crime rates go down because Latinos bring with them strong family and community values, and because they go out of their way not to bring attention from the police. Reality aside, the threat narrative persists in the imaginations of many of my participants:

> Mexicans are problematic. The majority like to drink and smoke, and they
> have bad language. The truth is that I'm not a saint, but the majority of
> Mexicans have obscene language, at least this is my point of view. And I do
> not want my children to grow up in this kind of an atmosphere. That's the
> truth. I may drink once in a while, like one or two or maybe three drinks,
> but when there are a lot of Mexicans around it's scandalous. They begin
> to yell, and, well, they cause a lot of problems. And when they are drunk
> and cause problems, then the police come. And then immigration comes.
> (Martín)

As Martín described his frustration with his Mexican brethren, he made clear that while he is not perfect, he has made a conscious decision not to be like "those Mexicans" who he believes cause problems. He places himself

in the minority, asserting that the majority of Mexicans are problem-caus-
ers. Similarly, Malia associates Montana with a peacefulness that is directly
connected to its small population, not only of Mexicans but also of other
minorities, which she associates with a variety of problems:

> I like the tranquillity here. In Florida *la gente morena* (dark-skinned) were
> always roaming the streets. Here it's good because there are not so many
> Hispanics. It also makes the Americans treat us better. Here they greet us
> and do not look at us so badly.

Jaime echoed Malia's sentiments, claiming that tranquillity is a product
of having a small Mexican population. "What I like is that the people
in Montana are good and *tranquilo*. It's not like in Florida or in Chicago
where there are many *Hispanos* which makes life very stressful because
of the delinquency of the *cholos*/gang members." Ingrid too decried the
prevalence of "bad things" that accompany having too many Mexicans in
one place:

> At first it was tough to be in Montana because there were so few Latinos.
> But now I realize that it is better that there are not so many Latinos,
> because, well, between Latinos comes a lot of bad . . . . In California it is like
> in Mexico. There are many Mexicans, many, many and there's delinquency
> also. In California, yes, it's really ugly. It's better here . . . . In California it's
> like in Mexico. There are Mexican dances and clubs, but there are also
> scandals all the time.

Ironically, there is a general sentiment that although racism clearly exists
in Montana, and most of my participants have experienced it, racism in
Montana is not as bad as in other places. Participants tend to characterize
those with racist attitudes to be the exception and not the rule, and they
credit Montanans with being generally kind and welcoming. Here again,
my research participants credit Montana's small Latino population with its
relatively low incidence of racism. Jaime said:

> There is not so much racism here. This is because there are only a few
> Latinos here. Perhaps it's just that they have not arrived here yet like they
> have in the big cities where there are so many gangs of delinquents. When
> there are a lot of us in one place, it seems that some [Americans] think that
> we are all the same . . . . Unfortunately when Mexicans cause problems we
> all get blamed.

Ernestina echoed Jaime's thoughts, asserting that in Colorado Latinos
were not welcome because there were so many of them. "There are so many
there that the people think bad of all of us." In Montana, participants cele-

brate that most of the Montanans they meet are friendly and greet them in the street. But they question the endurance of Montanans' kindness. Specifically, they fear that the generally warm welcome they have received will change if too many Mexicans move to Montana. This is another reason they would like to slow the migration flow into their adopted state.

My research participants are also concerned that a large Mexican community will inevitably bring more problems with the police. As I describe in Chapter 3, the police are already feared by many Mexican migrants, and they do not want the situation to be made worse. Here again, my participants conflate Mexican migrants with criminality. For example, Martín equates the crime that he says Mexicans commit with heightened vigilance and discrimination by the police. "Some Mexicans come with bad ideas and they begin to rob. They open a car and take the stereo. And when they do this the police become prejudiced against all of us." Victoria agreed:

> Our population here is growing, and that is good but it is also bad. Those of us who are here are afraid that if Montana fills with too many Latinos it is going to be like in other states where the police stop you just because you're Mexican and things like this. This is the fear. That if the Mexican population keeps growing, we are going to see more and more racism [by authorities].

Although Jose is a U.S. citizen, he has begun to fear the police because he believes they profile Mexicans. He thinks he will have more to fear in the future:

> Here we're still basically ok because there are not so many Mexicans. I think most of the police still think, "Well, there are not so many of them so we will leave them alone." But now there are a lot more coming. And if it gets to be like in California where the Mexicans are driving drunk and causing problems, crashing their cars, the police will be more and more vigilant. So this makes me worry that there will be more police watching us and more will be deported. When there are not so many the police just leave us alone. But already the police are stopping us more and more, they are watching us because more and more have arrived.

When most Mexicans initially migrated to Montana, the idyll of security, family well-being and tranquillity were not at the forefront of their minds. Few considered the actions of police or contexts of racism in their decision. Mexicans came to Montana because of the abundance of good jobs. My participants are economically savvy. They realize that in a state without a large surplus of migrant workers they can command higher pay. As such, a common concern among my participants, especially those who have been in Montana longest, is that a large influx of Mexican workers "will drive wages down." Jaime described the employment situation as he understands it:

> So in Big Sky there is a lot of construction, and although there are not so many of us here yet, many Latinos are beginning to arrive. What is going to happen is that Big Sky will become saturated like in other places, and when that happens our labor becomes worth less and less. When there are a lot of Hispanics, the employers have more power and can pay us less.

Jaime does not fault Mexicans for coming to Montana. It makes economic sense:

> The people are going to go where there is work, where there are more opportunities. And so I think that here will become like other places with a lot of Hispanos, and this will affect our work. I'm not saying that they will be illegals because not all of us are. I'm already seeing that this year there isn't as much good work as last year and that's because more people have arrived here to work.

Migrants' desire for good employment opportunities and wages have bred competition between migrants and discouraged network formation. Although I found a few narratives of Mexican solidarity within my transcripts and field notes, more common are narratives of envy and individualism. This resonates with findings from research in urban migrant hubs. Both Menjívar (2000), in her research with Central American migrants in San Francisco, and Mahler (1995), who researched Salvadorans on Long Island, New York, found high levels of individualism and competition among migrants.

Dorotea came to Montana after years of struggle in California, where she had even been in jail for a period of time because someone who was using her same false name and social security number committed a crime. She described her first experiences in Montana as "wonderful." She loved the small town feel of Bozeman and was happy and thankful when her husband immediately found a good construction job. She then relayed a story of a car accident she was in when driving from Bozeman to Big Sky. In the heart of the mountain canyon, they hit an ice patch and their car spun around hitting a guard rail. It was a terrifying experience. "I was so afraid that our car was going to explode," she recalled with emotion. "I grabbed the kids, and one was bleeding, and I dragged them out of the car . . . . Then, a car full of *gueros*/fair-skinned people stopped and helped us with everything." Dorotea was awed by the kindness of the people who stopped to help her. She had thought that, as they were Mexicans in Montana, no one would want to help, and they would have to walk to the nearest town. As such, even though the accident left her family without a car for the next few months, the accident served as a positive sign to Dorotea that her family was welcome in Montana.

Following Dorotea's positive narrative about the kindness of Montanans, her tone changed and she launched into a frustrated diatribe about the lack of solidarity within Montana's Mexican community. When her family was without a car, they received some help, she said, but once they got on their feet and began doing well again, their Mexican friends deserted them:

> It was like once we started to move ahead in our lives, people stopped talking to us. Always here I have found Latinos, our own people, who are really envious and they are envious of us. With the American people, I have no problem, I have nothing bad to say. To the contrary they have treated me well . . . . But it is my own people who are envious. It is like they do not like it when someone else gets ahead.

I asked Dorotea if this meant that most of her best friends in Montana were native-born Americans. She responded with a laugh. "Listen, honestly, friends? I don't have any friends here."[6]

Victoria offered a similar description of the lack of support that exists within southwest Montana's Mexican community. "We are special," she said with a tone of obvious sarcasm. "You know we all came to this country out of necessity and because we wanted to better our lives. Yet at times, instead of respecting each other and offering a helping hand, there is just envy among us." I prodded Victoria to explain what prompts the envy. She went on to talk about how many migrants she knows are concerned mostly about themselves. They believe that if someone else gets a better job, or a new truck, or obtains their residency or citizenship, it will hold them down. I was left wondering whether the lack of solidarity within Montana's migrant community is an organic symptom of a new destination in its infancy, or if the context of southwest Montana uniquely brings to the surface the antagonism that is common within and between minority groups that are struggling at the bottom of the social and economic hierarchy (Mahler 1995; Menjívar 2000; Perlmutter 2002).

Conclusion

When I began this research I was certain that my data would tell the story of the extraordinary difficulties associated with living as a Mexican labor migrant in rural Montana. I assumed that as jobs brought Mexicans to Montana, so they would be the major factor keeping them there. And yet my data tell a much more complex story. While it is true that work and wages brought Mexicans to Montana, they are not the only factors retaining them. My research participants tell me that they want to stay in Montana because of the area's tranquillity, security and natural beauty.

While the differences between labor and lifestyle migrants are many, throughout my research I was reminded of the important similarities that exist across class and ethnicity. Postindustrial society has spurred many in the United States, independent of race, class and ethnicity, to search for what has been lost, like job security and safe communities. Montana represents this. Additionally, the vast majority of migrants in my sample are from rural central Mexico. In Montana they feel a connection to the landscape and rural lifestyle, both of which remind them of home. And so despite isolation, the heightened threat of deportability and narrow employment niches, Mexican migrants have a strong affinity for Montana. They want to stay.

The experiences of Mexican migrants to Montana suggest that despite the formidable challenges of living as a migrant in the United States, migrants exercise agency. The migrants in this study have chosen Montana over other traditional destinations that in many ways are more amenable to a migrant population. Their agency is shaped in large part by gender and generation. Men, more often than not, made the initial decision to move to Montana. Yet women and children are often the ones who exert the most influence about staying. Mexican migration to Montana reminds us that the American Dream endures in the migrant imagination. No matter how porous its promise, migrants in this study are determined to consume whatever piece of the dream they can. Montana represents hope.

And yet, a limitation to my analysis is that I interviewed only those migrants who have stayed in Montana, or in a couple cases, left and returned. There are cases where migrants ultimately decide Montana is not best for them or their families. Similarly, whereas the vast majority of migrants told me they want to stay in Montana, increasingly I hear that they are contemplating a return to Mexico. Many are discouraged economically. Others have given up hope that immigration reform will pass in Washington, and they are tired of living in fear of deportation. Those contemplating return tell me that their savings will go further in Mexico than in the United States, and they would be happy to be near family and kin. If they return, their children will know Mexico and gain a stronger appreciation of their ethnic roots. While few migrants in my sample send remittances to support family in Mexico, many are sending money to support home construction. Having a house in Mexico is their safety net. As the American Dream withers in the hearts and minds of some migrants, they cling strongly to the hope that with savings, skills and ambition they can still achieve it in Mexico, a *Transamerican Dream* (see Schmalzbauer 2005). The Great Recession intensified contemplations of return. Is the Last Best Place "best," when wages and work have disappeared? I explore this question in the next chapter.

Chapter 5

Doing Gender: The Impact of
Economic Crisis on Household Dynamics

When we used to see news of the economic recession on TV in
2008, we thought, what are they talking about? My husband had
so much construction work . . . he couldn't keep up and we were
saving a lot of money. Then in June 2009 everything changed.
My husband didn't work for over a month. Now he just works
once in a while and when he does the pay is not good. (Victoria)

Work and good wages drew Victoria and Candido to Montana from Colorado in 2006 at the peak of the most recent construction boom. Candido
came first, recruited to join a team working on the development of an exclusive new ski resort. Victoria soon followed with their infant daughter. In
Colorado, both Candido and Victoria had worked for pay, as two incomes
were necessary there to make ends meet. In Montana, Candido's construction salary alone was enough to support them. Victoria welcomed her new
life as a stay-at-home wife and mother.

The Great Recession was relatively late to arrive to Montana and the
Rocky Mountain West. In 2007 and 2008, when migrants were leaving traditional hubs because of market saturation (Light 2006), the migrant population was growing in Montana. When the full impact of the Great Recession
hit southwest Montana in 2009, the construction industry came to a halt.
Candido, along with hundreds of other migrant men, lost his job. For the
first time in several years and since becoming a mother, Victoria was forced
to seek work outside of the home. Through her priest she found two part-
time jobs, one cleaning the private home of a parishioner and another caring
for an elderly church member. Victoria is ambitious and independent, and
she relished the feeling of accomplishment that her re-entry into paid work
instilled. Yet she was apprehensive about being away from her family. She felt
distressed not being with her young children, who were strongly attached to
her. But she was most concerned about Candido.

While Victoria went to work, Candido stayed home. He slept a lot and ate a lot. Victoria worried that he was depressed. Candido did not like to talk about the impact the recession was having on him or on his relationship with Victoria and their three children. His silence added to Victoria's stress. They began to argue more intensely and more often. Life was uniquely challenging as the roles in which they both felt most comfortable were disrupted, and there was no script to guide them across their family's new gendered terrain.

Gender, Immigration and the Great Recession

The Great Recession had a major impact on international migration trends (Migration Information Source 2008). Unauthorized immigration dramatically decreased with the recession's onset (Massey 2010), and scholars noted an increase in the voluntary repatriations of migrants to their home countries (Migration Information Source 2008). At the same time, migrants who stayed in the United States were among those most negatively affected by job loss (Hout et al. 2011). Whereas these macro trends have been well analyzed, little has been written about how the recession affected the daily lives of migrants in the United States, and specifically how migrant families dealt with the onslaught of unemployment and financial insecurity. Rural migrant families in particular have been absent from the discourse about the recession and its aftermath. As Victoria's and Candido's story exemplifies, the effects of the economic crisis rippled into relationships and households, and were likely intensified in places where families have limited social supports.

Jennifer Sherman (2013) finds that the Great Recession bore deeply into the emotional well-being of poor and working-class individuals, especially those who had dependents. Work is a large part of identity formation in the United States, especially for men. Workers reported feelings of stigmatization because they were not able to fulfill their caretaking roles within their families. Sherman finds that shame discouraged many of the poor and unemployed from pursuing public assistance and led to self-imposed isolation. Unemployed men in particular sought to avoid revealing their hardship publicly.

Although Sherman's research did not include migrant participants, her findings are helpful in understanding the implications of the recession for labor migrants in Montana. As was the case for native-born Americans, the "man-cession" brought gender to the forefront of migrant families. As I have detailed in earlier chapters, migrant men construct their identities around

financial provision. Most have worked in wage labor since they were teenagers. Work is at the crux of their masculinity and their identities as husbands
and fathers. Migrant women, on the other hand, construct their identities
around care and motherhood. The recession challenged both migrant men's
and women's identities and, as was true for Sherman's subjects, served to
further stigmatize and marginalize them.

During the crisis, demand for low-wage female labor, specifically in the
care and domestic services industries, sectors dominated by female migrants,
outpaced demand for low-wage male labor (Beneria 2010; Boushey 2009).
At the same time, the construction industry, which employs the majority
of migrant men in Montana, was hit particularly hard (Hout et al. 2011;
Schontzler 2010). Whereas international migration slowed with the deep-
ening of the recession in the United States, the labor demand that persisted,
particularly in the Mountain West, privileged migrant women. This changed
economic landscape had important implications for gender relations within
migrant households. In many families, women, such as Victoria, went to
work, stepping out of the role of intensive mothering for the first time since
migrating to Montana. While women went to work, many men, like Candido, stayed home, also for the first time.

The Great Recession did not impact all migrant families in Montana
equally. Most notably, the recession highlighted key differences between agricultural and construction families. Whereas construction workers earned
higher wages before the recession, the crash abruptly crippled them financially. Agriculture on the other hand, though not as high paying in most instances, has proven a much steadier and secure economic niche for migrants.
Boom or bust, dairy cows still need to be milked two or three times a day,
365 days a year. While the lives of construction families changed dramatically
with the Great Recession, the lives of agricultural families changed little if at
all. During the recession the typically less educated and more marginalized
agricultural families fared better than their more privileged Mexican peers.
Similarly, whereas gender relations were challenged within construction
families, they were not disturbed in agricultural families.

In this chapter I explore the implications of the Great Recession for gender relations within Mexican construction families in Montana. Assuming
the position that gender is performative (West and Zimmerman 1987), I
investigate how migrant women and men "do gender" in times of economic
crisis. Further, I look at how gender performativity influences rural survival
strategies and well-being. I show that, on the one hand, traditional gender
roles were disrupted by the crisis, as many migrant women entered wage

labor, while men stayed home. Yet simultaneously, gender ideologies were reinforced, as migrant women took on the additional emotional labor of protecting men's sense of masculinity by continuing to perform what they deemed to be a culturally appropriate gender script.

Whereas the paradoxical combination of gender transgression and tradition has been noted within urban migrant families (George 2005; Kibria 1993), its dynamics are different in rural contexts. Specifically, while urban migrants are more likely to look to networks for support (Hagan 1994; Hondagneu-Sotelo 1994), especially in times of economic crisis (Aguilar et. al 2010), in Montana I find that migrants, in the absence of strong networks, turned inward to their immediate families. This turn inward strengthened family solidarities in contexts of gender inequality.

Shifting Economic Structures, Rigid Gender Expectations

A rich body of sociological research shows that work opportunities for migrant women may transform or reaffirm gender relations depending on the context in which they occur (Menjívar 1999). Emerging forms of gender egalitarianism generated from women's paid work may coexist with entrenched forms of subordination (Gonzalez-López 2005). For example, when urban migrant women enter wage labor and contribute to family income, they typically gain autonomy in the domestic realm (Pessar 1999). In this sense, immigration may be empowering for women (Grasmuck and Pessar 1991). Yet whether increased autonomy in the household increases women's overall well-being is uncertain. Menjívar (1999) finds that power shifts within migrant households may heighten tension and stress, and that women tend to bear the brunt of the negativity. Domestic violence is one cited repercussion (Raj and Silverman 2002). And despite power gains in households, migrant women may continue to be subordinated in the public realm (Grasmuck and Pessar 1991).

Also uncertain is whether domestic power shifts, rooted in women's wage earning, alter gender expectations. Hondagneu-Sotelo (1994) finds that boosts in Mexican migrant women's wage work and autonomy in the household typically does *not* lead them to develop a feminist consciousness. Instead, the migrant women she interviewed devised meaning from their work because it supported their families, especially the social mobility of their children. To be sure, research suggests that while migrant women increasingly engage in wage work, they continue to maintain their time-honored responsibilities on the domestic front (Anastario and Schmalzbauer 2008; Deeb-Sossa and Bickham-Mendez 2008), and to embrace what they identify as traditional femininity (Hancock 2007). My data validates these findings.

I began to observe the effects of the Great Recession almost immediately following its onset in Montana. Visits by Mexican families to the food bank reached an all-time high in 2009,[1] while attendance at the monthly Spanish Mass dissipated. The latter signaled that temporary workers and some families were leaving Montana. The small Catholic Church, which used to fill every month, was less than half full for most of 2009, 2010 and 2011, and the church's beloved priest spoke of the possibility of having to discontinue the Mass entirely.

The rows of chairs toward the back of the church that were typically occupied by young single men were empty month after month. The majority of the men who used to occupy the seats were migrant construction workers on H2B visas. After their early departure for Mexico in 2009, they were not invited back in 2010 or 2011. I often wondered how the families of these workers in Mexico, who depend on remittances for their well-being, were making ends meet. A small core of families continued to attend Mass, but I noted a solemnity about them. Pedro and Candido, for example, who usually stood with their wives to sing in the small choir, instead sat stoically among the other worshipers. The crisis had penetrated the idyllic shield of the church, which for the past three years had been deemed by many of my participants to be a refuge of peace and happiness for Catholic Mexicans in southwest Montana.[2]

The public cloud of economic recession hung most visibly over migrant men, as women worked hard to maintain a cheery disposition despite the stress I knew they were experiencing. At Raul's third birthday, in the spring of 2010, for example, I noted a stark difference in energy between the segregated groups of migrant men and women in attendance. While Gaby and her friends bustled about the small trailer with smiles on their faces encouraging guests to indulge in more *tacos*, the men stood outside in the cold, dreary, spring drizzle nursing Coronas. My husband, Steve, whose green building business was also struggling in the midst of the recession, chatted with Abraham about the tough times in the construction industry. Later, as I bounced Zola in my arms while Micah swatted at Raul's birthday piñata, I overheard Abraham ask Steve whether he knew of anyone looking to buy some masonry equipment, including a couple of tractors and a truck. His business had gone bankrupt and he needed to liquidate.

It was obvious that migrant men's identities were dealt a terrible blow when they lost their jobs and, in a few cases, had to close their businesses.

The jobs that remained were in the low-wage service industry, which were much less prestigious than skilled work in masonry, roofing and dry-walling. Women told me that their husbands would feel too much shame to stoop to the level of cleaning houses or working in fast food kitchens. Instead, women took the jobs that their husbands shunned.

Inez, for example, whose husband, Jonathon, is a skilled mason, told me:

> My husband doesn't want to work in a kitchen. He has a lot of pride. Instead, he'd rather do construction work whenever he can and take lower pay. That means I had to find work . . . . I found a job cleaning a hotel. The pay isn't good, but it's something.

Similarly, Ernestina, who had been working part time in a community health clinic, talked the clinic director into giving her more hours. She began working full time in 2009 while her husband took small construction jobs when they were available. Still, she said, "life feels insecure." Victoria, as mentioned above, found a job cleaning the home of a wealthy family from her church, a job that allowed her to bring her baby with her, and to work while her older children were in school. Dorotea found fulltime work in a local hotel, and Ana, additionally burdened by her husband's deportation, began cleaning houses. In all of these cases women became, for the first time, the main income earners in their families.

Consistent with general trends in U.S. society (Heymann 2000; Jacobs and Gerson 2004; Schor 1992), I found that shifts in income-providing roles in migrant households were not matched with shifts in gender consciousness or a redistribution of domestic labor. Instead, women told me that in addition to their paid jobs, they continued to do all of the domestic work in their families. Inez continued, "I now have three jobs. I take care of the house and kids, I take care of my husband, and I clean hotel rooms. I work 10 hours a day outside of the home and 6 hours in the home. I'm always exhausted." I heard this theme consistently in my conversations with migrant women.

Similarly, when I asked the focus group of unemployed migrant men if they were using their time at home to help with critical domestic chores like cleaning, they all laughed, their eyes communicating that they knew this was not the appropriate response. "I know you are thinking that we are *machista*," Pedro said with a big smile, "but . . . . " He did not finish the sentence. I interpreted his silence to mean, "This is just the way we are," a sentiment validated by migrant women, many of whom told me with resignation that their husbands would never change.

Yet a few migrant men told me that they were undertaking select jobs around the house. A hierarchy of domestic tasks revealed itself in my interviews and observations, with child care, especially playing with children, and cooking, on the top, and cleaning and laundry on the bottom. Whereas migrant men expressed interest and willingness to engage at the top of this domestic hierarchy, they resisted doing the "dirty work." Pedro, for example, shared that the best thing about being unemployed was spending more time with Angela and his children:

> Being unemployed does have its good side in that for all of my life I have spent the majority of time working, only working, from the dawn until night. From the time I opened my eyes every morning of my life until now I was working, and also here I spent a lot of time driving to and from work. So I spent a lot of time working and only a little time with my family. Now it's different . . . . We are together a lot more. This is the good side. I get to see the kids when they get home from school and I get to go with them to the park . . . . I have a lot of stress in terms of the economic side of things. But there are really nice things about being home that before I didn't have.

Ángel, whose wife took a part-time hotel housekeeping job when he lost his job, began taking care of his children two days a week, the first time in his life that he had had sole responsibility in terms of child care. Like Pedro, he reported that he truly enjoyed this time with his children. When he lost his job Ángel also re-engaged with cooking, a task that he did regularly before his wife joined him in the United States. But Ángel made clear that his contribution to cooking did not include clean-up. "I like to cook and now that I'm not working much I cook more. But I will not wash a plate!" he asserted.

Gender inequality persisted in this regard as unemployed men, with a lot of time at home, engaged in the domestic jobs that they liked to do, such as playing with their children and cooking, yet seldom undertook household duties they did not enjoy. Therefore, women picked up the slack. This story is familiar. As has been noted in classic research on middle-class American households (Hochschild 1989; Schor 1992), migrant women's total workload increased as the household gender division of labor remained obstinate.

The nuanced intersections of gender and economic crisis also impacted migrant marriages. During my focus group with unemployed men, we talked in depth about the impact of the crisis on their partnerships. Men spoke openly and honestly about their challenges. I concluded from the conversation that the impact of the crisis was shaped in large part by the way power was organized within migrants' *relational contexts* (see Dreby and Schmalzbauer 2013) before the recession set in. In partnerships with the most rigidly defined gender roles and a skewed distribution of power, marital solidarity, although not necessarily marital satisfaction, was heightened. In these instances, with little or no outside support, couples leaned even more on each other and adhered more closely to a patriarchal script in which men made the financial decisions and women abided. To the contrary, in those marriages where there was more equality, tensions between partners intensified as they challenged each other more, especially over money matters. Yet, even in the cases where overt marital tensions intensified, I still found that the context of rural Montana ultimately mandated dependency, and thus couples stayed together.

Pedro, who, as I have mentioned elsewhere, forbids Angela to work and is the clear head of his household, told me, "My wife never challenges me, especially now. I make the decisions and we never argue." Abraham too, whose wife, Edith, remained at home during the crisis, said that his marriage had gotten stronger during the crisis because his wife needed him more and he needed her more. Ángel, whose wife went to work part time in 2009, shared that he had gained more respect for his wife during the crisis because he had learned through experience how difficult child care can be. He credited his newfound respect for strengthening his marriage. Still, Ángel made clear that respect for his wife aside, he still made most of the decisions in the household and his wife rarely challenged him.

Candido had a smirk on his face as the other men in the focus group shared their stories of enhanced marital solidarity. Unlike the other men in my study, Candido migrated to the United States as a teenager. He attended and graduated from high school in Colorado, is divorced from his first wife, and holds relatively progressive gender attitudes. His wife, Victoria, has told me on several occasions that Candido is supportive of all of her endeavors including learning English, looking for a job, and "dreaming big." They have a marriage based on respect and equality, and this nurtures Victoria's strength and independence. Never one to interrupt, Candido waited until everyone else was finished, then with a chuckle said, "Well, it's totally different in my house." He went on to say that Victoria challenges him more now than ever before, and, as I detail in this chapter's opening vignette, they argue more:

> My experience is really different . . . . We discuss things more now and as a
> result we argue more than before. This crisis has affected our marriage a lot.
> It's definitely more difficult now . . . . When there is money stress, we always
> have more problems, always. We argue over what the priorities are, and if
> Victoria doesn't agree with me she fights for what she thinks the priorities
> should be. It's not bad, because we always work it out. But it's certainly not
> easy between us when times are tough.

Thus as women gain autonomy, there can be greater household stress (see also Menjívar 1999). Victoria asserts power in her marriage where many of the other migrant women in this study do not. And yet in my interviews and conversations with Victoria during the time when Candido was unemployed, she consistently asserted a deferential commitment to him. Sure, she might challenge Candido, and they might fight, but ultimately, she assured me, her family and marriage are her top priority. Indeed, family solidarity reigned among the vast majority of families I met in my field research. I found that, in general, migrant women took it upon themselves to keep their families together despite whatever stress and frustration they might have with their partners. They believed it to be their responsibility, and part of their survival femininity, to maintain family well-being no matter what the cost. It is therefore no surprise that the cost was often women's own emotional well-being.

Added Burdens: The Emotional Costs of Economic Crisis

As I detailed in Chapter 2, Sara has long struggled with depression that until the Great Recession she blamed on loneliness and isolation. When I interviewed her during the second year of Reinaldo's unemployment in 2010, she told me that her depression had become worse than ever. It still emanated from loneliness but, more important, it came from the stress of keeping a semblance of normality in her family when they were barely making ends meet. For Reinaldo, one of the longest-standing migrant residents in town, and looked up to for his success as a supervisor and recruiter for a large construction company, losing his job was devastating to his pride and self-esteem. Sara told me that her duty, in addition to finding a way to keep food on the table, was to keep her chin up and his ego intact. The stress took its toll. She had persistent headaches, did not sleep well and struggled with back pain. Sara told me several times during my fieldwork that she would like to have a job. She is a permanent resident, and thus she has the possibility of working without the fear that unauthorized women have. Yet, as I detail in Chapter 2, Reinaldo refused to let her work. For many years, Sara did not push back, putting her marriage and loyalty to Reinaldo above her own ambitions.

I asked Sara to tell me what life was like during the time when Reinaldo had no work:

> For over a year and a half he was always here in the house. And when he was around there was so much tension . . . . And now he only works once in a while. We had some savings in the bank, so at first it wasn't difficult financially, but we knew the savings wouldn't last . . . . And it has been very stressful. He was, well . . . there were some days that he seemed happy, but there were more days when he was completely unbearable. On those days if I only looked at him he would get angry. I knew he was angry because he

didn't have work, and I tried to be understanding. He was so stressed. He slept a lot and he ate a lot . . . . And I couldn't say anything. He didn't want to talk, and when he did talk he was very aggressive. He never hurt me, but he was in a very bad mood, very aggressive.

"So how did you cope with this?" I probed. Sara continued:

It was so hard. It still is. For one, I do not have many Hispanic friends. I had my daughter but then she left and went back to Kansas. That was so difficult for me . . . . I have never felt so alone and so sad . . . . The thing is, Reinaldo always thinks I am happy and calm. But no. He never knows how I am really feeling . . . . It is my job to maintain harmony in the home. And it is a heavy weight. I always have to have the same face, smiling like everything is fine even when times are really difficult. He can be in bad humor, but I can never show it if I am. It all has made me physically sick. My knees hurt, my back hurts. And I know it's the stress.

We then talked about her son Brian. I asked how he was doing amid the stress that Sara had described:

I think Brian is sad. He does not really understand the situation, but he sees what's happening. I think he sees that his dad is sad and that makes him sad. Or he sees his dad angry or stressed and he gets stressed. But then I talk to him and I encourage him.

During the worst of the economic crisis, Sara worked hard to keep Reinaldo happy and supported. She put a similar effort into making sure Brian was all right. But no one was there to make sure Sara was all right, and so she suffered, but with a smile.

Angela took a similar approach to easing the stress within her family. Like Sara, she has never worked outside of the home. When Pedro lost his job, her emotional labor increased precipitously as she struggled to maintain peace and happiness within her family:

It's really hard when Pedro is around because he doesn't talk and he doesn't laugh. So I try to change my form to be in a really good mood so that he will feel better . . . . But we're both really tense, I know . . . . At times it's really difficult because I am someone with a strong character. So it's difficult. Because I am often tired and I don't want to hear noise, and then the kids scream or start to argue with each other, or cry. I want to just hide in my room, but it's my job to maintain the peace.

While Sara's and Angela's situations were not the norm among families in Montana, in that neither entered the workforce when their husbands lost their full-time jobs, the responsibility they both reported to maintain normality in their families during tough economic times was echoed in my focus group and interviews with migrant wives. Ernestina, for example, told me that her husband was "always distracted." Inez said that although he would never admit it, her husband was anxious. Victoria's reflections concurred. She described Candido as "very serious now, much more so than normal." She continued, "He never says anything about how he feels. I have to ask, 'Are you sad?' But he doesn't like to talk about it." In all of these instances, women felt it their duty to bolster their husband's self-esteem, to make sure they still "felt like men," and to make an extra effort not to make waves. This gender work was exhausting, but it was necessary to maintaining their families' well-being.

Migrant women who started to work outside of the home with the onset of the crisis carried different and additional burdens than those who remained at home. Most important, they told me that they felt the guilt of not being with their young children during the day. As a mother, I bonded with them on this issue, as I too feel constantly pulled between work and family. Of course, beyond that basic shared sentiment, our situations are very different. I love my job, which energizes and challenges me, and I have a feminist-identified husband and a financial safety net. The women in this study, without exception, had no choice but to enter into jobs that are exhausting, low-paying and low-status, most often cleaning hotel rooms or private homes, or working in fast food kitchens.

Whereas Victoria has told me on several occasions that "work is the best therapy," and other women reported that their confidence increased from earning a wage, and they felt it a relief to have some time away from the stress of their households, very few woman said they genuinely like their jobs. In this important respect, women's employment experiences are markedly different from those of their husbands, who report finding meaning and status in their skilled work. Most of the women I interviewed characterized their work as a necessary survival strategy, and those with young children resented, at least initially, that work took them away from them. For example, during a focus group with newly employed women, Inez explained, "Children need their mothers. They need us, period. And when we are not with them, they suffer." The other women in the group nodded in chorus. "Our children are suffering most from this crisis," Inez continued. "Before [the crisis], we could be with them. That was much better." The economic crisis chipped away at migrant women's socially constructed roles as caregivers, which added to their guilt and anxiety.

The emotional burden the economic recession generated for migrant families was not borne solely by wives and mothers. The significance that migrant men derived from their work entailed that without work their lives lost meaning. In one of our many conversations, Abraham told me that when he first had to close his company's doors, he wanted to sleep all the time, and he felt depressed. He also said that he worried most about his eleven-year-old daughter. She had gained weight because all she wanted to do was watch television and eat. "I know this is because she feels our stress," Abraham concluded. "She worries we are going to lose our house and have to move." When I asked Abraham what would help ease his stress and depression, he answered immediately and abruptly. "Work. That's the only thing that could make this better. I need more work." Without exception, all the men in my sample expressed the strain of not being able to fulfill their role as family provider.

Pedro confessed to me during the second of our in-depth interviews that

> it's really hard when one is accustomed to being productive, to doing things, and then all of a sudden you're not doing anything. It's a big frustration. It's like you feel, well, not invalid, but at times impotent. It's like I want to do something, and I can't and this stresses me a lot.

Much of men's stress is directly related to their responsibilities as family providers. When times were good, which spanned most of the time my participants had been in Montana, men were able to exceed their expectations for provision. Their wives did not have to work, and still they could buy superfluous things. Pedro continued:

> When my wife wants something I always want to be able to say, "Of course, you can have that." I can't do that now. And she depends completely on me, and that adds a lot of stress. I have all of the responsibility.

I had been nervous as I prepared for my focus group of newly unemployed migrant men. Having heard testimony from migrant women that their stoic husbands did not like to communicate what they were feeling, I worried that the men would not talk openly, and that our discussion would be short, disjointed and shallow. Yet the opposite occurred. Instead of being short and superficial, the focus group went on for almost three hours and ultimately ended only because the public library, where we were meeting, needed to close. I sensed that men felt comfortable sharing their struggles with each other in a space that was structured specifically for them to do so. My job was easy. They really wanted to talk.

When I asked them if they were feeling emotional distress because they were not working regularly, Ángel immediately replied, "Yes, I am feeling anxiety and stress, all the time." Candido spoke next. "Yes, I sometimes have a feeling of depression." Then Abraham summed up what I sensed to be the heart of men's suffering, the shattering of the American Dream:

> I always used to say that the United States was a dream, but now I say it's
> a nightmare. At times I am even dreaming about the nightmare that my
> life has become. What am I doing here, I wonder. Because it seems like my
> dreams have finished.

By the end of the focus group, I was both exhausted and exhilarated. I was
exhausted from hearing about the intensity of struggle in which the men
were immersed, and the inequalities that cut across most of their families. But
I was also exhilarated by the depth of reflection that the men in the group
demonstrated. I was left again to reflect on the many meanings of *macho*
(Gutmann 1996; Mirandé 1997).

Surviving

I chatted with Pedro following a Spanish Mass on a beautiful autumn Sunday in 2010. He told me that he and Angela were seriously contemplating
a return to Mexico. The successful masonry company that he had managed
with his brother Abraham for the past few years had gone bankrupt. There
was tension brewing between the typically close brothers. Indeed, they were
no longer talking to each other. Pedro told me that he had nowhere left to
turn for work. For the time being, his plan was to work short stints in other
states. He had heard of temporary opportunities in Oklahoma and Wyoming,
but he knew of nothing permanent. Mexico was looking more appealing by
the day, he said with a tone of resignation.

Pedro and Angela had been funneling savings over the years to Mexico to
build a house. They had originally strategized that the house would be their
safety net in case they were deported, and it would be their retirement home
whatever the case. While Pedro was not confident that he could immediately
find work in Calvillo, the small city in Aguas Calientes that he calls home,
he was comforted by knowing that his savings would last over a year there,
much longer than if he and his family stayed in Montana. The burden of providing for his family, which Pedro typically carried with great pride, weighed
heavily.

Several other families also contemplated a return to Mexico. Ingrid is a
widow who is from what she described as a violence-ravaged part of rural
Guerrero. She is in Montana with her son and daughter-in-law. She told me
that although she feared to return, she did not feel like there was another
choice:

> Well, I think that we would stay if we still had work. Like I always tell my
> children, you have to save, save, save money in Mexico for when the day
> comes that we no longer have work here. And here we are. What more can

we do here without work? We still have to pay rent, pay our bills. What are we going to do? We do not have another option but to leave.

Ultimately Ingrid did not leave. Like Pedro and Angela, her unauthorized status added intensity to the decision of return. With heightened border security, going back to Mexico would likely mean giving up the possibility of ever returning to the United States. Many unauthorized, unemployed migrants I met during the crisis were pained by the decision of whether to give up and go home or to try to weather the economic storm with the hope that the economy would rebound and President Obama would eventually follow through on his promise of immigration reform.

Other unauthorized migrants who contemplated return worried about taking their U.S. citizen children back to Mexico with them. In Montana, they had access to good, safe schools. In Mexico, especially in the rural areas where most originated, the schools were of poor quality, and some of their home regions were experiencing increasing levels of crime. With citizen children in the mix, survival strategies were complicated. In the men's focus group, Ángel shared that "because I have kids I do not know if it makes sense to return. For them to return to my small town would be very difficult." Pedro responded that in his family, his youngest children wanted to go to Mexico, but his oldest son, a freshman in high school, wanted to stay. "This makes it difficult," Pedro said with dismay. "Chaba wants to finish high school here and he wants to go to university. Do I take that away from him? Or do I leave him here alone? There is no good answer."

Jose sent his wife, Judith, and his infant son, Anthony, back to Mexico to live with his mother. Both Jose and Judith are U.S. citizens, which made the decision of return less daunting. While finances may prevent them from being together, illegality does not. Jose told me that by sending Judith and Anthony to live with his mother in Aguas Calientes he could cut his rent by 75 percent, sharing his small trailer with four other men. He found comfort in knowing that his separation from his family would be only temporary. "We just have to wait for the crisis to pass," he assured me. Later that month, Jose left Montana for Oklahoma where he found construction work on a large military project. The last I heard, Judith and Anthony still had not joined him there.

Abraham and Edith, who are both U.S. residents, thought seriously about following the same path as Jose and Judith. They own a house in Montana and their children are U.S. citizens. Because they have residency and thus the ability to travel to Mexico, their children know Mexico well and feel comfortable there. When Abraham talked to his oldest son about a possible return, he was open to the idea. Ultimately Abraham decided that splitting the family between Mexico and Montana would be even more expensive than remaining in Montana together:

> So at first I told Edith that if things got too bad here she could go to Mexico with the kids and I would stay here. Well, we would only do it because it would be an economic decision, a way to help us keep moving forward. But then I said, well if you go and I stay it will actually be more expensive because we have the house and I would have to keep paying it and sending you money. So I decided that we all should just stay . . . . And even though she has not worked, maybe Edith will have to start selling food, like tamales, from a truck.

Abraham and Edith weathered the crisis in Montana, managing to keep their house and family for the most part intact. Edith never sought formal work, nor did she sell tamales from a truck. They struggled, but they were able to stay put.

After Agosta's husband lost his full-time construction job he, like Abraham, found part-time work out of state. Agosta worked a cleaning job once in a while, but when I interviewed her, her optimism was beginning to wither:

> My husband told me that he found a good company, because at least they will pay enough for us to have food, housing and transportation. This is an advantage. He doesn't earn the same as before, but it's something . . . . But it's difficult to live not working. Really, we are barely able to pay for this modest trailer, and to pay for just the basic things . . . . So I said to him that I want to go back to Mexico because this is not the life that we hoped for in the United States . . . . I think we will go back in June after the kids are done with school. But I don't know. We will have to analyze what we need.

Unlike the other families who contemplated returning to Mexico, Agosta and her husband ultimately followed through on their plan. Because they both have permanent residency in the United States they left knowing that if the economy picked up in the future they could return. Although Agosta worried that moving back and forth would be difficult for her children, she and her husband ultimately decided that return was the best choice.

Like everything else that structures migrant life, survival strategies are gendered. Holding tightly to their role as economic providers, men during the crisis did what they could to re-enter the construction workforce. Every construction worker with whom I spoke took major pay cuts, as they went from working full time for one company, or in the case of Pedro and Abraham managing a company themselves, to working on small, temporary projects. The work they found during the crisis was sporadic and less than ideal, but it brought in some income and maintained a semblance of their self-respect. During the focus group Ángel provided a rich description of his daily efforts to make ends meet:

> Construction work has gone down a lot, so I try to keep going little by little looking for work wherever I can. Now I don't just work in one place. I work whenever I can and if I hear of someone who has work, I follow him, and if it's someone else, I follow him, hoping there will be something for me too. This is how we are surviving the crisis. The good jobs that we had before. They are gone. The guys I used to work with, well . . . we are no longer together. We all go our separate ways looking for work wherever we can. It's so depressing, working two days and then not for weeks.

In many of the cases where men worked sporadically or not at all for long stretches, migrant wives contributed to their households through paid work as hotel or house cleaners, or as kitchen help. In other cases men took temporary jobs out of state. For example, Pedro and Abraham finally made amends and spent much of fall 2010 doing construction work in Oklahoma. When that job ended, they returned to Montana and lived from savings for a while. They then found work in Wyoming, spending every other weekend with their families for a stretch of several months. Angela and Edith told me that it was difficult to have them gone, but they would have rather lived apart than suffer the anxiety of unemployment. As I was finishing my fieldwork in the spring of 2012, Abraham and Pedro were both unemployed again and living off savings, and Pedro and Angela were planning a move to Oklahoma before returning to Mexico for good. In a similar situation, in 2010 Sara's husband, Reinaldo, started to work sporadic stints in Iowa and North Dakota. The families of Pedro and Angela, Abraham and Edith and Sara and Reinaldo became translocal families.

Despite the pressure that migrant men feel to provide, migrant women told me that they bear the ultimate responsibility of keeping their families fed and healthy. During the peak of the crisis, Sara explained that this meant she had completely given up buying anything extra for herself. She obsessively watched the specials at Wal-Mart, bought food only from the discounted shelves and went with one of her migrant friends to the food bank when she had to. Indeed, the food bank had become a regular part of many women's routines. During an in-depth interview, one of the food bank directors in 2009 told me that migrants were their fastest growing demographic group. "It is the women who come, always the women." When I asked Sara about this, she explained that men would feel much too much shame to take handouts. "Many women don't even tell their husbands that they go to the

food bank. Yet, the money just doesn't stretch. We do what we have to do."
Angela detailed a similar survival strategy. She too frequented the food bank
and stopped buying anything extra. Her most important task was to make
their money stretch:

> We only pay our bills and buy what we absolutely need. We don't go out
> to eat. We only buy the food that is necessary and we don't waste anything.
> This is what I am focusing on. And with bills, well, there is nothing you can
> do. You have to pay them. Come what comes, you have to pay them. But
> anything personal, and even with food, we limit ourselves.

In addition to budgeting so that the family could make ends meet, women
working outside the home had to strategize free child care, since paying for
child care could wipe out their limited wages. When Victoria's housecleaning
boss told her that she wanted her to clean in the afternoons, when Victoria's
kids were out of school, Victoria swapped child care with Dorotea, who at
the time lived in the same trailer park. Similarly, Liliana, whose husband
was one of the few construction workers to maintain his job during the
crisis, watched the children of two other migrant women during the day. As
these examples suggest, the crisis marked the beginning of women's network
formation, as women reached out to each other, often for the first time, in
an attempt to navigate the crisis. Still, these networks were small, and they
tended to be centered in the Catholic Church. They were therefore difficult
to access by women who do not drive, are not Catholic or who do not attend
church regularly, and those who live outside of town, characteristics of the
majority of women in my sample.

In Montana, as I have detailed in other chapters, there is little in the way
of social support for migrant families who are living on the economic edge.
Whereas in traditional migrant hubs, social services and community organizations are structured to accommodate a migrant population, in Montana undeveloped informal networks are migrants' only semblance of social support.
This means that families look inward for survival, as family solidarity is the
most accessible means of getting through tough times. And so, although migrant women and men alike express anxiety from trying to maintain gender
norms in the face of tremendous structural opposition, their survival demands
this performance. Family always comes first for the migrants in this study.

Conclusion

The migrants in this sample have always struggled. They struggled first in
Mexico with poverty, unemployment and lack of opportunity. Many risked

their lives to cross the U.S. border without authorization. In the United States, they have struggled financially. They have withstood discrimination and suffered the deportations of friends and family. Through all of this they have clung tightly to a family division of labor that is based on gender expectations in which men are providers and women are caretakers. Family solidarity is their first priority, and the context of rural Montana both nurtures and demands it.

With the onset of the economic crisis, these rigid gender expectations have been challenged, as men and women have been forced to "do gender" differently in terms of household production. Migrant men's ability to provide lessened, and many rural migrant women transgressed their prescribed roles by stepping into wage labor and away from direct caretaking duties. This role disruption caused anxiety as both men and women felt that they were failing to fulfill their basic family responsibilities. While migrant men retreated into silence, migrant women struggled to maintain an air of normality in performing *survival femininity*, taking on the "second shift" of wage and domestic work (Hochschild 1989), while feeling culturally prohibited from complaint or protest.

In terms of reproductive labor, migrant women continued to do gender as they always have. But the dueling performance of tradition and transgression is grueling. Women's resulting physical exhaustion is compounded by the emotional burden of maintaining household routines and tranquillity in the midst of extreme stress. While the double burden faced by migrant women is not different from that faced by wage-earning women more generally (Heymann 2000), migrant women face additional burdens based on their social and geographic positions. Indeed, in Montana they take on a double shift in the context of isolation, lack of developed networks and marginal social and/ or unauthorized legal statuses.

In media depictions, Montana's mountains and large open spaces inspire a romantic vision of a simpler, happier time, when life was less complicated. This idyll of "The Last Best Place" focuses on family and fortifies patriarchal gender relations in spite of role shifts sparked by economic crisis. Constraints on mobility, both social and spatial, and fear of deportation and family separation, place the idyll at the center of rural migrant life. It fosters solidarity for migrant families who are struggling to survive. Children are the glue that holds families together and keep parents motivated to continue struggling. Children represent hope. In the next chapter I explore daily life in Montana through the eyes of the second generation.

Chapter 6

Through the Eyes of the Second Generation

It was a bright, cold March day in 2011 when I met up with Elena in the main reception area of the local hospital. It had been a year since I had last seen her, and I was struck by how different she looked. She was unusually thin and pale. On the phone the week before, Elena's mom had told me that Elena was so sick she looked yellow. Now that I was in Elena's presence, the accuracy of Ana's description was disturbing. It was difficult not to focus on the prominent scar at the base of her neck.

As we exchanged warm greetings, I was impressed that Elena was able to maintain a gracious smile and polite demeanor even though she was clearly nervous and not feeling good. Elena's four-year-old sister, Evelín, stood close by her side. Elena explained that following her appointment with the oncology social worker, she was going with Evelín to the Public Assistance Office to renew her Women Infants and Children (WIC) application.[1] Elena's parents, Ana and Rogelio, whom I introduced in Chapter 3, are both unauthorized. Although Elena spent much of her childhood in rural Jalisco, she was born in California. As such, she is a U.S. citizen and the public face of her family. She handles all of the family's interactions with social services and public authorities.

Elena, who had just turned nineteen at the time, was a straight "A" student in a rural school in the heart of southwest Montana's dairy region. She hoped to graduate in a few months. I knew her mom quite well, having been one of her regular tamale customers since 2007. We talked often and I had been to her home several times both to interview her and to buy tamales. The first time that I visited Ana in her trailer, she pointed out a framed certificate hanging high on their living room wall. The certificate boasted of Elena's selection to the academic honor roll. Ana, who has only a second-grade education, was visibly proud. At the time, Elena was a shy, quiet, young girl who was still quite homesick for Jalisco. She had found solace in school, where she had formed a special bond with her English teacher and was excelling in math and science.

Elena's younger sister, Carmela, did not like school. In 2009 she dropped out and moved with her boyfriend to a ranch in northeastern Montana. Soon thereafter she got pregnant. Ana cried when she told me the news. She wanted so much more for Carmela, and she clearly did not like or trust the boy who was soon to be the father of her first grandchild. Elena was Ana's hope and her strength—a good student, responsible, and a role model for her two younger siblings. She was the pillar of the family. Elena paid special attention to her younger brother Yerrick, the only child in the family born in Mexico and who was thus not a U.S. citizen. "I tell him he has to do good in school and he can't get in trouble. He has to finish high school. Then when I am twenty-one, I will help him get papers," Elena told me.

A lot changed when Elena got sick. She had not felt well for over a year. She had been persistently tired, yet unable to sleep. She kept her physical struggle to herself so as not to worry her mom, who was already burdened with depression and anxiety. "I'd lay awake all night long," she explained, "and I couldn't fall asleep until morning. Then one morning I just couldn't get up for school. I couldn't hide it anymore. So my mom went with me to the clinic." After blood tests and a biopsy Elena was diagnosed with thyroid cancer. That was in the fall of 2010.

Until her diagnosis, Elena did not know what cancer was. Ana was also ignorant of the disease. Forever etched in my memory is the phone conversation I had with Ana, during which she told me that Elena had cancer. "Where do you think she could have caught this?" Ana asked with despair in her voice. Before I could answer she followed up with a plea. ' I am so ashamed. Please do not tell anyone." Because of the shame and discomfort Ana displayed in talking about the illness, I at first thought Elena must have contracted a Sexually Transmitted Disease (STD). It only became clear to me that Elena did not have an STD when Ana finally used the word "cancer," a word that was clearly foreign to her tongue, and explained that it was located at the front of Elena's neck. I assured Ana that you cannot "catch' cancer and that it is nothing of which to be ashamed. Ana seemed surprised by my words. She had attended several appointments with different doctors by then, yet she still had no clear understanding of Elena's illness.

When I met up with Elena at the hospital, she had recently had her thyroid removed. She had called me a few days before, asking for advice about who might be able to assist her with a plan to pay off her hospital bills. Since she had turned nineteen she was no longer eligible for Medicaid.[2] Luckily her major surgery had occurred when she was still eighteen. Yet other bills were piling up, and Elena's family could not afford to pay even the smallest of them.

In response to Elena's request, I arranged for an appointment with an oncology social worker whom I knew to be a strong advocate for poor families in general and migrant families in particular. After I gave the social worker a summary of Elena's case, she assured me she could help. I hoped that her optimism was well founded, as Elena was scheduled to travel to a hospital in the medical hub in Billings, Montana, the next day. There she would learn the stage of her cancer and what her course of treatment would be. Elena was fearful of what the doctors would tell her, but she was more fearful about the financial stress the final treatments would place on her family. "I have thought about just not having the treatment. We don't have the money for this," she told me the day before on the phone, "but my mom says that I have to have it."

As the oldest child Elena takes on extraordinary responsibilities within her family. Before she got sick she worked part time after school in a research lab, a job she got with the help of her favorite high school teacher. She also worked on weekends in a local coffee shop. All of the money she earned went toward supporting her family. Before she got those jobs, Elena worked during the summers with her dad on a dairy farm. In Jalisco, before coming to the United States, it was Elena's job to care for her family's cows when they came in from pasture. Elena does not remember a time when she did not work. When her dad was deported in 2008 Elena helped hold the family together financially. She was just sixteen. Ana worked as much as she could during the nine months Rogelio was back in Mexico, selling tamales and cleaning houses, but it was Elena's income that was most stable. When Rogelio returned to Montana, again without papers, the recession had just taken hold and he was unable to find full-time work. Elena again helped hold things together.

When we arrived at the Cancer Center reception desk, I did most of the talking. When Elena piped in to answer one of the receptionist's questions, the receptionist interrupted her. Looking directly at me, she gruffly asked, "Does she need an interpreter?" I was defensive in my response. "No, she is fluent in English." Elena has a heavy accent, but she speaks well. I was frustrated by the woman's question and by her accusatory tone. I was also irritated because I knew that the hospital did not have interpreters. On-site translation is an issue that the community clinics have been pressing the hospital on for the past few years, as it is a major service gap for Spanish-speaking migrants in Montana.

In contrast to the hospital receptionist, the medical social worker was delightful. She immediately put Elena and Evelín at ease. Within an hour she had assured us that she could get at least half of Elena's bills forgiven and that she would keep working on the others. "For now, Elena," she said with a comforting smile, "I want you to focus solely on getting better. I have looked at your charts and I am confident that you are going to get through this just fine." I could immediately sense Elena breathing easier. Amid all the barriers that Elena and her family had confronted since Elena's illness began—language, knowledge, financial debt and Ana's and Rogelio's illegality—the social worker was a bright spot. Elena left her office feeling newly optimistic.

After exiting the hospital and entering the crisp mountain air, I followed alongside as Elena took Evelín's hand and walked with her through the parking lot to their pickup truck. After we said our good-byes, I watched as Elena helped Evelín into her car seat. I noted the mix of her youth, patience and maternalism. Exhausted by the appointment and the heaviness of my conversation with Elena, I was looking forward to going home, my workday complete. I knew Elena had another stressful meeting ahead of her. As Elena climbed into the driver's seat of her large, black pickup truck, I was struck by how small she looked. The family truck, which is registered under Elena's name, barely fit into one parking spot. As Elena pulled away my eyes were drawn to her pile of school books on the passenger seat.

Born in the United States to migrant parents, Elena is officially part of the second generation. Yet as Elena spent most of her childhood in Mexico before returning to the United States as a young teenager, she could also be considered part of the 1.5 generation, composed of those who came to the United States as children. Elena does not fit neatly into either category.

Elena's experience of adolescence, in relation to other children of the 1.5 and second migrant generations, has been both typical and extraordinary. It is typical in that she is one of 4 million U.S. citizen children who are members of mixed status families (Yoshikawa 2011). As such, although Elena is entitled to all of the rights and opportunities that citizenship entails, like other youth in her situation, because of her parents' unauthorized status, she has not sought all of the resources to which she is due (see also ibid.; Valenzuela 1999). For example, even though her income has at critical times supported her mother, father and younger siblings, Elena never counts her parents and unauthorized brother among her dependents, thus limiting her eligibility for certain kinds of assistance. Although Elena was a public school student, her parents never applied for free and reduced lunches for her, or for any other extracurricular support, so as not to bring attention to their unauthorized legal status.

Elena is also typical of other teens of the 1.5 and second generations in that she has taken on an important helper role within her family. Like many children in migrant families, Elena translates for her parents, serves as the family's interface with public authorities, and acts as a surrogate parent to her younger siblings (Valenzuela 1999). And like many children of migrants, Elena is resilient despite life's challenges. Elena's resiliency has been nurtured by the support of two adult mentors, both teachers. She met one of them on her first day of eighth grade. She met the other in high school. Elena's teachers are examples of what Portes and Fernandez-Kelly (2008) term *very significant others* (see also Ceballo 2004; Gonzalez 2011), individuals whose support makes a critical difference to the well-being of 1.5 and second-generation youth. One of these teachers helped Elena find her jobs and made sure her school absences were excused during the worst of her illness. She also helped Elena catch up with her homework following her surgery. Both teachers have been Elena's cheerleaders, urging her toward college.

While Elena's life, in the ways I mention above, fits the mold of contemporary 1.5 and second-generation youth, her life is also distinct in significant ways. Perhaps most important, Elena lives in a new rural destination, an exceedingly different environment in which to come of age than an urban migrant hub. In some ways this difference is beneficial. For one, rural areas tend to have lower levels of crime (Barnett and Mencken 2002; Maguire and Pastore 1995), thus giving youth a more secure environment in which to develop.[3] Additionally, rural communities may offer 1.5 and second-generation youth unique access to supportive role models and mentors, which can broaden their social networks (Marrow 2011; Silver 2012). Both were the case for Elena. She told me that she felt safer in Montana than she did during her family's short stint in California, and a few notable adults from the community have provided Elena with exceptional support and opportunities. And yet, despite the benefits of security and social support, legal exclusion still weighs heavily in daily migrant life, even in small towns (Marrow 2011; Silver 2012). To be sure, while Elena acknowledges her luck in being a U.S. citizen, the deportation of her father and her fear that her mother and brother could meet the same fate continuously burdens her. Therefore, despite being a citizen, Elena does not live freely (see also Dreby 2012; Gonzalez and Chavez 2012; Gonzalez 2011). And she recognizes that in terms of her parents' illegality, her family is even more vulnerable because they live in a rural, predominantly white state.

Elena's experience also deviates from the norm because, as a cancer survivor, she has had to negotiate the health care system from the unenviable intersection of rurality, poverty and parental illegality. Although Elena speaks English, albeit with a heavy accent, her parents speak only Spanish. Elena was burdened with negotiating her treatments and the financial aspects of her illness on her own. There are no formal medical interpreters in Montana to assist migrant families. Elena's mother was completely helpless to support Elena during clinic appointments and hospital visits. Not only was she helpless, she was constantly worried that Elena's health crisis would bring her own unauthorized status to light. In addition, Elena's family lives in a remote area far from the medical care that she needed. For her treatments, Elena had to travel two and a half hours from her home to the main Montana hospital. As her parents do not have licenses and are fearful of the police, Elena drove a few times on her own, even though she was sick, uncomfortable and exhausted.

There are still other factors that make Elena's experience as part of the second generation unique. When Elena arrived in Montana she did not speak English. She enrolled in a rural public school where only one adult, the Spanish teacher, spoke Spanish. Elena did not have access to an ESL program, and she and her younger sister were the only minority students in the school. Aside from the muted contentment she received from a friendly teacher and from the feeling of familiarity she got from the mountains surrounding her home, Elena experienced life to be mostly hostile. Although she eventually made a few good friends in high school, and was even nominated to be prom queen her senior year, Elena has always felt out of place and quite alone in Montana.

In the remaining sections of this chapter, I explore in further detail the ordinary and extraordinary facets of childhood and adolescence among the 1.5 and second generations in southwest Montana. I highlight the lives of both U.S. citizen and unauthorized youth, the majority of whom live in mixed status families. I find that, as has been the case for Elena, many of the issues that impact children's lives are issues that would impact them if they lived anywhere. Illegality, social marginalization, fear and extraordinary familial responsibilities shape childhood and adolescence in Montana just as they do in other migrant destinations (Abrego 2006; Dreby 2012; Gonzalez 2011; Vasquez 2011). Yet Montana's rurality, specifically its expansive geography and homogeneity, shape these daily life phenomena in inimitable ways, often intensifying their effect.

Extraordinary Responsibilities

The 1.5 and second-generation children and adolescents in Montana are above all resilient. Young children love to play, and to laugh and to spend time with their families and friends. Adolescents embrace the partnering joys and struggles of coming of age in America. They enjoy social media, fast food and pizza, and most dislike homework. Yet the resilience that contextualizes the mundane parts of new destination childhood and adolescence is often times partnered with unusual stress and responsibility. As the children of migrants, most of whose parents do not speak English, and many of whose parents are unauthorized, the lives of the youth in this study are anything but carefree. For those children and adolescents who are unauthorized themselves, more stress abounds. Southwest Montana's rurality and specifically the service gaps that rurality entails, generates extraordinary responsibilities for youth within their families.

CHILDREN AS INTERPRETERS

Vera was born in California and moved to Montana when she was eight years old. She remembers the relief she felt upon arriving in the small, peaceful agricultural community that would be her home for the rest of her childhood and adolescence, and the excitement of seeing snow for the first time. Vera and her family came to Montana to escape what her parents believed were imminent dangers of growing up in urban California. Even though she was still a little girl, Vera felt the presence of these dangers too, and though the transition to Montana was not easy, she was happy to move. Vera's dad had secured a job, via his brother, as a ranch hand. Vera's mom, for the first time in her adult life, stayed at home to take care of the house and the children.

Vera and her family were one of only a few Mexican families, at the time, who had settled in an agricultural community of four thousand residents about two hours west of Bozeman. As such, there were few if any resources in the town to support migrant families. There were no ESL teachers at the school, no interpreters at the hospitals or public offices and no social service workers who had knowledge of the special challenges facing migrants. Since that time a migrant clinic has opened in the town to serve the growing population of seasonal farm workers in the area, yet when Vera was growing up she and her family were on their own. Even though both of Vera's parents are U.S. residents, they do not speak English and have low levels of formal education. They arrived in Montana ill prepared to maneuver an underfunded, English-based public sector. As the oldest daughter, and fluent in English, Vera was the one who guided them.

When Vera was thirteen years old, her mother began having health problems that eventually led her to seek medical care. Vera accompanied her mother to her appointments at a local clinic, doing her best to explain to her mother what the doctor was saying. This was a difficult task for Vera, who at thirteen was obviously not trained in medical translation. The doctor deemed Vera's mother's problems to be rooted in her reproductive system. As a young teen, Vera did not understand exactly what the reproductive system was. She certainly did not understand the psychological and emotional aspects of reproductive issues for women approaching middle age. Vera did her best to relay all the critical information the doctor gave her. Finally, there came an appointment when the doctor determined that Vera's mom would need surgery, a hysterectomy. Having no idea what a hysterectomy was, Vera again did her best to explain to her mom that the doctor needed to perform an operation to take out the things that were causing the pain and discomfort. Her mother agreed, not understanding the extent of the operation.

Vera's mom went into surgery not knowing she was having a hysterectomy. It was not until weeks later during a routine check-up that she learned she no longer had a uterus or ovaries. Vera, now in her twenties, still feels guilty about her incomplete and inaccurate translation. For Vera, translating in difficult situations was a normal part of her youth. She translated for most of her parents' medical appointments. Her older brother translated too, though Vera was typically the one they looked to in health situations. Additionally, Vera translated at her own parent-teacher conferences, and she helped her parents file their taxes and complete other public forms and registrations that are part and parcel of living in the United States.

More than ten years after Vera had translated for her own mother's health crisis, I called on her to assist me in translating for another family, ironically from her hometown. It was the spring of 2010 when I received a call from Courtney, an outreach worker at the migrant health clinic there. Joaquina, the wife of a migrant farm worker and the mother of three children, was at the regional hospital in critical condition. She had gone into the hospital three days earlier for a mastectomy following a breast cancer diagnosis. Courtney had worked with the hospital to have the surgery done without cost, as Joaquina was unauthorized and the family had no health insurance. The entire family, composed of her husband, three children and her son's pregnant fiance, accompanied Joaquina for the surgery. The surgery seemingly went well and, initially, she was recovering nicely. Then tragedy struck. Joaquina had a massive stroke and fell into a coma. The family had been sleeping in the hospital waiting room for two days when Courtney called to ask if I might check in on them. Vera, then a graduate student with whom I was working at the university, came with me to the hospital. We brought donuts and juice.

When we arrived in the waiting room, it was clear that the situation was dire. Francisco, Joaquina's husband, was on his cell phone in the corner. He was crying. When Vera and I entered the room, Francisco tried to hide his tear-drenched face. Joaquina's three children were hovered together on one of the generic hospital couches. Hesitant at first, Vera and I approached the family explaining that we were friends of Courtney and that we were there to help in any way that we could. They thanked us for taking the time to visit. Alexia, Joaquina's young teenage daughter, explained that she had been translating for the doctors throughout the night. The news was not good. Joaquina had had four more strokes. Francisco was on the phone with Joaquina's mother in Mexico telling her that her daughter was dying.

The neurologist who was overseeing Joaquina's case entered the waiting room, his face foreshadowing the terrible news that was to come. Vera and I introduced ourselves to the doctor as he approached the family. He told us that he was relieved to meet us and asked if we could interpret for him. We asked the family if that would be all right. They graciously agreed. We then sat down together as the doctor proceeded to tell us that Joaquina was brain dead, that she was not going to get better. He recommended, with empathy in his voice, taking her off life support. Vera, who for years had translated for her own family, now found herself translating this devastating news for another migrant family from her hometown. The irony was not lost on me. Francisco, his arm around his eight-year-old daughter, Lucía, looked to Lucía for clarification. "Dad, he is saying she is going to die," Lucía sobbed in response.

In this moment, I became intensely aware how heavily the hospital's lack of translation weighed on migrant families, especially children. Even though Vera was translating for the doctor, she struggled to explain the complexities of brain swelling and the body's response to it. And although Vera was doing a tremendous job explaining everything, while simultaneously expressing empathy and support for the grief-stricken family, Francisco still looked to his daughters for clarification and validation. I did not blame him. He did not know us, and even though Vera is a native Spanish speaker, she is not trained in medical translation.

It was a full twenty-four hours before Francisco agreed to let the doctors disconnect Joaquina from life support. We were with the family for most of those twenty-four hours. I sensed that their strong Catholic faith was at the heart of their struggle. "There might be a miracle," Francisco told me. "This happens and people come back. God does not want us to give up." In phone calls he received from family in Mexico, relatives pleaded with him not to let Joaquina die. And yet, there was more going on. When the neurologist had relayed the grave details of Joaquina's situation during his meeting with the family, it was clear to all of us who spoke English that even a miracle would not save Joaquina. I understood this. Vera understood this. Lucía and Alexia understood this too. Yet Francisco did not have the full information that we had. Lucía, Alexia, Vera and I were unable to communicate Joaquina's medical reality effectively. Thus Lucía, only eight years old, and Alexia, thirteen, found themselves in the unenviable situation of trying to persuade their dad to trust them, that they knew best, and it was time to let go.

Although none of the other youth in my sample shared with me experiences of the same level of intensity as those of Vera, Lucía and Alexia, most told me that they regularly translated for their parents. They mentioned health appointments and parent-teacher conferences as the most common situations in which their translating services were required. Because there are few educators or service workers in Montana who have even a rudimentary knowledge of Spanish, 1.5 and second-generation youth carry the burden of filling this service gap for their parents.

Lucy, a teacher at one of the local high schools, and one of the only teachers in the area who is fluent in Spanish, told me that if a Spanish-speaking parent needs to enroll a child in school, or to fill out a school form, "There is no one there to help them." Until Lucy's Advanced Spanish class translated all of her school's registration documents into Spanish, the forms were available only in English. When I asked Lucy how families managed, she told me that in some cases she translated for the families, but in most cases she assumed that children translated the documents for their parents. She told me that the same holds true for parent-teacher conferences. My interviews with children and teens validated Lucy's hypothesis.

I talked to many children who told me they translate for their own parent-teacher conferences. Some told stories related to the embarrassment of both translating a teacher's praise and a teacher's criticism, an awkward situation for a child. Olga, for example, who lived in rural Alaska before moving to Montana, shared a memory about when she had to translate during conferences:

> It was kind of like, well it was hard because of the stuff that they would say, and I would tell my mom . . . . I'd just be laughing and stuff, and the teacher would say: "Be serious." . . . There was this commercial where the teacher tells the daughter who knows English and Spanish to tell the parents who don't know, and then says: "Your daughter is not doing so well in school," and then she's like: "Mom, dad, I am doing really good." It was kind of like that. One teacher was like: "Did you make sure you told your parents?" and I was like: "Yeah."

Olga's story exemplifies the power that children have when they are put in the position of translating for their parents. For most of the children in my sample their ability to speak English, and their parents' dependence on them for translation, flipped the typical parent-child power relationship on its head, an example of what Portes and Rumbaut (2001) term *dissonant acculturation*. The same role reversal between parents and children can be seen in terms of negotiating school work and general language learning.

CHILDREN AS TEACHERS AND TUTORS

In addition to helping their parents as interpreters, several of the children I met told me that they are teaching their parents English or teaching their parents to read. Max's parents, Juan Carlos and Julisa, have only primary school educations. The region where they grew up in Jalisco is so remote that they would have had to ride a mule for three hours to get to the nearest town that housed a secondary school. Thus school beyond the primary years was pragmatically difficult and seemingly useless in their subsistence agricultural community. Now that they are in the United States, they both want to learn English. But before they can learn English, they have to learn to read and write in Spanish. Max, who is nine, has taken on the responsibility of making his parents literate. In our interview he proudly told me, "I'm teaching my mom and dad how to read. We're working on the abc's in Spanish and English. I really like school because the more I learn the more I can help my mom and dad."

Similarly, Chiara told me that what motivates her most in school is her desire to pass her knowledge on to her mom. Every day after school Chiara and her mom practice English. Chiara enjoys playing teacher. She is unusually close to her mom, Liliana, who is prone to anxiety attacks and bouts of homesickness for Mexico. Chiara feels happiest when she can help her mom. She thinks that learning English will help her mom feel more at ease in Montana.

There are limited opportunities for migrant adults in Montana to learn English or to study basic literacy. The region lacks a community center or organization dedicated solely to the migrant community. While a service learning program initiated via the Latino Studies Program at Montana State has tried to fill this service gap, and the Adult Learning Center has been a useful resource for some, the needs of the migrant community far outweigh university faculty and students' time and ability. In addition, lack of public transportation outside of Bozeman partnered with large geographic distances make it difficult, if not impossible, for migrants in the most rural areas, and for those everywhere who do not drive, to access language and literacy classes. As such, the job often falls to the children of migrants.

It is also common for older siblings within migrant families to act as tutors for their younger siblings. Because most parents in my sample have relatively low levels of formal education, and because most do not speak, read or write in English, they are ill equipped to assist their children with homework. Whereas I was not surprised to learn that working with siblings on class assignments, or to better their reading and writing skills, was the norm for older 1.5 and second-generation youth, I was surprised to hear a few of the teens I interviewed talk about how hard they are working to help their younger siblings improve their Spanish. All but one of the children I interviewed, five-year-old Junior, asked to do their interviews in English. Similarly, they all said that they prefer to speak English over Spanish in all settings of their life and are often frustrated when their parents make them speak Spanish at home. Several said that they do not speak Spanish very well.

Older siblings, and especially those who spent some of their childhoods in Mexico, have come to find the value in retaining their Spanish. Similarly they are motivated to pass that value down to their younger sisters and brothers. Olga, who was born in the United States but spent her early childhood years in Mexico, feels it is her responsibility to teach her younger brother, who has never lived in Mexico, Spanish. She finds it challenging that her brother and her parents have a difficult time communicating:

> It is frustrating . . . and they tell me or my sister to tell each other what they found. I am like: "He understands, tell him." It's like, if you don't do it, he's going to forget it [Spanish] and stuff. And it's true. My mom, what my mom would think, if she wouldn't have stuck with the language, we wouldn't have learned Spanish. So it's kind of like, I guess, win–lose situation, because she never learned it [English], but we would have lost Spanish. And I am trying to get that across to my little brother, you know, it's really important, and I try to talk to him in Spanish, but then sometimes . . . I just start talking to him in English.

Even though Olga's mom or dad would seem the obvious ones to teach their son Spanish, Olga and her older sister Juliana argue that they are the better teachers. They feel it is better to be bilingual in order to teach someone another language. More to the point, they feel that in their experience it is necessary to be bilingual in order to serve as the bridge that allows Spanish-speaking parents to connect with their English-speaking children. Both Juliana and Olga feel it is their responsibility to be that bridge in their family.

CHILDREN AS LABOR

In addition to their jobs as family interpreters and tutors, most 1.5 and second-generation teens, as well as some children I met, work outside of the home to help their parents. For teens, this phenomenon is less extraordinary, as many teens in the United States work for wages. Yet fewer native-born, middle-class teens in the United States work because their families' well-being depends on it. Working for gas money, or to save for new clothes or going out, were common reasons teens worked in the middle-, working-class Midwestern town where I grew up. The reality for the children of migrants, especially during difficult economic times, is very different. As I detailed in the vignette that opens this chapter, Elena's income was crucial for her family's survival, especially after her dad was deported. Many of the teens I met worked with their parents, if their parents had jobs. For example, teenage girls worked with their moms cleaning houses when the recession set in. Teenage boys commonly work with their dads in construction or agriculture.

Even a few of the youngest children in my sample work with their parents outside of the home. Zelizer (1985) theorizes that childhood is socially constructed; it means different things depending on context. In postindustrial societies children have little economic worth, as they are not expected, and in most places are forbidden by law, to work. My own children are classic examples of those whom Zelizer describes as "economically worthless" but "emotionally priceless." Now ages five-and-a-half and seven, and thus with their class consciousness still in its infancy, they continually grappled with why it was that they saw so many young children in our temporary home of Oaxaca selling gum and candies on the city's streets, or leading burros through the mountain roads near their school. Their questions would prompt discussions about unequal childhoods. Furthermore they would prompt me to explain that children are essential labor in many agricultural families, and that this is true in the United States as well as in Mexico.

In Montana, it is common in agricultural families for children to work. For this reason Montana's U.S. senator John Tester was one of the few voices of protest to 2012 legislation that would have bolstered protections against child labor in the United States. Many of my university students who grew up in ranching families were laborers on their family ranches from a very young age. Likewise, I found that 1.5 and second-generation children who live in agricultural families are expected to work throughout childhood. Max, for example, informed me, "My brother is ten. He works at the dairy with my dad. I'm going to start working with them soon." Similarly, Junior, who is only five, is already helping his dad, Ernesto, with the cows. Not even in kindergarten yet, Junior is well versed in the daily routine of a large dairy farm. Elena's younger brother too, still in elementary school, recently began helping their dad in his job on a dairy farm.

In addition to formal work, 1.5 and second-generation children and teens help their mothers with child care and with the normal workload within their households, such as cleaning, cooking and doing laundry. In the early stages of my fieldwork, I hypothesized that a rigid gender division of labor would direct the labor of boys and girls in migrant families. Yet I soon learned that gender was only one variable in the child labor equation, and it was not the most important one. Elena, for example, helped with the cows in Jalisco and worked on a dairy with her dad in Montana. Her call to labor was based most importantly on her being the oldest child of an agricultural family. Among the families in my sample, gender roles appear to be most flexible in agricultural families. As I detailed in Chapter 2, although all of the children and wives in agricultural families told me that their dads/husbands made the rules and were clearly the heads of the households, and although in all cases women in the families did the majority of the domestic work, agricultural migrants also told me that men accepted and indeed encouraged their wives and daughters to work. Julisa theorized this to be a holdover from life in rural Mexico, where everyone—boys, girls, women and men—has to work. I found that flexible gender divisions of labor within agricultural families can coexist with *ranchero masculinity* (see Smith 2006), in which men maintain patriarchal authority and women bow submission. And so in Montana, both boys and girls whose parents work as ranch- or farmhands are expected to follow suit. Both boys and girls work, but both also know their place within the gender hierarchy of the household.

Emotional Burdens

The extraordinary responsibilities of 1.5 and second-generation youth in southwest Montana are typically partnered with emotional burdens connected to their membership in vulnerable migrant families. Children of migrants in Montana often take on their parents' stress. They are savvy about the unique dangers of living without authorization in a new rural destination.

When I first met Victoria's oldest daughter, Samantha, she had just entered kindergarten. She was shy and extremely attached to Victoria. I witnessed several episodes at Victoria's house in which Samantha started to cry when Victoria did nothing more than leave the room. As Samantha has gotten older her timidity has dissipated, and she has become more confident and outgoing. When I interviewed Samantha formally, she was nine. I was impressed by her thoughtfulness and her maturity. She seemed a happy, well-adjusted child, excited about school, her friends and piano lessons. Yet the complex layers of her emotional state were revealed as our interview progressed. Most important, I realized that Samantha is hyperaware of her mother's unauthorized status and the danger that it poses to the family's well-being.

During our interview I asked Samantha if she knew what an immigrant is and what she thought life was like for Mexican immigrants in Montana. Samantha was clear on the meaning of "immigrant" and immediately focused her response on her mom. "It makes me really sad that my mom's an immigrant because she can't go to Mexico to visit her parents." Victoria had talked with me in depth about her frustration about not being able to visit her parents, especially her father, who was elderly and diabetic. Victoria wanted to help with his care, and she carried a heavy guilt for living so far away. Samantha is sensitive to Victoria's grief and guilt, and she provides her emotional support, a heavy responsibility for a nine-year-old. As our conversation continued, I asked Samantha if her friends know that her mom is an immigrant. She made clear that her mom's immigration status was nothing to share outside of the family's inner sphere:

> I don't want people to know that my mom's an immigrant because it's private. It's safer if they don't know. Because if you don't have a green card you have to be careful who you tell. They could arrest you and take you back to Mexico . . . . I haven't told anyone that my mom's an immigrant.

Dreby (2012) suggests that we consider the impacts of illegality on children in terms of a pyramid. The most damaging impact of illegality, a deportation in which children are separated from their parent(s), is situated at the top of the pyramid. Although, relatively speaking, the numbers of families who face this are few, for those that do experience deportation and separation, the harm that is done is grave. When Elena's dad was deported, for example, Ana almost had a breakdown. Elena suffered not only from missing her dad but also because she had to support her mom and her younger siblings emotionally and financially.

On the base of Dreby's pyramid are the large numbers of children who endure the persistent anxiety that is rooted in an ongoing fear of the deportation of a parent. In my own research I found that, like Samantha, most of the children of unauthorized parent(s) are positioned on the base of the pyramid. They are aware of their parent(s)' vulnerability and, as such, they live with chronic fear and anxiety. Samantha, for example, told me that she is afraid of the police because she knows they could arrest her mom, and she knows that driving is the most dangerous activity an unauthorized migrant in Montana can do. Therefore, whenever she is in the car with her mom and they see a police car, she knows to sit up straight immediately and not to move. She told me that her six-year-old and three-year-old sisters know to do the same. When at the end of our interview I asked Samantha what makes her happiest, she told me, "Having my family together makes me happiest." Her biggest fear is separation.

Chiara, like Samantha, was a smart, charming, soft-spoken nine-year-old when I interviewed her in 2011. Like Samantha, she is extremely close to her mom. It was clear throughout our interview that Chiara worries about her mom, Liliana, a lot. Liliana is in an unhappy marriage to Chiara's step-dad. She told me on a few different occasions that she would leave her husband if she could afford to, but, as of the time of our interview, she depended on him for financial support. Liliana is also extremely homesick. She misses her mother, siblings and her home in Vera Cruz. Her homesickness is so extreme that it has at times made her physically ill. Liliana told me that she would go back to Vera Cruz, but she fears the brewing violence in her hometown and she wants her children to have the benefit of a U.S. education. Liliana, like her husband, is unauthorized. All of her children are U.S. citizens. She knows that if she returns to Vera Cruz with her children, she would have a difficult time ever returning to the United States. She cannot imagine living apart from her children. And she knows that her children would not do well living apart from her.

Chiara wears her mother's sadness like a second skin. During our interview, she started to cry when I asked her if there was anything that scared her. I turned the tape recorder off and we stopped the interview when her tears began. I stayed with the family during lunch, during which Chiara opened up about what had made her cry. Her most looming fear is being separated from her mom. She does not know how she could survive even one day without her. Some days she does not even like to go to school, even though she loves to learn and is an excellent student, because she fears coming home and finding that her mom has been arrested. Chiara continued to say that she likes Montana and would not want to live anywhere else in the United States (she spent the first few years of her life in Florida). But she would rather move to Mexico than stay in Montana, because she knows how much her mom misses her family and her home. Chiara also knows that although in many ways Montana is "safe," it is also a place from which many Mexicans have been deported. It is a place where Mexicans are safest when they stay at home. As I listened to Chiara speak both eloquently and honestly about her struggles, I could not help but think that returning to Mexico with her mom would alleviate much of the weight of worry and fear that she carries on her young shoulders.

Like Chiara and Samantha, Pedro's and Angela's daughter Catalina is a U.S. citizen. And so, like Chiara and Samantha, Catalina is immersed in the colliding worlds of citizenship and parental illegality. Whereas Catalina is a good student and she told me that she has many friends, she also has learned that she can never share all of who she is, nor can she ever let down her guard with them. When I interviewed her in the spring of 2011, her family was preparing to move temporarily to Oklahoma, where Pedro had found a construction job. They were then planning to move to Aguas Calientes:

> It's hard that my parents don't have papers. I'm worrying all the time about my parents getting caught by immigration and us getting separated. My parents don't talk about it much. But I know . . . . We're planning to go back to Mexico in a year. If we do go back to Mexico it's one less thing to worry about . . . . My Mexican friends know my parents don't have papers, but no one else knows. You don't know if their parents might work with immigration . . . . You know, me, I have papers and I am legal and it's better. But you still worry a lot about your parents.

Adriana and Gabriela also struggle with the anxiety associated with illegality. Sisters, they are among the few in my sample who are unauthorized themselves as well as having an unauthorized parent. Adriana, who is twelve, has had many problems adjusting to life in the United States. I surmise that her struggles have roots in Mexico, where she lived until she was eight. As a young child in Mexico City she was a daily witness to her parents' tumultuous marriage, and she was scarred, according to her mom, by her dad's eventual abandonment of the family. When Lourdes, her newly single mother, decided to take Adriana and Gabriela across the border without papers, Adriana was old enough to internalize the danger the trip entailed. Adriana has vivid memories of the physically strenuous and terrifying border-crossing, during which she and Gabriela were separated from Lourdes for several days. Of all the girls I have met, I worry most about Adriana. I sense depression brewing, rooted in a painful sense of insecurity.

Unlike Adriana, Gabriela does not have clear memories of their border crossing. Nor does she remember her father very well. Still, she struggles in Adriana's unhappy shadow, absorbing her experiences and her memories as if they were her own. Although she was only nine years old when I interviewed her, she too was aware of the insecurity of being unauthorized and of the intensified insecurity of being unauthorized in Montana.

When I arrived at Adriana's and Gabriela's apartment for my interview with Gabriela, I could immediately sense that something was wrong. Jennie, a community organizer who works closely with Latino youth in the area and did several of the youth interviews with me, was already there. Lourdes's boyfriend at the time, who lived with them, was standing outside. He and Jennie approached my car before I had the chance to get out, telling me that the family had moved out of the apartment that afternoon. There had been a raid at the Mexican restaurant where Lourdes worked, and ICE had obtained a list of the addresses of all of the restaurant's employees. When I inquired where they had gone, he directed Jennie and me to the house of one of Lourdes's friends. He assured us that the friend was expecting us and that Gabriela was ready for the interview. He thought it would be a good distraction. We drove to the house and knocked on the door. Lourdes's friend answered and ushered us inside. She pointed to Gabriela, who was sound asleep on the couch. A television was blaring in the background. Jennie, who knew Gabriela well, approached the couch and gently began talking to her. It took Jennie at least five minutes to rouse her.

After a few minutes of conversation, Gabriela, Jennie and I started the interview. The first few minutes were like pulling teeth. Gabriela did not have much to say. Just when I was about to suggest we end the interview, Gabriela shed her protective shield and started to open up. When I asked Gabriela if she knew what an immigrant was, she said she did not. Even after I explained the concept, she did not identify herself as an immigrant.[4] Yet Gabriela did know that her family was in danger of being found by the police, and she knew that she did not like having to hide at a friend's apartment.

Unlike Gabriela, Adriana knows what an immigrant is, and she is aware that she and her mom and sister are immigrants. Adriana is also aware that no one in her immediate family has papers, which puts them in perpetual danger. In the longest, and most lively, of all the formal interviews I did with preteen children, Adriana spoke openly about how difficult it is to live precariously in the United States. Although she has never lived anywhere else in the United States except Montana, she imagines that in Montana it is more difficult to be an immigrant because "there are not many of us here." Adriana's family came to Montana because her uncle owns a restaurant and promised her mom work in the kitchen. Otherwise they probably would have moved to a place where there are more Mexicans, or they would not have migrated at all.

Yet Adriana likes Montana. When I asked her where she wants to live when she gets older she told me that she wants to live in Montana, in the same place they live now. She likes Montana because it is "calm." Then she paused and said, "Well (I would like to stay) that is as long as they don't tell us to go, go, go!" I paused, waiting for her to go on. When she did not continue, I asked, "Who do you mean by 'they,' Adriana?" She responded without hesitation, "Immigration. As long as that doesn't happen, I will be so happy."

The testimony of the U.S. citizen children I met who are part of mixed-status families, as well as those who are unauthorized themselves, supports research that finds increased immigration enforcement to be detrimental to children's well-being. Survey research conducted by Santos, Menjívar and Godfrey (2013), among middle school students in Arizona, finds that children's awareness of SB1070, the most punitive anti-immigration legislation in the United States, is correlated with a weakened sense of American identity. They also find that children who are aware of the law perceive greater discrimination on behalf of public authorities, thus weakening their trust in the legal system and civil society. These findings suggest that even when children themselves are not directly affected by antimigrant laws, the symbolic power of the law can weaken their sense of belonging and security.

Paradoxical Partnerings: Belonging and Exclusion in the Lives of Youth

As a mother, I often reflect on how nice it is to be raising my children in Montana, where the crime rate is relatively low, we are surrounded by natural beauty and small, tight-knit communities and good schools provide an idyllic environment where kids can thrive. As I detailed in Chapter 4, the Mexican mothers and fathers I met in my field research celebrate these same things. Even when the economy crashed and households lost their livelihoods, many found a way to stay in Montana for their children. And yet the idyllic haven that cradles my own children is less comforting and reliable for the children of Mexicans.

The children of migrants are clearly marked as different from the other students in their classrooms and the other children in their communities. They have few peers who share a similar life history, skin color and native language. Because there are no migrant enclaves in southwest Montana, and because school boundaries are determined by neighborhood or geographic zone, Mexican children typically find themselves isolated from one another.[5]

Some scholars would argue that the lack of a Mexican ethnic concentration in Montana's public schools should benefit Mexican youth, as it means they have fewer barriers to assimilation. Carola Suárez-Orozco and Marcelo Suárez-Orozco (1995), for example, find that 1.5 and second-generation youth in Boston and San Francisco who have just one friend who is fluent in English are more likely to succeed academically than those who do not. Mexican youth in my sample are immersed directly into Montana's English-speaking school system, and they have no choice but to create relationships with native speakers. Even children, like Elena, who arrived in Montana from Mexico speaking no English learn English quickly. In Montana there is little hand-holding for non-English speakers within public schools. Most of the children I met in this study are resilient, and they cope as need be. Not only do they cope, in many cases they thrive. Yet in other cases, racism and alienation wear youth down. I find that the daily lives of 1.5 and second-generation youth in Montana are characterized by paradoxical partnerings of belonging and exclusion, hope and frustration.

SCHOOL AS A HAVEN

Most of the young children I got to know during my field research said that they like school. Many actually told me they "love school." They like to learn, they like their friends and they like the diversion that school represents. Above all, young children highlight their teachers as keys to their comfort in and enjoyment of school. They told me that their teachers make them feel welcome, special and safe.

When eight-year-old Dalia took a two-week trip to Mexico in the spring of 2011, her first time visiting the homeland of her unauthorized parents, Roberta and Ernesto, her teacher gave her a beautiful travel journal before she left. She encouraged Dalia to use the journal to write about her "special trip" and to include pictures and mementos from her visit with her Mexican family. Her teacher, knowing that Dalia was traveling not with her parents but with her uncle, also wanted Dalia to have something that she could share with her parents upon her return to Montana. When Dalia returned to school, her teacher helped her prepare a presentation in which she shared highlights of her trip with her second-grade classmates. Dalia told me that she felt special and proud because she has family in Mexico and because she was able to visit a place that most of her peers will never have the chance to see. She smiled when she added, "Also, I know that my teacher and my friends really missed me when I went to Mexico." Dalia feels that she is a valued member of her school community.

When I asked Dalia and the other preadolescent children I interviewed if they want their classmates to know they speak Spanish and have a Mexican heritage, they all responded in the affirmative. Samantha, for example, told me, "I am proud that I speak Spanish. All my friends know that I speak Spanish." Dalia said that even though she speaks English with her friends, "I teach them words in Spanish." Gabriela said that she has friends who like to hear her speak Spanish because it is so different from English. Children told me that many of their native-born Montanan classmates are fascinated by the fact that they speak two languages, and they proudly described commonly getting requests from friends to say English words in Spanish. Although all but one of the children I interviewed preferred to do their interview in English, and they correspondingly asserted that they were much better speaking

English than Spanish, most expressed an interest in and a commitment to speaking both languages.

In 2010 Samantha wrote a song that her teacher encouraged her to enter into a districtwide contest. Samantha's song, which she called "Peace and Love Everywhere,"[6] won first prize in the contest, and she performed it at a communitywide festival. Already a role model among her peers, Samantha loves school, has aspirations of becoming a scientist and a singer and has only positive things to say about her educational experiences. "I love my teacher!" she exclaimed during our interview. In addition, she has many friends who think it is "really cool" that she speaks two languages. School has been a haven for Samantha, and it has helped transform her from a shy, insecure little girl into a confident preteenager. Although all of the children I interviewed are aware that they are "different," which they most commonly explained in terms of skin color and bilingualism, most do not see their difference as a deficit. The elementary school teachers of the young children I met have been passionate advocates for the children of migrants, celebrating the importance and value of knowing two languages and having family in two countries. At least through their elementary school years, school seems to serve as a sanctuary for children, even for those whose families are marginalized in the larger society (see also Gonzalez 2011).

The ways in which bilingualism is treated as an advantage and something to be lauded in rural Montana is strikingly different from what has been found in urban contexts. In cities with large Latino populations, speaking Spanish can lead to stigmatization by teachers and other students (see Vasquez 2011). In Montana's elementary schools, even though there are few bilingual students, teachers nurture what Portes and Rumbaut (2001) term the *selective acculturation* of Mexican-American youth, encouraging them to simultaneously assimilate *and* maintain strong ties to the language and cultures of their parents.

This has been especially true for the few children who attend an international-themed public elementary school in town. When I first met Dorotea, she was preparing ingredients for *tortillas* and *tacos* that she was scheduled to bring to her daughter's third-grade class the next day. Her daughter's teacher had invited migrant parents to share food from their homeland. The Mexican students at the international school, unlike the children who attend other regional elementary schools, say they do not feel especially different from their classmates, as most of their classmates have parents from other places. Brian, for example, told me that he has two best friends at school, one who is Chinese but who was born in England and the other who was born in Jamaica. The international school is also the home base for the region's only formally licensed ESL teacher, who serves as an important bridge between migrant parents and teachers. Whereas the international school in Bozeman is exceptional in the ways in which it celebrates diversity and welcomes 1.5 and second-generation youth, I gleaned from my observations and formal interviews that all of the region's elementary schools are doing quite well in making 1.5 and second-generation Mexican youth feel at home.

In addition to serving as a positive forum in which youth are encouraged to embrace their Mexican and Spanish-speaking identities, my data suggests that school is an important social outlet for Mexican children, structuring their days and giving them meaning. This is an especially important function for the children living in isolated rural areas, who are geographically removed from other children, as well as from parks and community resources. Without school, they would have little to no contact with children or adults outside of their families.

For their first three years in Montana, Max's family shared a trailer with Roberta, Ernesto and their three children. When Roberta and Ernesto moved into their own house, as I detail in Chapter 2, Max lost his built-in playmates. During the summers, Max's older brother, who is ten, works every day with his dad on the dairy. Max spends most of his time alone. When I asked him if he had other friends with whom to play, he told me that he had one good friend from school, but that this friend lived too far away to see during the summer. This is a common challenge for many children in rural Montana, both the 1.5 and second generation as well as the white native born. Those who live in agricultural areas live far from other dwellings and do not benefit from neighborhood networks of children. Yet this challenge is accentuated for second-generation youth, many of whose parents are un-authorized and whose mothers do not drive. The school year provides them with activities and socialization that they do not get during the summers. I interviewed Max a few weeks after the school year ended in 2011, and he told me, "I miss school when I'm not there . . . . I can't wait for it to start again."

Only three of the migrant children I met during my fieldwork were in-volved in extracurricular activities. Samantha and her younger sister Olimpia take gymnastics and piano lessons, and Brian plays the violin in the school orchestra. Most children come home after school and watch television, play video games or, when the weather is conducive, play outside. Money con-straints and lack of transportation make after-school activities impossible for most. As such, it is the school day itself that structures children's lives, adding to its value and importance.[7]

Although most young children do not participate in extracurricular activities, all of those I formally interviewed attend church at least once in a while. Most attend the Catholic Church, which offers a monthly Spanish Mass. For some, church is an important weekly ritual. For example, Brian, Samantha and her sister Olimpia regularly attend a Friday prayer group with their parents. They also sing in the choir during the monthly *misas*. Brian, Samantha and Olimpia were the only children who told me they like church. While most of the other children I interviewed said they dislike church because "it is boring" or "you have to stand up a lot," they also acknowledged church as the one place where they have friends who speak Spanish and English, and who are Mexican, and they said it is a place where their parents also have friends.

RACISM AND EXCLUSION

Whereas school is a haven for most young 1.5 and second-generation youth, it can be a scary and lonely place for some. Adriana and Gabriela shared with me painful stories of bullying and racism, which they felt was targeted at them because they are Mexican. Gabriela and I talked about her school and about her connection to the other children in her school. As was the case for the vast majority of children I interviewed and met in my field research, Gabriela is the only Mexican in her class. That, though, does not bother her. She told me that for the most part school is "ok," but then she told me that there are a few kids whom she does not like. "Tell me about them," I encouraged. "Well, some kids at school say, 'Do you speak Mexican?' and they call me names . . . . My sister gets teased a lot. They call her names. They call her crazy Mexican and stuff like that."

When I interviewed Adriana the next week she validated Gabriela's testimony. Except for her creative writing project in English class, she does not like school. I probed her to talk about what it is about school that she does not like. She went on to offer a detailed analysis of the compounding intersections of race and class that make getting through the school day an often painful endeavor. She told me that while life in Montana felt more financially secure than she remembers life in Mexico City, she struggles with other things:

> I have a good life here, but also bad. Sometimes at school kids say, "No you can't do this because you're a Mexican. You can't do this and you can't be with our group because you're a Mexican . . . . They act out running across the border and they tease me."

Later in the interview while talking about her friends at school, it became clear that Adriana is targeted not only because she is Mexican but also because she is poor. Adriana is smart and savvy. She knows that no matter what she does, even if her mom gets papers, she will not fit in with rich "American" girls who have "really blonde hair, and really, really blue eyes":

> Adriana: "There are rules, you know, like cool people can hang out with cool people and nerdy people can only hang out with nerdy people."
>
> LS: "So, what makes someone cool?"
>
> Adriana: "To have money. They have an iPhone and they bring it to school. They wear cool clothes and all that stuff. And they like to blame things on the kids who are low, who can't say that much. Like they know I don't have money. Sometimes, they, well sometimes I'd try to sound like 2 percent rich because my uncle owns a [Mexican] restaurant, and then they say, 'Well, their food stinks.' . . . There are kids at school who are racist to me. Like they would blame stuff on me and they would say bad stuff about me, like . . . [long pause] saying, 'She's a Mexican and she can't do anything. She's not rich.' Yeah [with a sarcastic laugh] I have the rich problem."

Adriana further demonstrated her class consciousness when she told me that most of her friends, although none of them are Mexican, are also poor. "How do you know they are poor?" I asked. "Well, I know they are poor because they live in apartments like me. The rich kids live in houses." Despite the bullying that Adriana confronts at school, her girlfriends make her happy. Like a typical "tween," Adriana told me, "you know, we just love to talk. We love to talk about ourselves. We talk and talk." She also assured me that her friends stand up for her when she gets picked on. They make school tolerable. Thus, whereas Adriana does not have the opportunity to slip unnoticed into an elementary school enclave of Mexican 1.5 generation youth, she does find herself at least semiprotected by a clique of poor and working-class girls (see also Bettie 2003). While all of the children in my sample are disadvantaged, I found that it is only children who attend schools that are rigidly stratified by class who faced overt hostility. The majority of these children are members of construction families who live in or close to town in the areas that are in the process of gentrification. Here inequality and insecurity breed competition and divisions among children.

While Adriana and Gabriela are unique in terms of the persistent and overt racism they have confronted, there were a few other elementary-aged children I interviewed who said they had had at least one experience of being teased or excluded because they are ethnically Mexican. Max, for example, shared with me the story of being the only one in his class not to be invited to a birthday party:

I had some friends in Manhattan, [Montana], where we used to live, but they aren't friends anymore because their dad doesn't like Mexicans. They told me that I couldn't go to Cody's party because his dad doesn't like Mexicans.

Max went on to explain that Cody's dad works on a dairy like his own dad and had blamed Max's dad unfairly for something, he was "not sure what." He did not seem to have had his feelings hurt by the incident, as he told me in a matter-of-fact tone that there are just some people who "don't like Mexicans."

And Catalina, who had just finished eighth grade when I interviewed her, told me that there are some racist kids in her school who "say things behind my back, like 'You skipped the border.'" Additionally, a few children reported being called "ugly," while others said that there were kids who were "mean" to them for no reason. These children did not identify their taunts with their migrant status. Rosa, who is seven, for example, told me that some girls at school say that "they won't be my friends, but they don't say why."

Roberto Gonzalez (2011) theorizes that the marginalization of unauthorized 1.5 and second-generation youth discourages them from identifying as "American." My data supports his supposition. I found that even those children who are U.S. citizens, born in the United States, who have never visited Mexico and who prefer to speak English over Spanish, still do not identify as American. Instead, they identify as Mexican. When I asked them to describe an American, the children tended to focus on skin color. In the minds of the young 1.5 and second-generation youth in Montana, Americans have "tan" skin and hair, or "blonde" hair, and they speak English, while Mexicans are, as Max said, "dark like me," and they speak Spanish. Thus, while I am heartened to know that most young Mexican youth in Montana feel safe and happy in their schools and in their communities, I am disheartened to know that not one of them identifies as a member of the country in which they live and in which most of them were born. This is not to suggest that an American identity should be the ultimate goal of incorporation. It is, though, to critique the context of social marginalization in which Mexican-American youth do not find an American identity an option because of their skin color and native tongue.

UNIQUE CHALLENGES OF ADOLESCENCE

The exceptional incidents of racism and exclusion that appeared among elementary school–aged children appear to intensify and become more frequent as the 1.5 and second-generation youth in Montana move into adolescence. Additionally, as the 1.5 and second generation come of age, gender plays an increasingly critical role in determining one's experience of belonging or exclusion, success or failure. Whereas the teenage girls I interviewed, as well as the other girls I got to know informally in my fieldwork, shared few stories of struggle, all of the teenage boys I met highlighted struggle as a central part of their lives.

Born in Arizona, Juliana and Olga, sisters and best friends, spent their early childhood in Aguas Calientes, Mexico. When Juliana was six and Olga was five, they moved with their mother, who had finally attained her U.S. residency, to Arizona and then to Alaska to join their dad, who was working in a fishery there. Their little brother came to the United States as a baby. Both Juliana and Olga told me how difficult it was to leave Mexico, where they were surrounded by grandparents, aunts, uncles and cousins. After fifteen years in the United States, both sisters still consider Mexico home. Juliana and Olga spent most of their youth in Alaska. They moved to Montana the day after Juliana graduated from high school.

Juliana and Olga now both laugh when they describe what it was like to arrive in Alaska from Mexico. "It was like, wow, where have we landed? My dad wanted to take a picture of us by this stuffed grizzly bear. It was like we were on a different planet." Olga and Juliana did not speak English, and Alaska, as is still true in most of Montana, had no ESL support in the public schools. They both learned English quickly and became stellar students. But they never liked Alaska. They felt like outsiders and they suffered teasing and bullying from a few of the American Indian students in the school, the other "others." Their parents kept them on a tight leash. They were not allowed to attend slumber parties or sleepovers at friends' houses. To be sure, they rarely went out. They did not drink alcohol or attend parties, and they were quite naive about typical teen life. To this day they spend most of their free time together or with their immediate family. They pay special attention to their younger brother, trying to teach him Spanish and keep him in line, as he is quite rebellious.

When Juliana's and Olga's parents informed them that they were moving to Montana to join their aunt, uncle and cousins, they were thrilled. "It was like we were moving to the big city." Juliana laughed. "You know it's not like Phoenix, but it was a lot better than Alaska . . . . There's a mall! It is small, but it's a mall." They did not shed a tear when they left Alaska. They were happy to arrive in a place where they had family and where there are more Mexicans. Life was not easy, but they both excelled in school. I asked Olga to talk about what her transition into high school in Montana was like.

Olga: "For me, just talking to my cousin, before this whole economy thing started, [the recession] you know, she told me that there were so many

Mexicans and stuff, and I seriously, my first year of school, like, I expected so many to be there, and I was like, oh my god . . . . There was seriously . . . I guess there was four with my cousin and five with me. But I expected so many other people to be there. Like just what she talked about. But . . . with the economy, more people were leaving to . . . other states or Mexico. But I was just completely, like . . . oh my gosh . . . . At the beginning it was really hard, just being new and stuff. But then towards the end, I made new friends. Like for graduation, yeah, it was nice."

LS: "And did you have any problems? Did you have any bad experiences?"

Olga: "At school no. Not really. I kind of, I think it got better, I never had problems at school . . . . But, there was the one time at Wal-Mart."

LS: "What happened at Wal-Mart?"

Olga: "I was talking to my mom in Spanish and this girl, I could feel it, she was like standing like in the corner with a magazine and she was glaring at me."

LS: "How old was she, do you think?"

Olga: "Maybe in high school. Maybe a junior. I mean, a high schooler for sure. I could tell that she had something against me, or something. But I was still talking to my mom, when . . . talking to her in Spanish. And then she was, I can't remember, but she was looking at me and she's like: 'Why don't you go back to your country?' and I . . . I said something in Spanish, because in English I didn't know what to say. And I just felt, it was, I felt like it was the most horrible thing in my life. And in Alaska I never experienced that. And I was just like: 'Cabrona!' I was so mad. And then . . . I didn't have the strength to go after her . . . and be like: 'You don't have the right to be saying that.' I was born here and I know English too, just because I am speaking a different language . . . but my sister . . . Juliana, she went after her."

LS: "You did? Tell me about it, what did you say?" [turning to Juliana, who as sitting with Olga].

Juliana: "The funny thing is, I didn't hear her, I didn't see her when this whole thing happened, but I was right by her, I don't know how I missed it . . . so my little sister told us what she said, and so I said, 'Which girl?' And then she's like, 'The one that's right there.' And she was hiding. Yeah, you know, hiding . . . by the manager and then she went over by the jewelry section, so I actually saw her and I went back over there and I am like: 'What did you just say to . . . go back to our country? You know you don't even know what you're saying. You know this is America, everybody is here for a reason, and you know, just because I am talking in a different language doesn't mean anything. I am free to talk and you know, speak to whoever I want, you know. I was born here. You know, I can speak another language.' . . . People were looking at me and like the workers were there, they didn't say anything. It was like a couple of people that were walking by. And they were just like in shock.

And I'm just like, why does she, why is she saying that, you know. 'We speak two languages, we were actually born in the U.S. so you can't say anything about us, so in a way if you tell us to go back to our country, why don't you go back to your country, wherever you came from.'"

Juliana and Olga demonstrated confidence and resilience in the midst of what I could tell was a traumatic experience. They did not cower. If anything, Olga later told me, the experience made them more determined to do well in school and in their lives. Despite experiencing overt racism, both Juliana and Olga thrived in high school and they both went on to thrive at the state university. As I am writing, Juliana is finishing a graduate degree in community health. She is also organizing students around Montana to support the Dream Act and Immigration Reform. Juliana and Olga are both optimistic about their futures and are proud to be a symbol of upward social mobility in their family and community. Their cousin Magali is also now at the university, studying in the natural sciences. She too is a straight A student.

Whereas most teenage girls have done well both in school and socially, the story is different for the teenage boys. As I detailed in Chapter 3, both of Gaby's sons dropped out of school and struggled with alcohol, drugs and depression. Pedro's eldest son, Chaba, a good student with aspirations of being a nurse, did not finish high school. When I interviewed him in the spring of 2011 he had plans to finish his General Education Degree and had hopes of going to nursing school. Yet when I spoke to him six months later his school plans were on hold and he was working full time with his dad in construction. Ernestina's son, Adolfo, graduated from high school, but it was a struggle. He got picked on a lot. I was surprised by this, as he is a handsome, strapping young man, the physical stereotype of a popular teenage boy. During the worst episode, three boys from his class tried to hit him with their car in the parking lot. He reported the incident to the principal and his mom followed up with administrators, but nothing happened to the boys. To the contrary, Adolfo was made to pay for the damage that was done to the car when he hit it with his fists in order to protect himself.

When I interviewed her, Lucy was a Spanish teacher and informal migrant family advocate in the high school that houses the largest number of 1.5 and second-generation teenage boys, the same school that Chaba and Adolfo attended. In our interview she told me, "There's a lot more pressure on Mexican boys than Mexican girls .... They have to deal with a lot of stereotypes." I asked her to explain in further detail what the stereotypes are and how they affect the boys.

There are mostly Mexican boys at the school and they all hang out together because, well, they are Mexican and some of them only speak Spanish. And they kind of had the stereotype going of gangs. And I tried to tell the other students, "Listen if you were in Mexico and there were only five of you from the U.S. you'd probably hang out together too." . . . But the stereotype kept coming from the students and from the administrators. The students would say, well they always hang out at their lockers together and they are always in their little group . . . . And I suppose the Mexican guys personify it. I mean they have the baggy pants, they look the look.

Lucy's analysis was confirmed by Gaby when, in theorizing why her son Bruno started to get into trouble, she told me, "Well, everyone thought he was a *cholo*/gangster, so he finally started acting like one." None of the other boys I met spiraled as far down as did Gaby's sons, both of them ending up in legal trouble and eventually being deported. But the vast majority are not on a path to upward mobility. To the contrary they are continuing in the footsteps of their uneducated fathers, working in agriculture or construction. This point was highlighted when I attended a college information session for Latino youth. Ten adolescent girls attended the session, many of them with their mothers. No adolescent boys attended.

Robert Smith's (2006) work is helpful here. He suggests that 1.5 and second-generation boys, when they do not fit into U.S. youth culture, cling more closely to the *ranchero masculinity* of their fathers. Ranchero masculinity does not encourage academic achievement. Instead it celebrates physical labor, alcohol consumption and men's control of public space. *Ranchera femininity,* on the other hand, which is based on women's passivity and submission and which prioritizes motherhood, does not threaten the school success of 1.5 and second-generation girls.

There are exceptions to the discouraging trend I observed among 1.5 and second-generation boys. César is a soft-spoken nineteen-year-old who was born and raised in a Montanan ranching community. Both of his parents are unauthorized, a fact of which he was not aware until he applied for university. He told me that he had some really tough years in middle school when a couple of boys at school gave him a hard time because of his dark skin. César felt down for a while, as he grappled with being different from everyone else. But he bounced back. He was a great student, a varsity athlete and active in his community. He credits much of his success in high school as well as his involvement in the community to having one really good friend who made him feel like he belonged, who always supported him. César is now one of only a few Mexican males at the local university. He is thriving.

Conclusion

In many ways the lives of the 1.5 and second-generation youth in Montana resemble the lives of those in traditional migrant destinations. While they are resilient in many ways, they also carry the burdens that come with being the children of migrants. They often serve as interpreters and tutors for younger siblings, and they often worry about the vulnerability of their parents, especially when their parents are unauthorized. As they grow up, their burdens intensify as they become more conscious of their legal status or that of their parents, and the vulnerability that comes with it. They feel the stigmatization of their migrant roots more.

Yet the lives of second-generation youth in Montana are also extraordinary. Because of the rurality of Montana and the dearth of support for Spanish-speaking migrants, children's helper roles take on more urgency. Often children are put in situations that strain their maturity, such as having to interpret in health situations whose details and implications are beyond the comprehension of their young minds, and acting as the public face of the family because the authorities do not recognize the special needs of non–English speaking migrants.

Mexican youth in Montana are also extraordinary in that they do not live in ethnic enclaves. Nor do they attend schools with significant minority populations. As such, they experience a forced assimilation of sorts. Whether this is ultimately beneficial or harmful is still uncertain. Young 1.5 and second-generation youth learn English quickly and have non-Mexican friends. They typically like school, which serves as an important haven and diversion in their otherwise isolated lives. And yet, my data also suggests that life gets more difficult as the 1.5 and second generation come of age. Boys especially begin to experience more bullying and stereotyping, which leads most to embrace the *ranchero masculinity* (ibid.) of their fathers. In this construction of masculinity, the emphasis is on physical labor and "macho" behavior, notably alcohol consumption, and not on education. Second-generation girls, on the other hand, do well in school and do not suffer the teasing, bullying and stereotyping of peers. As I write, the gender imbalance of second-generation youth attending the local university is great. Teen girls are thriving. Teen boys are struggling. Of course, as I note in this chapter, there are exceptions. But the patterns are striking and deserving of concern.

In the typical migrant narrative, children represent hope. I have yet to interview a migrant parent who does not cite the desire of giving their children a better life as the reason they migrated or the reason they struggle to stay in the United States despite economic crisis and the threat of deportation. Parents are especially appreciative of the unique opportunities that Montana gives their children. To them, rurality offers more security and tranquillity, and better schools, than do traditional destinations. They stay in Montana, despite the challenges that staying entails for them personally, because they believe it is best for their children. Only time will tell whether their sacrifice has paid off, and whether Montana's idyll has meaning and depth beyond its romantic promise.

Chapter 7

Hope and Opportunity in the New West

> This ethos of getting along, as well as the tremendous growth
> in immigration, has given rise to the emergence of what I call
> cosmopolitan canopies—settings that offer a respite from the
> lingering tensions of urban life and an opportunity for diverse
> peoples to come together. Canopies are in essence pluralistic
> spaces where people engage one another in a spirit of civility,
> or even comity and goodwill. Through personal observation,
> they may come casually to appreciate one another's differences
> and empathize with the other in a spirit of shared humanity.
> Under the canopy this sense of familiarity often breeds comfort
> and encourages all to be on their best behavior, promoting
> peaceful relations.
> —Elijah Anderson, 2011. *The Cosmopolitan Canopy:*
> *Race and Civility in Everyday Life*

In his most recent book, Sociologist Elijah Anderson introduces *cosmopolitan canopies* as places where people of different races, classes, genders and ethnicities mix in a spirit of civility. Anderson takes his readers to Philadelphia, a city with a long history of segregation. There canopies provide multicultural shelters under which cosmopolitanism supersedes ethnocentrism. The Reading Terminal and Rittenhouse Square are primary examples of Philadelphia's cosmopolitan canopies. Underneath these canopies people connect in ways that are uncommon on Philadelphia's streets and in its neighborhoods, both of which continue to be demarcated by race and class. In the Reading Terminal, a white college student engages in conversation about a local professional sports team with a black customer at a popular diner, and street musicians, business professionals and migrants, rich, poor, black and white, engage each other with respect and without fear.

According to Anderson, cosmopolitan canopies take on special significance for those living on society's racial and ethnic margins, offering them safe entree into spaces that have long been colonized by white privileged classes. Under the canopy, even those with racist attitudes and those who are typically uncomfortable with difference and diversity are motivated to exercise civility. To act any other way would be to breach the canopy's unwritten rules.

Outside of the canopy the *color line* persists, reminding us that, despite popular discourses that boast of a postracial society, race matters in America, a lot. Skin color still privileges and subordinates. But under the canopy, the racial boundaries that bitterly divide urban populaces are blurred and de-emphasized. Canopies thus offer us glimpses of what it could be to live in an urban society characterized not by racial hierarchies but by *racial peace*.

Of course, cosmopolitan canopies are not utopian spaces immune to tears and ruptures. There are times when the color line is unexpectedly drawn underneath the canopy. At these moments, people are reminded of the fragility of contemporary cross-race relations and how far we have yet to go to achieve racial democracy. As Anderson explains:

> The most problematic aspect of the social relations under the cosmopolitan canopy appears when the color line is suddenly drawn, and an issue that people had assumed mattered little comes to dominate the whole situation. Tensions may arise over turf and territory, particularly when a member of one group considers a member of another group to be out of place, or even threatening. In these circumstances, the "gloss" that people put on to smooth their interactions can wear thin. The celebration of diversity, the practice of civility, and even the pretense of tolerance itself can all break down, exposing the racial fault lines that still exist in contemporary American society." (154)

These moments of rupture alert us that racial wounds still fester. Through their intensity and impact, the ruptures emphasize how much work must be done to create a society that does not promulgate new wounds. Canopies are human spaces and, as such, they are flawed. Still, they offer hope and inspiration as well as respite.

Southwest Montana is anything but cosmopolitan. As I detailed in this book's introduction, Montana is an exceptionally white and rural state whose counties and towns, like Philadelphia's neighborhoods, are segregated. While linked migration into Montana has increased the state's racial, ethnic and class diversity, it has also intensified social segregation. As is the case with urban gentrification, rural gentrification has pushed the poor and working classes out of historical town centers into regional outskirts and rural hinterlands. Mexican migrants to Montana typically find themselves either isolated in trailers on the large ranches or farms where they perform agricultural labor, or in trailers or town houses in the low-income developments that have sprouted up on former agricultural lands in the semiperiphery. Commonly, native-born whites, many of whom have come to Montana as lifestyle migrants and who live in town or on hobby ranches in the pristine wilderness outside of town, are shocked when I tell them that Latinos are the fastest growing demographic in the state, for their paths rarely cross. As I have described in detail in previous chapters, most of the Mexicans in my sample live socially and geographically isolated lives. They are isolated from the white native born. They are also isolated from each other.

In the summer of 2011, after hearing Elijah Anderson speak about cosmopolitan canopies at the annual meeting of the American Sociological Association in Las Vegas, I returned to Montana with my head spinning. "Do cosmopolitan canopies exist in Montana?" I pondered. Anderson's ethnographic account is an urban account, and yet I could not help but think about the concept of the canopy in relation to my research. As Anderson describes them, canopies are safe spaces, and safe spaces are critical, it seemed to me, to the well-being of marginalized groups anywhere, rural or urban. Similarly, it would seem they are critical to the well-being of all multicultural societies.

My immediate response was a resounding "no." In Montana we do not have places analogous to the Reading Terminal or Rittenhouse Square, where people come together across race, class and gender in a mix of civility and goodwill. There are few if any places in Montana where *everyone* feels safe and welcome. Montana is often grouped with other states in the New West that are infamous for their racial homogeneity, lack of cosmopolitanism and violent enforcement of both the color line and the gender line. Montana is not that far from Laramie, Wyoming, where Matthew Shepard was left to die, tied to a fence post. His crime, being gay. Montana is also not that far from Coeur D'Alene, Idaho, infamous for its contemporary white supremacist activity.[1] As I detailed in Chapter 4, as recent as 2009 white supremacists organized in Bozeman, spreading racial hate literature and organizing public demonstrations. I know well from my research participants as well as from my black, Latino, Asian and American Indian students that it is often difficult, and at times frightening, to be a person of color in Montana. Indeed, I can think of no public place in southwest Montana, outside of certain (but not all) university spaces, that is characterized by a depth of race, class and gender diversity partnered with civility.

And yet there are canopies of a different sort emerging in Montana. In addition to expatiating on the significance of cosmopolitan canopies, Anderson touts the importance of canopies in which diverse elements of the same race or ethnic group may "mingle peacefully and express themselves fully" (93). While not representative of multirace, class and gender groups, these canopies serve an important purpose in building ethnic and racial community within marginalized groups. Whereas cosmopolitan canopies still do not exist in Montana, canopies that provide a safe space for marginalized groups do exist, or at least they are emerging.[2]

Throughout my research I have noted the important role that local churches play, for example, in offering Mexican migrants not only a spiritual home but also a physical gathering place where they do not have to fear the police, ICE, or racist neighbors.[3] I have noted the important role that community health clinics and the food bank play as places where migrants can obtain critical social services without being stigmatized, and where materials and some services are now offered in Spanish. I have also noted the ironic positioning of Wal-Mart in the lives of migrants. It is the only place in the region where they can find and afford everything they need to prepare a variety of Mexican food, and where they are likely to be shopping among people from diverse race and class backgrounds.

And yet, with every rural canopy that I have noted in my field research, I have noted overt ruptures in the canopy caused by regular occurrences of racism and hostility to difference. In Montana's emerging canopies, ruptures are part and parcel of the canopies themselves. As such, in Montana canopies do not offer full or even consistent protection. In addition, because of the rural context of Montana, many migrants have difficulty accessing the few canopies that do exist.

Although Montana does not have fully developed cosmopolitan canopies, I am encouraged by the civility and comity I have observed between *individuals* from different race, ethnic and class backgrounds. Meaningful human connections have developed underneath Montana's partial canopies, and I have watched them persist and even grow stronger outside of the canopies. I have witnessed diverse individuals move beyond civil and respectful public interactions, like those Anderson describes within Philadelphia's cosmopolitan canopies, into the realm of trust and friendship.

Thus, paradoxically, I hypothesize that rurality, while fostering the exclusion and marginalization of migrants in general, may actually facilitate relationships between Mexican labor migrants and the white native born. Underneath the few and partial canopies that exist in Montana, there are individuals, both Mexican and white native born, who serve as *bridges* across race, class and ethnic difference. These individuals nurture and strengthen canopies and offer hope for a more peaceful, welcoming and tolerant rural America.

Rurality breeds the potential for cross-culture connections between individuals. Because there are no ethnic enclaves in Montana, when migrants enter public space they cannot help but encounter individuals ethnically, culturally and linguistically different from themselves. Depending on luck and context, cross-cultural connections may ensue. In the stream of lifestyle migrants into Montana people exist who, while seeking the tranquillity and natural beauty of Montana, tell me they miss the ethnic and cultural diversity of the city. I have found that these individuals are uniquely open to connecting across difference, and that they often seek out opportunities to form new relationships. My good friend Heidi, a lifestyle migrant from Seattle, hired Ana to clean her house when Rogelio was deported and became one of her regular tamale customers. Heidi theorizes that the relatively small size of Montana's migrant community encourages bridge-building. She believes that in Seattle and other large cities, segregated enclaves and the sheer size of the migrant community are intimidating to individuals, both migrants and the native born, who want to connect across race and cultural differences. And when paths do cross, they often do so in an impersonal way. In Montana, Heidi jumped at the chance to get to know Ana, and even though Heidi does not speak Spanish and Ana does not speak English, she felt that she and Ana both made an impact in each other's lives. "That wouldn't have happened in Seattle," she told me.

There are also native-born Montanans who are committed to welcoming newcomers in their midst. Some have lived away from Montana for parts of their adult lives. In their time away they came to appreciate cosmopolitanism and brought this appreciation back to Montana. There are also native-born Montanans who have never lived anywhere else, and some who have never even traveled outside of the West, who have a family history of working in agriculture and who have a deep respect for the work ethic and rural values they associate with Mexican labor migrants. I have observed these individuals, too, reach out across difference. When diverse individuals meet, genuine connections may take root.

In this chapter I explore the symbolic canopies of southwest Montana. I highlight the importance that canopies have in the lives of a uniquely isolated migrant community, and the ways that rurality and gentrification have contributed to the structure and function of each canopy. I also interrogate the social ruptures that both characterize and threaten the integrity of these canopies. Finally, I bring to light the stories of key individuals who have served, so importantly, as bridges across Montana's growing race, class and ethnic divides. These are the people who have worked tirelessly to strengthen rural canopies and nurture tolerance and acceptance among all people.

The Catholic Church as a Canopy

On the first Sunday of every month, one of the Catholic churches in Bozeman offers a Spanish Mass. The monthly *misa,* the first of its kind in Montana, began in the summer of 2007 as a result of an impressive organizing effort by Victoria, Gaby and Rebeca, who had been sporadically attending an English Mass in Bozeman. There Gaby had learned from one of the parishioners that there was a new priest in town who spoke Spanish. Motivated by the hope that she could have Raul, then a baby, baptized in Spanish, Gaby rallied Victoria and Rebeca to go to the church to meet the priest. The priest welcomed them with warmth and enthusiasm. What followed was an exciting challenge. Not only would the priest baptize Raul, he would also perform a monthly Mass in Spanish *if* they could assure him that one hundred people would attend. Victoria, Gaby and Rebeca, thrilled by the prospect of a monthly misa, accepted the challenge joyously.

They were uniquely positioned to make the misa a reality. At the time, they all lived in or near town, and both Gaby and Victoria knew how to drive and had access to a vehicle. Most important, they all felt passionately that a church service in Spanish was needed for their own spiritual health, as well as for the spiritual development of their children and the well-being of their Catholic Latino brethren. So they went to work. They made fliers and posters and distributed them everywhere they knew Mexicans go—Wal-Mart, the laundry-mat, the food bank and the Western Union stall within a local grocery store. They carried fliers with them and approached people they saw who appeared Latino to tell them about the misa. Despite the geographic dispersion and social isolation of the migrant population, word spread. On the day of the inaugural misa, well over a hundred people were in attendance.

The church is housed in a simple, contemporary structure. The entrance expresses humility, and the church's interior space follows suit. The space is quite plain, with folding chairs instead of pews and smooth white walls. Yet the high, vaulted ceiling and the majestic mountain views from the church's large front windows give the otherwise humble building a feeling of grandeur. Before the misa was initiated, the church was attended primarily by students, faculty and Catholic families living near the university. The congregation has a youthful, progressive energy that I have been told is unique. The priest is a middle-aged, swarthy-skinned, genteel-looking man with a delightful presence. Although not completely fluent in Spanish, he speaks the language with grace and confidence. And although not Latino, he has an immigrant history. His parents migrated to the United States from southeastern Europe and instilled in him an understanding and appreciation of the migrant dream and corresponding migrant struggle. Before coming to Montana, he spent years in California with a diverse parish. He has a strong social justice conscience, and a warmth and charisma that are overtly welcoming.

The priest and Victoria clicked immediately, supporting each other in their roles as *bridges* between the native-born and migrant members of the church community. Speaking English well, and possessing confidence and energy, Victoria was an ideal candidate to become the assistant for the misa. Since the inception of the misa, Victoria has worked tirelessly to translate materials into Spanish, prepare the misa bulletin, and organize a plethora of fundraising efforts. Victoria has also been a regular lector during the misa, reading from the Bible, sharing announcements and concerns and encouraging migrants to be strong in their faith and struggles. Perhaps most important, Victoria was the organizational force behind a Friday prayer group for which several migrant families gather to study the Bible, encourage each other in their faiths, and support each other during difficult times. The prayer group forms the core of the Spanish choir.

Victoria has also taken the lead in reaching out to the nonmigrant Catholic community. Most notably, for the past several years she has been the lead organizer of a bilingual celebration of the Virgen de Guadalupe. During the celebration migrant members of the parish sing songs in Spanish and perform indigenous Mexican dances. The ceremony is followed by a meal of tamales, *atole* and sweet bread. The sanctuary fills with community members of all ages and social classes, Latino and native-born white. One cannot help but leave the celebration inspired by the sense of community it instills.

The church was the first place in southwest Montana to offer a gathering place for Mexican migrants. Migrants commune monthly to worship and socialize. During the summer months, migrant women sometimes offer lunch following the misa, replete with tamales, *posole* and tostadas. These communal lunches offer migrants the rare opportunity to socialize in a semipublic space, on the church lawn. Migrants also use this space and time to celebrate birthdays, baptisms and first communions. I have even attended a wedding that was held following a misa.

At the church, parishioners make conscious efforts to make all attendees feel welcome. Here it does not matter if one is authorized or not, or whether someone is rich or poor, single or married. Whereas most Mexicans in Montana are labor migrants, there are a select few who own their own businesses, and there are others who are in Montana on graduate student visas. In the church all mix as equals.

As another example, whereas most Mexicans in southwest Montana migrated with their immediate family members, many single young men on

H2B visas also live and work in the region seasonally. Although the H2B workers live in employee-sanctioned housing in Big Sky, over an hour's drive from the church, they make extraordinary efforts to attend the misa, waking up before dawn to catch a bus that travels an hour through the canyon to the Gallatin Valley Mall. From the mall they walk a few miles, arriving at the church over two hours before the Mass begins. They then make the same journey home. During and after the misa, these young men, many of whom are separated from their wives and children, find rare moments of community.

In addition to serving as a spiritual gathering place, the church has become an important place for immigration-related social justice organizing and community outreach efforts. Individuals within the church have been critical to making this happen. As I have mentioned, Victoria is one such bridge, utilizing her bilingualism to support community organizing efforts. There are other individuals who have played key roles in strengthening the church's canopy and supporting the migrant community.

Jennie, a native-born Montanan, is an extraordinarily critical bridge between the native-born and migrant communities. Jennie credits her parents for gifting her with a love of Spanish and a commitment to community building. Her parents met as Peace Corps workers in Latin America and then moved to a ranch in Montana. They both pursued either paid or volunteer work aimed at helping others upon their return to the United States. Jennie's mom, before her untimely death from cancer, was one of the only ESL teachers in Montana. She was loved by migrant families for the meaningful work she did with Mexican youth and the support and friendship she gave their parents. Jennie has in many ways followed in her parents', and especially her mother's, footsteps. She studied Spanish at the state university, spent her junior year abroad in Mexico, and, when she returned to Montana, sought opportunities to speak Spanish and connect with Latinos.

At the university's Annual International Food Bazaar in 2007, Jennie met Antonio, a graduate student from Mexico City. Although bilingual and highly educated, Antonio is from a working-class Mexican family. He credits his academic success with a scholarship he was awarded to study at the prestigious National Autonomous University in Mexico City (UNAM) and the University of California Los Angeles. Antonio's mother migrated to the United States when he was young, and he was raised by his grandmother within a large extended family. He understands the difficult reality of migration. Antonio's Catholic faith is at the core of his identity, and he was one of the original members of the church's Friday prayer group.

Jennie and Antonio became fast friends, and Antonio introduced Jennie to the Mexicans he had met through the church. Jennie's family, Catholics, in turn began attending the church. Jennie and Antonio soon became central figures within the Catholic Mexican community. Both bilingual and with social capital, Jennie and Antonio are able to be effective advocates and to provide support for migrants in times of need. They have also become close friends with many migrants. Indeed, both of Antonio's and Jennie's social worlds are now centered on the Mexican migrant community.

The university-based group Latinos y Salud (Latinos and Health) and more recently the Montana Immigrant Justice Alliance (MIJA), developed around Jennie's and Antonio's central role in the migrant community. A new immigration lawyer to Montana, Shahid Haque-Hausrath, is the director of MIJA, and, although he does not speak fluent Spanish, he has become a critical advocate for migrants throughout Montana. Jennie has worked with each group as a community organizer, paid at times, but doing most of her work as a volunteer. With essential organizing help from Jennie, both groups have held "know your rights" forums at the church, during which they up-date migrants on immigration law and inform them about what to do if they are pulled over by the police. They also host annual visits by the Boise-based Mexican consulate to renew and process Mexican passports and national identifications. Latinos y Salud has also established a Community Action Board, composed of native-born white and migrant community members. They organize in support of immigration reform and against anti-immi-gration bills in the Montana legislature. As one of the few bilingual leaders, Jennie has been central to these efforts, uniting migrants and native-born activists and raising awareness about immigration throughout the greater Montana community.

Also using the church as a base is the university-based student group Tías y Tíos (Aunts and Uncles), which organizes activities and tutoring for 1.5 and second-generation Mexican youth. The organization's student leaders, Jenna and Jessa Thiel, who founded the group in the spring of 2010, fol-lowed by Jessica Cartwright, Frances Moore and Ashley Piper, have served as bridges between the university and the migrant community. Every other Sunday throughout the academic year, service-learning students from Mon-tana State University's Sociology and Latino Studies programs gather at the church to meet up with Mexican and non-Mexican youth for a group activ-ity such as playing soccer, going to a museum, bowling or sledding. For most migrant children, Tías y Tíos is the only extracurricular activity in which they participate. In addition to organizing activities for youth, volunteers for Tías y Tíos tutor and mentor Mexican children, encouraging them academ-ically and often serving as a sounding board for problems in their personal lives. Students also participate in language exchanges with migrant parents, a forum for university students to practice their Spanish and migrants parents to practice their English.

Tías y Tíos serves another critical purpose. The majority of Montana State students are white, native-born Montanans. Most have never traveled outside of the country and a significant few have never ventured outside of the Mountain West. As such, studying Spanish and connecting with migrant children and their families can be a life transforming experience. As a professor of these students and one of the advisors of Tías y Tíos, I have witnessed shy, politically ambivalent students, unsure about what to make of the demographic transformation occurring in their community, turn into social justice activists, friends and advocates of the migrant community. Three students with whom I have worked in Tías y Tíos have gone on to work in law enforcement in the Gallatin Valley. They have told me that the human connections they made with migrant families through Tías y Tíos, in addition to the language and cultural competency they gained, have given them a critical, social justice based perspective on immigration that they have brought into the police departments they have joined. I am hopeful that the student bridges that have grown out of Tías y Tíos will help give rise to future cosmopolitan canopies in southwest Montana.

Tías y Tíos has also offered a forum for native-born children and 1.5 and second-generation Mexican youth to play together and form friendships. My own children as well as children of other faculty and community members attend Tías y Tíos events regularly. When children play together, parents meet each other. In this way, children have become critical bridges across culture and difference. My hope is that these youth bridges too will nurture cosmopolitanism and a stronger community.

In further support of migrant families, Professor Bridget Kevane, the director of Montana State University's Latino Studies program, has held multiple information sessions encouraging 1.5 and second-generation youth to attend college. Raised in Puerto Rico and linguistically and culturally fluent in Spanish, Professor Kevane has reached out across race and class creating trust and forming friendships with many Mexican families. Through her advocacy, Professor Kevane has also found herself serving, like Jennie and Antonio, as an informal social worker of sorts, translating for migrant parents at dental appointments and school conferences, as well as at migrant forums. Additionally, she has become a faculty advisor for Tías y Tíos, institutionalizing engagement learning as part of the Latin American and Latino Studies program at Montana State. Juliana, Olga and Sandra, all of whom have appeared in this book, and who have now graduated from Montana State University, note Professor Kevane as one of their primary inspirations, crediting her for giving their studies meaning and direction beyond the classroom.

On a beautiful, warm Sunday morning in September 2009, my husband, children, mother and I laid out a blanket on the church lawn to participate in the first bilingual Mass in Bozeman's history. The lawn was covered with blankets occupied by both native-born and Mexican families. Some attendees were dressed in their finest, but most donned casual late summer fare. The priest welcomed everyone, focusing his homily on the importance of inclusion and tolerance. I took note on this special day that many of the people in attendance were not traditional church-goers. I assumed that many, like me, are not Catholic. They were there to support the construction of a cosmopolitan canopy. And yet a church, because it follows a strict doctrine, cannot welcome all. In the Catholic Church compulsory heterosexuality excludes those who do not fit the church's gender prescriptions. I have observed the church canopy's gender-based ruptures come into stark relief on a couple of different occasions over the last few years.[4]

Although only a partial canopy, the church has been critical to the health and well-being of many Mexicans in Montana. I cannot overemphasize the strength and support that participants tell me they get from attending the prayer group, the monthly misa and other church functions. For many women, attending the monthly misa is the only time they regularly leave home. It is not an exaggeration to say that for some, the church has meant spiritual and emotional survival. Additionally, by offering a monthly religious service in Spanish, an annual bilingual Mass, and by serving as a platform for race and class-based social justice organizing, the church has helped bring a slice of cosmopolitanism to southwest Montana. For many native-born white Americans, natives of Montana and lifestyle migrants alike, the church has provided a space in which cultural, linguistic, class, ethnic and racial diversity can flourish. To be sure, despite its ruptures, buds of cosmopolitanism are emerging underneath the church's canopy.

Although the Catholic Church is the largest and most notable religious canopy in the region, other churches too have reached out to the Mexican community. There is a robust Mormon, Jehovah Witness and Evangelical presence among my participants. In all cases, migrants talk about religion, and specifically their church homes, as providing them solace, strength and a sense of community. Whereas the vast majority do not have access to weekly services in Spanish, they look forward to the regular opportunities they have to commune with other Latinos along with the native born. Because the Mexican community in Montana is too young to have yet developed hometown associations or other migrant organizations known to be beneficial to migrant well-being (see Levitt 2001), churches serve a critical role in maintaining and strengthening community ties.

The Food Bank: A Basic Needs Canopy and a Bridge of Friendship and Support

The food bank was among the first social service entities in southwest Montana to note an influx of Mexican migrants to the region. The first migrants who came to the food bank were construction workers on H2B visas. Because of the stringent regulation within the H2B program that ties workers' visas to the employers who brought them to the United States, workers do not have the flexibility to seek work elsewhere during slowdowns or stoppages. Unfortunately, both slowdowns and stoppages are common occurrences within the construction industry. I heard from several of the H2B workers I met during my fieldwork that employers typically bring in more guestworkers than they will likely need on a daily basis. The extra workers serve as a safety net so employers are prepared if a new project unexpectedly presents itself or a project takes an unforeseen turn that demands more laborers. As such, H2B workers, though legally guaranteed certain wage and hour protections, told me that when there is no work they are out of luck. In these situations they do not get paid, and, not uncommonly, they find themselves hungry. Donna West, a full-time volunteer at the food bank who has gone out of her way to cater to the needs of the growing migrant community in southwest Montana, told me that when the H2B workers first came to the food bank they were visibly famished. She recalled several of the men, who had traveled together in a large pickup truck, ripping open a bag of bread in the parking lot and eating voraciously.

With the arrival of Mexican laborers to Montana, word spread quickly that the food bank had a daily bread room that was open for the distribution of bakery items and produce to families and individual workers in need. To pick up food from the bread room, one did not have to fill out any paperwork, or sign anything or answer any questions. Thus it did not matter if one had papers or not. Everyone was welcome. Slowly at first, but gaining momentum as word got out, the food bank became a gathering place for migrant women, many of whom told me they risked driving without licenses when they heard that there was a place where they could supplement their wages with free food. The food bank played an especially critical role during the worst of Montana's economic crisis, from 2009 to 2012, when many construction workers were unemployed.

The food bank is housed in a 10,000-square-foot contemporary loft-like structure that is made from a mix of corrugated metal and wood. It is located, literally, on the other side of the tracks, a couple of miles north of downtown Bozeman in a rundown industrial area that is slowly being gentrified. One of the largest nonprofits in the region, the food bank relies on committed staff and many volunteers to keep the shelves stocked with food and to manage the paperwork of the hundreds of families who are qualified to receive monthly food distributions.

Despite its being one of the largest organizations in the region, before 2006 no one who worked at the food bank spoke Spanish. Thus when the first truckload of H2B workers arrived, staff and volunteers were at a loss about how to assist them. Whereas food bank staff members were able to use hand signals to motion the workers toward the daily bread room, they were not able to inform them about the other programs the food bank offered, most importantly the distribution of monthly food stocks that include canned goods, meat, dairy and dried grains, beans and rice. As it became clear that the workers would continue to come back when in need, and then as migrant women began to utilize the daily bread room as the economy faltered, the English-only standard and cultural homogeneity of the food bank became increasingly problematic. Donna took it upon herself to find a way to service the growing Latino community.

Donna grew up in a poor Jewish family in Cuban Miami. Most of her childhood friends were Latinos, and her brother married a *Cubana*. Donna grew up respecting the migrant struggle, which to her was symbolized by the strong values and work ethics of her Latino friends. Donna also remembers being hungry. She can recall moments when she could have turned to the streets but made the decision instead to finish high school and try to go to college. Donna did go to college. She married a successful attorney and she moved to Montana. In her new community, she dedicates herself to serving and empowering society's poor and marginalized. Donna sits on several social service boards in Montana. Head Start, the Human Resources Development Council, and the Help Center are just a sample of the organizations to which she contributes. But Donna's passion, and the place where she spends the most time and exerts the most energy, is the food bank.

I met Donna at the inaugural meeting of the Coalition of Resource Organizations (CORO) in the late fall of 2006. CORO was started by Buck Taylor, the chief operating officer of Community Health Partners,[5] when the community clinics under his directorship found themselves unprepared to meet the needs of their growing Spanish-speaking clientele. CORO began as a network of service providers from around the region who were eager to share information and ideas about how to cater to this new population. In addition to the twenty or so service providers who attended the first meeting, there were a few concerned community members who had an interest in working in whatever way they could to support and welcome Latinos to Montana. One of those concerned community members, Hunt McCauley, would become one of the central bridges between southwest Montana's social services and the growing migrant population. He would also become a dear friend of many Mexicans he met through his advocacy work. At the first CORO meeting Hunt and I both volunteered to help with translation at the food bank. As such, I got to see Hunt in action, and through our work together, he became a close friend and research collaborator.

Hunt is a retired rancher and veterinarian. He has worked extensively in Mexico and Latin America. He speaks fluent Spanish and is committed to using his retirement years to making a difference in his community. Hunt's wife, Sue, who is English, shares Hunt's commitment to community service. In addition to being a talented artist, Sue sits on the board of the Bridger Clinic, which specializes in providing low-cost reproductive health services to women and men in the Gallatin Valley. Hunt and Sue are vibrant community members, known and loved by many across the race, class, ethnic and gender spectrum.

Whereas my volunteer stint at the food bank lasted only six months over the course of a pretenure sabbatical, Hunt continues to spend a couple of hours each Monday through Friday, rain or shine, at the food bank. When a new Mexican client comes to the food bank, Hunt welcomes her (the vast majority of clients are women), explains how the bread room functions, and encourages her to sign up for monthly food deliveries. Very importantly, Hunt makes sure that everyone feels welcomed, emphasizing that documentation status does not matter.

Although the food bank's mission is to feed the hungry, it has developed into a canopy under which information is shared and friendships are made. In the fall of 2007, when I was volunteering there with Hunt, I met Giselda, a Mexican migrant who had come to Montana from Colorado. At the time she was living with her husband and toddler in a rundown motel about a mile's walk from the food bank. Giselda first came to the food bank after her husband lost his landscaping job. They were desperate. Hunt and I set Giselda up with an emergency food ration and signed her up for a monthly food pickup. We also explained to her that she could come and get bread and produce every day.

Within a few weeks of her visit to the food bank, Giselda's husband found a new job, and they were no longer in need of the food bank's services. Yet

Giselda and her daughter continued to come to the food bank every day. Giselda rarely took food, but she chatted with Hunt and with me while her little girl played on the food bank's expansive front lawn. Through our daily chats, Hunt and I got to know Giselda well. We were the first to learn that she was pregnant. We were also the first to learn that she had miscarried and had been treated poorly by a nurse at the hospital. Pregnant myself at the time, and having miscarried two years earlier, we bonded over our shared experiences. Giselda told us about her husband's struggle with tuberculosis, and about the pros and cons of living as an unauthorized migrant in Montana. While Giselda was exceptional for her regular visits to the food bank, visits that were made possible because of her proximity, other women, too, came to find the food bank as a place where they could meet their family's emergency food needs and engage in friendly conversation and access other important social service information.

During his time at the food bank, Hunt has become a trusted friend of many Mexican migrants. He has earned this trust via the generous support and advocacy he offers. In addition to translating at the food bank, Hunt has spent hundreds of hours translating for a local dentist who has treated the severe dental problems of several agricultural families, ferrying women and children to health appointments, and assisting families with taxes and passport applications. Hunt has also taken it upon himself to deliver food to struggling agricultural families who live in remote rural areas and do not have easy access to the food bank. The trust Hunt has established among Mexicans in Montana is symbolized by the invitations he has received to birthday parties, graduations, baptisms and even private funerals.[6]

As is true with the church, the canopy of the food bank has suffered tears and sporadic ruptures. While Donna and Hunt have worked tirelessly to make the food bank a canopy for all people who are in need of food, there have been times when the color line has been drawn in violent and hateful ways. Many women I talked to while volunteering at the food bank, and others I interviewed after I completed my stint there, talked about confronting the hateful words and faces of white food bank clientele. Ana, for example, told me that during a visit she made to the food bank a white woman looked at her, scowled and then pretended to vomit. Julisa similarly told me that when Juan Carlos lost his job and she went to the food bank for emergency help, a man stuck his tongue out at her and said what she interpreted to be, "Go home illegal." Donna validated their stories. To be sure, she told me that many of her white clients had complained to her and other staff that the food bank was serving foreigners. They were especially bothered that "illegals" were taking food that they felt was rightfully theirs. "How did you handle these situations?" I asked Donna during our formal interview. "Well," she replied, "I didn't put up with it for a second. The minute anyone complained, I told them to shut up. 'Listen,' I'd say, 'everyone deserves to eat. I don't care who they are or where they are from.' End of discussion."

The most frightening rupture in the food bank's canopy occurred when a white client threatened to call ICE on a Mexican client. While ICE ultimately did not come, soon thereafter the same client called the police and reported that an "illegal" had damaged his car. The police came and demanded to see the paperwork for all the food bank's clients. While most of the food bank staff cowered upstairs in the office, unsure of how to handle the situation, Donna stood firm in the food bank parking lot, refusing to let the police officers see any of the organization's private files. Finally the officers left. Whereas a potential deportation crisis was abated, it was weeks before migrants returned to the food bank. Word had spread that ICE and the police had their eye on migrant clientele, and it no longer felt like a safe place.

Donna and Hunt worked hard to repair the rupture. They arranged to increase the food bank's stock of rice and beans, they got a supply of children's books in Spanish, and they educated staff and white clients about the social justice commitment they had to the migrant community. After a while things settled and migrants in need began to return. While I am not so naive as to think that the racism of individual white clients was erased, I do think that through education and example, Donna and Hunt created a new expectation of civility. Donna told me that clients now understand that "whatever they think about immigration, they better keep it at home. At the food bank all are welcome, and if you want food you must check your hate at the door."

Facebook: A Virtual Canopy

In the spring of 2013, I was invited by Sociology Professor Hung Cam Thai, an expert in transnational families and gender and migration, to present my research at Pomona College. I spoke to a mixed audience of faculty, students and staff about the intersections of illegality and gender in the lives of Mexican migrants in Montana. In the lively and engaging discussion that followed my talk, the conversation turned to the unique isolation of migrants in rural America. The students in attendance, some of whom were migrants themselves, talked about the importance of networks to the well-being of migrants, especially women. As I detailed in Chapter 2, Montana's geography limits traditional network formation, adding challenge to the already difficult lives of women. As I finished my analysis, an unassuming young man raised his hand and asked, "So, what about social media networks? What role do they play in the lives of migrant women in Montana?" His question gave me a new perspective. Whereas traditional migrant networks are undeveloped in Montana, and canopies are few, often inaccessible and incomplete in their coverage, I realized in that moment that women's social networks were blossoming over social media, Facebook in particular.

In 2008 I received my first invitation, from Victoria, to join Hi5, a social media site that was popular at that time among Mexican and Central American migrants. Whereas I joined the site, I did not visit it regularly and did not recognize it as an important communication platform for the migrants I was getting to know in my fieldwork. In the summer of 2012, as I prepared to move to Oaxaca with my family for our sabbatical year, I decided it made sense to re-engage with social media. I joined Facebook. I soon learned that many of the Mexicans I knew in Montana, and even a few who had been deported and had returned to Mexico, had become regular Facebook users. Following my light bulb moment at Pomona I realized that Facebook had become a virtual canopy for some Mexicans in Montana.

My students now announce all Tías y Tíos events over Facebook. The Community Action Board of Latinos y Salud and the Montana Immigrant Justice Alliance (MIJA) use Facebook to organize against antimigrant legislation and to share information about immigration reform. Whereas migrants have been hesitant to gather to organize in opposition to anti-immigration legislation in Montana, Facebook is a canopy under which they feel secure enough to voice their political thoughts. In the fall of 2012, when my official fieldwork was completed and I was in Mexico working on this manuscript, the first antimigrant initiative, LR121, The Montana Proof of Citizenship Question, made it onto the Montana ballot. I watched with awe and inspiration as many of the migrants I knew well spoke out against the initiative over Facebook, posting social justice slogans and engaging with each other as well as native-born Montanans interested in the same issue. When LR121 passed with overwhelming support, MIJA immediately posted information detailing what exactly would change when the initiative went into effect. Of course, MIJA's limitation is that it posted the information in English. The vast majority of migrants speak only Spanish. Jennie again served as an important bridge translating information for the anxious migrant community.

In addition to the growing political engagement I have witnessed under the Facebook canopy, I have observed women in particular use Facebook as a platform from which they give each other comfort, advice and support. In the winter of 2013, Victoria's brother died tragically, not yet forty years old.

Victoria was distraught. Unauthorized, she was unable to return to Zacatecas to grieve with her family. Over Facebook Victoria was able to express her intense grief and receive support from a plethora of friends and family both in Mexico and in Montana. She posted pictures of her brother. She posted prayers. Friends and family responded with their own photos and prayers. Victoria also used Facebook to post a political proclamation, condemning the broken U.S. immigration system for breaking apart families and denying humans their dignity and social rights.

Two months later, Victoria's father died from the diabetes that had been ravaging his body for years. Again, Victoria was distraught, grief-struck, and far from her family. Over Facebook, I witnessed Victoria again express her sadness and her anger, and I observed the love and support she received from family and friends. Using Facebook, Victoria was able to grieve in Spanish, across borders and without fear of being detained. Victoria has a strong network in her life and, as has historically been the case, this network is critical to her well-being. But unlike traditional migrant networks, Victoria has built and nurtured her network in cyberspace.

Similarly, under the Facebook canopy, I have observed Gaby reconnect with her deported sons, and I have witnessed her sons nurture a connection with their younger brother, Raul, who was only a toddler when they were deported. Through regular photo postings and updates, Gaby's transnational family can now safely stay connected. In the spring of 2013, Gaby posted pictures of the three beautiful birthday cakes she made for Raul's birthday. I smiled as I noted the loving messages her older sons sent applauding Gaby's handiwork and acknowledging the special day. Special celebrations and times of intense grief aside, every day migrant women exchange encouraging words over Facebook. Most common are the Spanish postings emphasizing the importance of being thankful and appreciating each day's blessings. Many of the postings that women share have a religious sentiment. Rarely a day goes by that an image of the Virgin Mary or Jesus on the cross is not posted. Women also use Facebook to invite friends to birthday gatherings, children's graduations and religious festivities. Facebook has provided a Spanish forum for otherwise isolated migrant women in Montana to connect with each other, as well as to connect with friends and family in the states where they lived previously, as well as in Mexico. Facebook has nurtured translocal and transnational women's networks. Whereas several migrant men I know are on Facebook, they rarely use it as a communications forum. In my observation, for migrants in Montana, Facebook is a highly gendered space.

Although in many important ways Facebook represents new opportunities for network building, it also brings to light social divisions and hierarchies within Montana's migrant community. For example, while it is used widely and regularly by literate migrant women, many women are excluded from the forum. I have realized, in large part through observing communications over Facebook, that the wives and partners of construction workers, who tend to live nearer to town and to have secondary educations, are those who participate in social media. The agricultural workers in my sample, who are the least educated and many of whom are illiterate, are excluded. Their illiteracy, in addition to the fact that they do not own computers or have access to a public venue where computers are available, blocks their access to the on-line migrant community. The agricultural families struggle most to access Montana's canopies, while the construction families show the most promise of establishing networks underneath and outside of the canopies.

It will be interesting to see what role social media comes to play in the lives of the 1.5 and second generation in Montana. As of this writing, several of the elementary school–aged children of migrants who live near town and whose parents are on Facebook utilize the site. The majority of all adolescent children and young 1.5 generation adults are also regular users. Excluded are preteenage, and a few teenage, children from agricultural families, most of whom do not have home computer access. I hypothesize that this will change as the agricultural children grow up and are socialized through school into the on-line social world. I imagine that, as this happens, owning a computer will become a priority within migrant households. Roberta has already expressed interest in her children learning how to use a computer. Before I left for Oaxaca, I gave her my old laptop. As I was leaving the field in summer of 2012, Hunt was helping Roberta decide whether getting wireless in the old farmhouse they are renting was a possibility. If it does turn out to be feasible, Roberta's children may expand their own networks despite their geographic isolation. Roberta, though, along with other migrant women in her situation, will be excluded until she learns how to read and operate a computer.

Conclusion

I end with this chapter because for me it represents hope. Despite the extraordinary challenges of living in geographically and socially isolated spaces, the symbolic bridges and canopies of southwest Montana encourage the incorporation of migrants into the larger community. What is not known is what will happen to these canopies in the future. Unlike the cosmopolitan canopies celebrated by Anderson, which are institutionalized in urban space, Montana's rural canopies are in their infancy. Whereas they are ripe with potential, they are also implicitly vulnerable to being dismantled or trans-formed.

The dispersion of migrants in southwest Montana makes it difficult to conceptualize them as a community. To be sure, many migrants I met avoid the canopies I mentioned and have little interest in becoming a more visible ethnic group. For them, a large part of Montana's appeal is the feasibility it presents of living off the radar screen. This presents a challenge for those who are trying to organize and unite Mexican migrants. For now the canopies I mention serve as welcome places for those who are seeking support and connection. And they remind me of the unique place that the New West has in the ever-evolving migrant story.

Chapter 8

The Last Best Place?

As I complete this manuscript, *Outside Magazine* has just nominated Boze-man as a contender for the "Best Town Ever." The nomination has caused quite a stir as Bozemanites and those living in the areas surrounding Boz-eman express both pride in the attention the nomination has garnered and regret about the increased influx of people that it may generate. Southwest Montana's acknowledgment by *Outside Magazine* is based principally on its access to hiking, skiing, mountain-biking, climbing and fly-fishing. Bozeman has also garnered recent media attention for its "postcard quaint" downtown and its growth as a sustainable high-tech business community.[1] The word is out. For people looking to combine lifestyle and opportunity, southwest Montana is the place to be. For sure, Montana has entered a period of vast cultural, economic and demographic transformation. Lifestyle migrants and tourists flock to Montana in search of the idyll of natural beauty, tranquillity, simplicity and amenities. And labor migrants follow. Whereas populations are declining in much of the United States, towns and communities in the Mountain West are growing rapidly, their economies booming in compari-son with other regions (Wilkinson 2013).[2]

The "Best Town Ever" has resonance for the labor migrants I met in this study. As I detail throughout this book, Mexicans in Montana tell me that if they have a choice, they do not want to live anywhere else in the United States. Their fondness for Montana highlights their agency as pioneers on this new frontier of immigration. Even through the difficult years of the Great Recession, the vast majority of migrants I met struggled to maintain a foothold in Montana. Whereas some ultimately left, many stayed. And those who decided to leave told me they did so with a heavy heart. Mexicans mi-grated to Montana for economic opportunity, but they have stayed for much more. They connect with Montana's rural landscape; with the mountains, rivers, wide open valleys and the big sky. Their narratives suggest that Montana nurtures their *geographic habitus* that was born in the *campo* and *pueblos* of central Mexico, and was under siege in the urban hubs where the majority lived before moving to Montana. Place matters in the lives of migrants I met. It matters in terms of their sense of security, their level of contentment and the hope they have for the future.

When Mexican migrants speak of Montana, they speak about struggle but they also speak of tranquillity. Their narratives suggest a paradoxical partnering between the unique challenges of being among the first nonwhite, non–English speaking migrants in southwest Montana, and the intimate relationship that migrants are developing with Montana's natural and cultural landscapes. In addition to feeling an immediate connection to Montana's natural and built environment, migrants have consumed the palatable narrative that in Montana crime is low and people are good. "In Montana one can leave their doors unlocked," encapsulates the delight that labor migrants experience in coming to Montana from urban areas they deem dangerous and morally corrupt. For almost all of the migrants I interviewed, Montana signifies that the American Dream of jobs, security and natural beauty is still alive.

Ultimately, both lifestyle migrants and labor migrants seem to be searching for the same thing—the collage of spiritual, economic and cultural well-being that is lost in advanced American capitalism. The rural idyll represents their quest. Longing for an era of security, tight-knit families and communities, neighborliness, low-crime and clean air inundate the psyches of the Mexican migrants I met. Even for those who have never experienced the things for which they are nostalgic, the sentiment is powerful, and Montana nurtures it. Women celebrate the ways in which Montana bolsters their capacity to be good mothers, offering their children their presence in addition to safety and good schools. Men celebrate that Montana offers them the enhanced ability to provide and protect.

Social Ruptures

Yet peering below the surface, it is clear that the transformation of the West is not truly idyllic. A growing inequality has accompanied the region's demographic and cultural change. Migration into Montana has intensified spatial and social segregation. As happened in the 1990s in gentrifying urban spaces around the country (Slater 2011), in rural spaces, too, the in-migration of wealth has led to the out-migration of the poor and working classes.

Lifestyle migration into southwest Montana has further intensified the gap between rich and poor. Mexican migrants work and live in what Chavez (1998) terms "the shadows" of the wealth that demands and depends on them. Mexican migrants to Montana have joined poor and working-class native-born Montanans in the social margins, a space fraught with tension and insecurity.

Gender is a powerful indicator of how migrants experience the paradox of southwest Montana. A landscape that is liberating to the eye can be oppressive to the soul. Mexican women find themselves uniquely isolated by the distances and rugged terrain that characterize Montana. Their social position in a masculine economy means they are often constrained to the home. In some ways this isolation may ironically provide women refuge in their roles as mothers and wives. But the gendered context of their lives is also brutal. It is unduly challenging to live day after day away from supportive kin. And while some canopies, both real and virtual, offer temporary respite, migrant women most often find themselves alone in their gendered responsibility as their families' caretakers. Unauthorized women struggle most, carrying the constant fear of deportation and family separation. And when men are deported, it is women who must pick up the pieces, by holding family together in a hostile context.

Migrant men struggle too. Whereas they celebrate good work and wages, they also confront the insecurity of their daily commutes, which take them over treacherous terrain on roads where they are perpetually vulnerable to accidents and traffic stops. When the Great Recession crushed the construction industry, migrant men's sense of manhood took a terrible hit, their ability to provide and protect eroded by economic factors outside of their control. As the recession lifts and they return to work, the economic landscape has brightened once again. Yet the threat of deportation still encapsulates daily life for men whose gendered responsibility as providers demands they traverse public space in which it is impossible for most Mexicans to be anonymous.

Children of the second generation, who are U.S. citizens, experience Montana differently than their parents. Their incorporation into the local environment through school and friendships gives them a deep social rooting. They speak English and consider Montana home. But their identity as Montanans precludes an identity as American. To be sure, every one of the youth I interviewed, while preferring English over Spanish, and expressing a love for where they live, identified not as American but as Mexican. The youth here would more aptly be characterized as Mexican-Montanan than Mexican-American. They still feel the mark of being different, of not being totally accepted by the larger society, even though, like their parents, they feel a deep connection to the rurality of Montana. Additionally, those whose parents are unauthorized live with the daily fear that a parent could be deported and their family thus divided. At a young age children of unauthorized parents learn that they can never be totally open about who they are and where they come from with anyone outside of their inner circle. Stress is implicit in the childhoods of the Mexican Montanan second generation, and they experience life as more hostile as they age.

Boys especially find it difficult to come of age in a place in which general societal knowledge of Mexican youth is based on gangster stereotypes that inundate popular media and culture. And so the *ranchero masculinity* (see Smith 2006) of their fathers takes hold, as hard labor replaces education as central to the construction of Mexican manhood. Young Mexican women experience more supportive and flexible expectations. School is encouraged, and young Mexican women more often than young Mexican men grow into roles that deviate from those of their parents' generation. Sandra, Juliana, Olga and Vera have all successfully finished university and are motivated by their dreams for the future. At the same time, Chaba, Adolfo, Bruno and Mateo confront futures that are less clear and less bright.

Trends that Transcend Place

The story of Mexican migration to Montana is unfolding on many levels. In important ways this is a local story about migrants' relationships to the specifics of place. But in other ways this is a global story. The structural transformations that drew Mexicans to Montana are connected to economic shifts that are happening on a macro level (Hirschman and Massey 2008). And the ways in which Mexicans experience Montana are as much about the transnationality of their lives and the ways in which migration has been constructed in U.S. law and culture as they are about how they interface with Montana's law, culture and economy. Whereas there are barriers to migrant well-being that are specific to southwest Montana, there are others that transcend place.

Illegality, for example, penetrates the daily lives of migrants everywhere. Even those who are authorized feel the stigmatized conflation of migration and criminality in the broader society (Chavez 2008). The threat of deportability is felt by migrants in Los Angeles, Arizona and New York City as well as in rural Iowa and Montana. The gender implications of illegality also transcend place, as unauthorized mothers in urban as well as rural and suburban destinations report feeling the constant fear of being separated from their children (Abrego and Menjívar 2011). Similarly, the tensions and inequalities that exist in mixed status families persist across space (Dreby 2012). And in most places if an authorized child has unauthorized parents she is less likely to access the entitlements for which she is due than a child whose parents have papers (Yoshikawa 2011).

Gender may be constructed differently depending on local context, but it is a major axis of inequality wherever migrants settle. Gender is fluid. Still, across space, it is central to the ways men and women experience privilege and subordination. For example, whereas in Montana, Mexican women report liberation from the violence to which they were vulnerable in the urban destinations where they lived previously, many experience new struggles with boredom, isolation and economic vulnerability resulting from Montana's rurality. And while in Montana, women report empowerment as mothers and subordination as individuals, they tell me that when they lived in urban destinations, this equation was flipped. Men's identities and experiences shifted less dramatically with migration to Montana. Still, men's gendered responsibilities as providers weigh more or less heavily depending on the economic and geographic landscapes of their lives. Men told me that they feel more economically secure in Montana than in other places, but also more vulnerable to deportation and discrimination. This study shows the importance of analyzing how intersections of landscape, the organization of space, economy, legality, marriage and transnational cultural expectations shape the ways in which gender is experienced for, and performed by, men and women. When any of these variables shift or are transformed, gender may be transformed too. This ethnography highlights the place specific trade-offs that men and women must negotiate in the process of transnational and translocal migrations.

Evolving Lives and Identities

Over the seven years that I have been immersed in this project, six years in the field and one year finalizing my data analysis and writing this manuscript, the lives of the individuals I introduce in this book have continued to evolve. Through their evolutions, the complex entanglement of social position and place continues to influence the ways in which they experience daily life. The question mark that punctuates this book's title is accentuated by the paradoxical partnering of struggle and opportunity and the iterative journey forward for the migrants in this book. Below, I leave you with a window into the lives of this book's lead characters as they look toward the future, and I analyze each story in the context of immigration more broadly.

GABY

Raul is now in first grade. Although Raul struggled throughout his kindergarten year, both academically and socially, his teacher and the school's
administrators provided him support. Gaby has been impressed with the
school and with Raul's progress. Just a few years ago she feared that the abuse
Raul sustained from her former boyfriend would scar him forever. She is
now optimistic that a happy childhood is not only possible but likely.

Raul is a friend of my son Micah. Here again, my position as a mother has
opened up ethnographic opportunities, in this case to observe Raul through
Micah's eyes. Raul has played at our house several times since the school year
began. He is a smiley and energetic child. He is also extraordinarily athletic.
During Raul's last visit to our house he and Micah played basketball against
Micah's closet door for hours. Micah and Raul also play football and soccer
outside of school hours. According to Micah, Raul is one of the best players
he knows. Despite his talent, he is the only one of Micah's friends who does
not play on an extracurricular sports team. Tight finances and Gaby's rigid
work schedule limit his participation.

Raul's success on the playground does not follow him into the classroom,
where he is in trouble often for talking out of turn and not paying attention.
When I recently asked Raul if he liked school, he adamantly responded,
"No." Aside from recess, gym and lunch, he finds it both boring and difficult.
I was not surprised by his response. Gaby has never been in a position to
encourage Raul's intellectual development. She has called me a couple of
times since school began to see if I might be able to explain Raul's homework assignment. Although Gaby is learning to speak English, she struggles
to read basic homework directions. It seems that this struggle will only intensify as Raul progresses through elementary and into middle and high school.
Despite Gaby's dedication to Raul's development, Raul lacks the academic
support that most of his middle-class peers get at home.

Raul is close to his mom and yearns to be close to his deported brothers.
The last time he was at our house he told me that all he wanted for Christ-
mas was to go to Mexico to visit Bruno and Mateo. Gaby's unauthorized
status prevents this. Even if she had the ability to travel legally, she could
not afford to do so. And so their separation will remain interminably. In the
meantime, Gaby fosters her family connections transnationally. I am always
thrilled to see the photos Gaby posts of Raul on Facebook, his smile big and
bright, to which Bruno and Mateo always respond lovingly and with enthusiasm. To me, Bruno's and Mateo's engagement indicates a desire to remain
an intimate part of their brother's and mother's lives. It suggests that despite

being divided by borders, and prohibited from a safe and legal reunion, family and love can endure.

While Raul is doing well, Bruno and Mateo are struggling with returnee life in Monterrey. Mateo is doing better than Bruno. He has a job working for a call service company, his bilingualism proving a valuable resource in the Mexican marketplace. He has a girlfriend and plans to get married soon. Bruno, on the other hand, has slumped into another depression. A year ago, while walking home at night, he was mugged at gunpoint, beaten up and robbed of his wallet and watch. Since that time he has literally been afraid to leave the house that he shares with his grandmother. His fear and depression have blocked him from pursuing school or employment.

Carrying the responsibility for Raul's, Bruno's and Mateo's well-being, Gaby also struggles. She continues to be anxiety-prone and emotional about the risk of her own deportation. While she has maintained the same minimum-wage job for the past few years, she can still barely make ends meet and fears she will have to move again at the end of this year. She loves her cozy basement apartment on the outskirts of town. In it she and Raul feel comfortable and safe. In addition, they are now in one of the most lauded elementary schools in the region. Gaby worries that Raul, who is just starting to find his first grade groove, will be negatively impacted by having to move houses and schools again. Only six years old, he has already lived in a half-dozen homes. The idyll of Montana includes small neighborhood schools, to which the majority of attendees can walk with their parent(s). This has been a wonderful community builder for those whose lives are stable and secure. But for those who do not have the privilege of putting down roots in a home that they own, and whose economic and legal insecurity means they must move often, the neighborhood model means that their children are denied the attachment the model was created to support. As a single, unauthorized mother, Gaby is more vulnerable than her peers. And thus, so too is Raul.

Gaby continues to hope for a partner, but she is also confident in her ability to manage the world on her own. Her moods tend to be volatile. At times she is happy and optimistic about her life, certain that immigration reform will open up new opportunities. She was involved for a while in the community advisory board of Latinos y Salud, which motivated her and made her feel part of a broader community. This group has since dissipated, but Gaby remains involved in the prayer group at the Catholic Church. Following the Friday prayer meetings, after her friends go home, Gaby goes to a cleaning job, a new employment gig that supplements her wages. While she cleans, Raul sleeps in the corner. It is no surprise that Gaby is often exhausted and at times depressed and overcome with fear about what the future will bring.

As a single mother she feels especially fearful of what her deportation would mean for Raul. He has no one else in the United States on whom to rely if something were to happen to her. And though she cherishes the Facebook relationship that she has created with Bruno and Mateo, and that they maintain with Raul, she grieves that her family cannot be together. Both the threat and reality of deportation are burrowed deep in her consciousness and are central to her daily life.

And yet Gaby plans to stay in Montana. When LR121 passed in November 2012, barring unauthorized migrants from accessing local social services, Gaby panicked and contemplated a move. An email that she sent me at 3:30 a.m. began: "Leah, pardon me, but I am unable to sleep so worried about what will happen tomorrow. Should I leave Montana? Will I ever be safe here?" Ultimately Gaby decided to stay, realizing that it would likely be no better somewhere else. Although her support network in Montana is small, she has one. She will stay in Montana for Raul, trying her hardest to give him the opportunities that she, as a child, was denied.

Gaby's story highlights the ways in which gender, illegality and rurality intersect to impact migrant life. Because Gaby does not have access to the higher paying jobs of her male peers, a function of the gendered economy of southwest Montana, she has failed to achieve financial security. The precariousness of her financial situation is intensified by her illegality. She is not positioned to ask for a raise or to complain if her work conditions seem unreasonable. Indeed, she is even hesitant to ask for a day off if Raul is sick, as she is terrified of losing her job. Finally, Gaby's vulnerability is accentuated by living in a place where she must traverse large geographic expanses to manage daily life, and that offers few social supports to ease her care burden. Gaby will stay in Montana, and yet all indications are that her life will not get any easier.

VICTORIA AND CANDIDO

After seriously contemplating a return to Zacatecas last spring, Victoria and Candido have decided, for now, to stay in Montana. As political conversations have begun to focus on the importance of Latinos to both the Democratic and Republican parties, they have regained hope that immigration reform will someday become a reality and that Victoria will finally be able to join the rest of her immediate family as an authorized member of society. When Olimpia, Victoria's youngest daughter, entered Head Start, Victoria began working more, cleaning houses and saving money for the future. As an unauthorized woman in Montana, she will never have the possibility of earning as much as Candido, but she is determined to make the most of her decision to stay in the United States. She has joined her oldest daughter, Samantha, in taking piano lessons, and she has enrolled all of her daughters in gymnastics and swimming lessons. She attends each lesson.

Victoria's path forward has been iterative. When Victoria and I exchanged emails last December while I was in Oaxaca, Victoria told me that her life was full and she was inspired about the future. Then her brother died and her world collapsed. She shared her grief with me in several email exchanges, simultaneously venting her anger about the U.S. immigration system, which denied her the possibility of grieving her brother's death with her family in Mexico. Through her emotional emails I could envision her tears and hear her screams. Victoria told me that Samantha was also struggling with grief. Having met her uncle only once, and when she was too young to remember, she absorbed her mother's sadness. Only eleven years old, she has come to understand the injustice of the U.S. immigration system. Legal violence framed Victoria's and Samantha's grief and delineated their options to cope with it.

Just after Victoria told me that she was beginning to believe she would someday be happy again, her father died. Whereas his death was not unexpected, it shook Victoria to her core. "I may be a good mother," she told me, "but I have failed as a daughter." I have heard this sentiment from Victoria a few times over the course of our relationship. She is angry and distressed that because of her social position, she has been made to choose one role over the other. She chose motherhood, a decision that brought tremendous guilt when her alcoholic, diabetic father passed away. Although he was a complicated figure in her life, absent and at times violent during her childhood, Victoria loved him. Distance and guilt intensified her longing to be with him as he aged and grew sicker. But she was most distressed about not being able to support her mother, who was devastated by the consequent deaths of her son and husband. Again, legal violence ravaged Victoria's life.

Candido does not feel the same guilt in living far from members of his family. He feels it is his responsibility to send money when there is a need. Yet he does not experience regret that he is not there to care for aging or sick relatives. Candido sees his role as that of provider, not a caretaker. Candido is a U.S. citizen. As such, he is able to visit his family regularly. He tries to make the trip to Zacatecas every few years. Because of his social position as a male U.S. citizen, Candido has been spared the suffering that at times envelopes Victoria.

Illegality has prevented Victoria from achieving her ideal of femininity, which includes caring for her family and striving for her own life goals. It is a curse that would impact her anywhere she settled in the United States. In

Montana, the curse is intensified by the lack of resources Victoria can access to push her immigration case forward, and the vulnerability she has come to expect in negotiating public space. At the same time, because of the good wages that pre- and postrecession Montana offers Candido in his construction work, partnered with the tranquillity that both Victoria and Candido associate with rurality, she continues to prefer Montana to other places.

As I write, Victoria has just received her General Education degree, a long-standing goal that has beckoned since she arrived in the United States from Zacatecas thirteen years ago. She would like to start classes at the local community college and is working with an immigration lawyer to figure out how she might do so without being burdened by international tuition. Once again, her illegality poses a major barrier to her aspirations. Still, she is determined not to give up. Candido, for his part, has once again found steady work. The construction industry in southwest Montana is rebounding, and this has given him a greater sense of security and optimism. Wages and employment opportunities matter a great deal in terms of how he and his family experience Montana. With a healing economy, Candido's and Victoria's marriage has become less volatile, and they are enjoying more outings and trips as a family. They try to spend each weekend camping, hiking and embracing Montana's natural splendor.

Only a few of the migrants I interviewed requested a special pseudonym. Victoria was one. I believe "Victoria" encapsulates her spirit, and her family's spirit, perfectly.

ROBERTA AND ERNESTO

Of all the families I have gotten to know well over the past six years, Roberta's and Ernesto's lives have proven the most steady. The major reason is Ernesto's employment in agriculture and not in construction. No matter the state of the economy, the cows still need to be milked. While many families lost income during the recession and had to separate temporarily, as men sought work out of state, Ernesto's job continued without a blip. What is more, Roberta's and Ernesto's family actually gained income as Roberta joined Ernesto milking cows in addition to sorting potatoes seasonally. All three of Roberta's and Ernesto's children are doing well in school, and Junior spends his breaks from school helping at the farm.

What *has* changed for Roberta and Ernesto is that they have been joined by kin from Jalisco. Recently, Juan Carlos's brother, Leo, whom Ernesto has known since childhood, arrived in Montana with a friend, after Juan Carlos picked them up in Las Vegas. The two men arrived in bad shape, battered from a difficult border crossing. One had infected blisters on his feet. Hunt

McCauley visited with them at Roberta's and Ernesto's house soon after the two men had arrived. He was awed by the lackadaisical manner in which they talked about their infected feet and traumatic border crossing. Ernesto and Juan Carlos are helping to connect their friends with work, and Juan Carlos and Julisa are housing them during their transition. One of the men will work in construction and the other in agriculture. Unlike Ernesto and Juan Carlos, these newcomers have arrived in Montana directly from Mexico and alone. Their families are in Jalisco awaiting their first remittance check. If Montana continues to grow as a migrant destination and the border militarization continues to intensify, both of which are likely, the demographics of migrant families here may change to include more single unauthorized men.

Roberta and Ernesto were dealt a blow in the spring of 2013 when they received word that Roberta's brother, Carlos, who was working on a dairy farm in Wisconsin, had been killed in a tractor accident. His wife had been killed in a car accident the year before. Therefore, Carlos's death orphaned his two young daughters. Although Roberta and Ernesto were open to taking in their nieces, the family ultimately decided that they would go to Las Vegas to live with another aunt. Roberta worries about their well-being. In addition to dealing with their nieces, Roberta and Ernesto were charged with figuring out how to get Carlos's body home to Jalisco, abiding by his mother's wish. Hunt organized the shipment of the body, an expensive and emotionally taxing duty that Roberta and Ernesto could not have handled without his help. The grief from Carlos's death has since subsided, yet Ernesto is reminded every day of the dangers of agricultural work and the responsibility he carries for his family's provision and well-being.

When I first met Roberta and Ernesto six years ago, they both asserted that they would stay in Montana for three years, maximum. Then they would return to their *ranchito* in Jalisco to raise their children there. Their plans have changed. Whereas they both continue to long for their Mexican home, their roots in Montana have grown deeper. Their children are thriving in elementary school, and they have found peace away from their ancestral home. Ernesto, especially, cannot imagine walking away from his dairy job. Despite the hard labor that demands he awaken at 4:00 a.m. every day, rain, snow or shine, Ernesto enjoys his work. It nurtures his geographic habitus, which is oriented around agrarian work in a mountainous countryside. Roberta enjoys the life too, waking with Ernesto without complaint every day either to make him breakfast or to join him in work. It has been a pleasure to watch them move toward greater financial stability and happiness in their lives. Although they are part of a growing immigration network, they still celebrate that the number of Mexicans in Montana is small relative to other places. They continue to prefer their position off the public radar screen. They have created their own little world in an isolated rural outpost. For Roberta and Ernesto, Montana has made all the difference. Although they are both unauthorized, illiterate and far from loved ones, here they feel a sense of security and upward mobility.

ELENA AND ANA

In the spring of 2012 I called Elena to share with her a scholarship opportunity that I had read about in the Montana State University daily announcements. The American Cancer Society had a new program for cancer survivors who wanted to attend university. I was giddy reading the email, thinking it absolutely perfect for Elena. I was certain she would be an ideal candidate. My giddiness was shattered when Elena responded to my news of the scholarship opportunity with unexpected news of her own. She had decided not to pursue college. She was returning to Jalisco to get married.

Whereas I was truly disappointed by Elena's news, both worried that she was marrying someone with whom she had only spent a month over a holiday visit to Jalisco and discouraged that she was forgoing more education, I was struck by the happiness in her voice. I was reminded as she spoke, about her homesickness for Mexico and how socially marginalized she had always felt in Montana. I concluded that for Elena, at that moment in her life, Montana represented cancer, struggle and the trauma of deportation. She wanted out.

Elena returned to Jalisco, and I did not hear of her for many months. In the meantime, though, I spoke a few times with Ana. Her life had changed somewhat. For one thing, she was without another of her daughters. She was sad and disappointed that Elena had returned to Mexico and was not pursuing university. Ana's tone of voice suggested that she remained anxious and a bit depressed. Ana is working now, sorting potatoes. She is thankful for the work. She prefers sorting potatoes to having to drive into town to clean a house every once in a while. Like Roberta and Ernesto she still feels safest in the shadows. The further removed she can be from public space, the better. For Ana, home continues to be a refuge of sorts, despite the loneliness that encapsulates her there.

Recently, I received news that Elena is returning to Montana. The announcement caught me by surprise. I had assumed that Elena would find happiness in her return to Jalisco, her homesickness finally alleviated. And yet, the transnational context of her life complicated her reincorporation into Mexico. Instead of feeling at peace in Jalisco, Elena found that she missed

Montana. Soon after arriving in Jalisco she began the tedious process of ap-plying for a visa for her new husband. Elena hopes that they will find work on a ranch, continuing their rural lives close to her parents and her younger siblings. Elena is thankful for her U.S. citizenship, which has given her the possibility of safe (re)return.

SARA AND REINALDO

Of all the women I met in my field research, Sara was the most socially isolated. She also appeared the most depressed. Right before I left the field in 2012, I saw her at a graduation party. As people danced, ate and socialized, Sara sat alone. Reinaldo was working in North Dakota. She told me that she felt at her wits' end.

Things have changed. Two months after I saw Sara at the graduation party, while Reinaldo was in North Dakota working for a long stretch, Sara got a job cleaning at a hotel. As I write, she has held this job for more than a year. Once with more time on her hands than she knew what to do with, Sara now has a busy life. She gets up early every day, gets her youngest son ready and off to school, then hustles out the door to work. She drives her-self, another seemingly mundane life change that has boosted her autonomy in immeasurable ways. What is more, she has helped two other authorized migrant women in the community to get cleaning jobs at the hotel. At one time, not too long ago, Sara was the most isolated. She is now the hub of a new women's employment network.

With her new job, Sara's attitude about life has changed. She has become more involved in church. She not only attends *misa* but also helps organize events and celebrations. During the recent bilingual celebration of the Vir-gen de Guadalupe, Sara performed in the dance and choir ensemble and organized the meal that was served afterward. Additionally, she now sells her ornate baked goods to individuals celebrating weddings, graduations, birth-days and baptisms. Her dream of having a catering business, which seemed far-fetched just a year ago, now seems possible.

Of course, Reinaldo is an important part of this story. His attitude about women's work seemingly changed following months of his unemployment during the Great Recession. Reinaldo found work at the end of 2010, but it was in North Dakota and Iowa, which took him away from home for long stretches. During one of these stretches Sara got her cleaning job, working in secret for a while and then eventually winning Reinaldo's approval. This story serves as a reminder that as economies shift, often so too do gender relations (Gutmann 1996). Reinaldo still holds tight to his *machista* ways, but they are different than they at first appeared. He is more accepting now of

Sara's outside activities. Gender is fluid, and because of its fluidity home is
no longer Sara's prison.

Of course, it was not only a shift in gender attitudes that spurred the
change in Sara's life. Social position mattered too. Perhaps most important,
Sara is authorized. Unlike Gaby, Victoria and Ana, Sara does not have to fear
deportation. Because Reinaldo is also authorized and her children are U.S.
citizens, illegality does not pose an imminent threat to their well-being. Of
course, as a Mexican in Montana, she still fears profiling and discrimination
because of her skin color and because she does not speak English. But ultimately she knows that she is one of the most privileged among Mexicans in
Montana.

Toward the Future

Is Montana "The Last Best Place"? It depends. I have learned through my
research that place is vitally important to how migrants experience daily life.
And yet place means different things depending on one's social position and
the transnational and translocal context of their lives. Gender, illegality and
social class have intersected with geography to shape the stories I have shared
in this book.

The migrants in this study have a unique connection to Montana. This
is due in part to the comparative context of their lives. Most migrated from
other places in the United States that are hostile toward immigrants and have
high levels of crime and violence. In addition, the vast majority of migrants
in this study are from rural parts of Mexico that approximate the mountainous and arid region of Montana in which they have settled. This does not
mean that life is easier in Montana. In many ways life is more difficult. Social
position is central to the equation. Mexican migration to Montana showcases the complexities that shape the agency of migrants in deciding which
areas of their lives to prioritize in choosing a destination. It also suggests that
depending on one's position in the family, the list of priorities may look
different. In this way, Mexican migration to Montana also reveals the way
power is organized within migrant families.

Ironically, as I finish this manuscript my family and I have made the difficult decision to leave Montana. Like many of my participants, I still feel a
strong connection to Montana, and my heart feels heavy as I imagine making
a home somewhere else. For nine years I have felt that, for me, Montana is
"The Last Best Place." Yet I have also always felt unsettled about rooting
my life in a place shaped by an idyll that is only fully accessible to the well
resourced. As is true for the migrants in this book and others, my choice to

move was initially prompted by an employment opportunity, as I was offered what for me is a dream job at Amherst College in western Massachusetts. And yet other lifestyle factors weighed heavily in our decision. While we grieve leaving the mountains of Montana and the idyllic context of our Bozeman lives, my husband and I are enthused about the opportunity, natural beauty, diversity and proximity to major metropolitan areas that western Massachusetts will offer us and our children. Through the lens of grief and excitement, I am left to reflect yet again on how my social position has bolstered my agency to choose where and how I will live. I leave Montana hoping that my family and I can create our own best place. Because of our privilege, I am confident we can.

For my migrant friends and research participants, place is more difficult to create. In Montana, migrants' feelings of belonging paradoxically coexist with experiences of marginalization. They espouse adoration for Montana, and yet most recognize that their existence in Montana is tenuous. Job loss, anti-immigration legislation, and deportation can limit migrant agency. Indeed, social position influences how and where one can live, and the tradeoffs one must weigh in the process of deciding how and where to live.

For this reason I end this book reiterating the theoretical point that places are not objective. The meaning of Montana does not exist detached from the social positions of its inhabitants. We experience place through our own social histories, which are in turn shaped by the natural, cultural, political and economic landscapes of our lives. For this critical reason, the story of Mexican migration to Montana mandates that the question mark at the end of this book's title remain.

Notes

Chapter 1

1. As a contrast to the romantic works of Doig and Kittredge is *Breaking Clean*, by Judy Blunt (2002). This book, written from a gender perspective, details the difficulty of being a woman in rural Montana.

2. Montana is distinctly segregated, which intensifies its aura of homogeneity. Although the state has a relatively large Native population of 52,000 (www.montana.gov), Native communities are geographically and socially marginalized. Until the recent in-migration of Mexicans, there have been no other minority groups of significant numbers who call Montana home.

3. See Gail Schontzler, *Bozeman Daily Chronicle*, April 18, 2010.

4. In 2010, Donna West, volunteer director of the food bank, told me that the numbers of working and middle-class Montanans visiting the food bank have been increasing steadily over the past ten years.

5. See Werwath Associates (2012).

6. I struggled over whether to use the term "migrant" or "immigrant" throughout this book. Ultimately I chose "migrant" as it better encapsulates the process by which my participants came to Montana. The vast majority migrated to Montana from other U.S. states, not directly from Mexico. I use the term "migrate" to highlight their movement both across international borders and within the United States.

7. According to Odem and Lacy (2009) Central Americans outnumber Mexicans in Virginia, and Puerto Ricans outnumber Mexicans in Kentucky.

8. See Wilkinson (2013), who writes about the business growth in the New West, driven by young entrepreneurs looking for places where they can partner lifestyle and ingenuity. He labels the New West the "green coast," home to sustainability-focused high-tech and outdoor industries.

9. Whereas linked migration and rural gentrification constitute the con-

textual point of departure for this study, this book is not about gentrifiers. It is about labor migrants—construction workers, agricultural workers and their families—and what daily life is like within a gentrified context of inequality.

10. See Wilkinson (2013) for a description of this process in Bozeman.

11. Although my family and I originally came to Montana for work, we decided to stay because of the natural beauty and amenities.

12. Throughout this book I use "geography" and "geographic" to signify physical terrain and the organization of physical space.

13. An important exception is Deeb-Sossa and Bickham-Mendez (2008), who researched the experience of Latinas in Williamsburg, Virginia, and the Research Triangle, North Carolina.

14. By translocal, I mean the social field that connects places within the United States, whereas by transnational I mean the social field connecting the United States and Mexico.

15. I use the terms "authorized/unauthorized" instead of "documented/ undocumented" to suggest the social construction and malleability of migrant legality. Whereas many of my participants do not have and have never had documents, others have false documents and some arrived in the United States on tourist visas and then became unauthorized when those visas expired. Several participants who are now U.S. residents did not have legal documents when they first arrived in the United States, and still others are trying to become residents.

16. I further expand on the impact of motherhood on my research in a book chapter, "Motherhood and Transformation in the Field: Reflections on Positionality, Meaning, and Trust" (Schmalzbauer 2013).

17. Guestworkers to Montana, both H2B construction workers and H2A agricultural workers, break the mold of family migration. The H2A and H2B workers in my sample are all transnational fathers.

Chapter 2

1. *Campesino* translates as peasant in English, yet it does not have the same negative connotation in Spanish. *Campesinos* are small farmers.

2. The vast majority of Mexican migrants I interviewed live in nuclear families.

3. See also Ivan Light (2006), who argues that market saturation and low wages pushed Latino migrants out of California.

4. The expansion of care and domestic industries is credited for large increases in female migration (Ehrenreich and Hochschild 2002). According to the 2011 U.S. Census American Community Survey, women now constitute 51 percent of all migrants to the United States.

5. The gender composition of the migrant labor force changed during the period of the Great Recession, which I detail in Chapter 5.

6. The community health clinics were the first social service places in southwest Montana to hire bilingual staff. They have Spanish-speaking staff in all of their clinics and have taken the lead in pressing other social services to follow suit.

7. Not all of the couples in my sample are legally married. Having children prompts the use of "husband" and "wife" even for those who are not legally married.

8. Roberta's son was treated for dehydration, given some antinausea medicine and released.

9. There is debate about the malleability of one's habitus. Whereas there is ample research showing how migration can alter attitudes about sex and gender (Hirsch 2003; Gonzalez-López 2005), I find that the context of departure and reception in part determine the level of malleability of gender norms and expectations.

10. H2A workers come to the United States on visas that cannot exceed one year. The most (in)famous U.S. guestworker program, the Bracero program, was formalized in 1942. Until its end in 1964, more than 4 million Mexican agricultural workers came to the United States to work on temporary visas (Hahamovitch 2003). When the Bracero program ended, the H2 guestworker program, which had been begun in 1952 to bring Jamaican cane cutters to the U.S., was expanded to include Mexican and other Latin American workers. In 1986, the H2 program was revised into the H2A and H2B program. H2A visas were designated for agricultural guestworkers, and H2B visas for service guestworkers.

Chapter 3

1. Geographer Rachel Silvey (2006) encourages migration researchers to look at the intersection of place and social position in their analyses of gender and migration. Few sociological investigations of immigration have included place in their intersectional analysis. As such, much of the gender and migration literature is rooted in urban empirical analyses. Geographers have been at the forefront of bringing place into analyses of new destination migration. See also Nelson and Hiemstra (2008) who argue that local context shapes migrants' identity as well as interactions between migrant and receiving societies.

2. The most infamous recent antimigrant law is SB 1070 in Arizona, which mandates that police determine the immigration status of those who are arrested or detained if there is "reasonable suspicion" that they are in the United States without authorization. The Supreme Court upheld this section of the bill in 2012. Five new destination states have adopted laws that mimic S.B. 1070. They include Utah, Indiana, Georgia, Alabama and South Carolina.

3. As I write, the Montana Migrant Justice Alliance has submitted an appeal to LR121 to the Montana Supreme Court.

4. I first introduced the concept of the "impossibility of anonymity" in the

article "Gender on a New Frontier: Mexican Migration in the Rural Mountain West," *Gender and Society* 23(6): 747–67.

5. During my fieldwork there were only two ICE agents in Montana. In a meeting with social service workers in 2008, these two ICE agents told us that they concentrated their efforts in southwest Montana, especially in the area around Big Sky ski area, where most construction jobs are located.

6. In the case of voluntary departure, an unauthorized migrant agrees to leave the United States at his own expense and in exchange does not have a formal removal order on his record. If an unauthorized migrant has a removal on his record, he is barred from re-entering the United States for ten years.

7. I learned via my direct exposure to arrests and deportations that when migrants are arrested in Montana, they are typically transported to Billings and eventually to Idaho before being tried or returned to Mexico. Rarely do they stay in Bozeman for more than a couple of days. As Billings is two hours away, visiting those who are detained is a difficult task for family members. Adding to the challenges of detention, because there is no one in the Montana jails who speaks Spanish, it is difficult to determine when or if a family member has been moved.

8. See also Dreby (2012), who found that one of the most difficult aspects of deportation for women was suddenly becoming a single mother.

9. At the time of this writing, Joe Arpaio was appealing a civil suit alleging civil rights violations, and had just narrowly escaped being recalled by voters (Greenblatt 2013).

10. Since that incident the Montana Human Rights Network has made migrant rights one of their main platforms.

11. I detail Jennie's relationship to the migrant community in Chapter 7.

Chapter 4

1. Ghose (2004) writes about the gentrification of Missoula, Montana, three and a half hours northwest of Bozeman. Missoula has experienced growth in lifestyle migration similar to that of Bozeman, yet Missoula has yet to see an influx of Mexican labor migrants.

2. Eleven of my adult interview respondents come from this part of Jalisco. In addition I talked to many others who originate from Jalisco.

3. Poverty in Mexico is concentrated in rural areas. More than half of Mexicans living in rural areas live below the poverty level, and 25 percent live in extreme poverty (Burstein 2007).

4. Beginning in the 1990s Montana saw a decline in the number of farms and ranches of 100 to 1,000 acres, which were replaced by "ranchettes" of 10 to 100 acres. Much has been written about the cachet that Montana ranchettes have for wealthy Californians (see Flores 1999).

5. According to USA.com (2013), Montana's crime rate is lower than the

national average, ranking fifteenth out of all U.S. states with number one having the lowest crime rate.

6. Interestingly, over the period of my field research I observed Dorotea to develop close friendships with Victoria and Gaby.

Chapter 5

Parts of this chapter appeared in Schmalzbauer, Leah. 2011. "Doing Gender, Ensuring Survival: Mexican Migration and Economic Crisis in the Rural Mountain West." *Rural Sociology* 76(4): 441–60.

1. This was reported to me by Donna West, who has worked at the food bank since 1993.

2. In Chapter 7 I detail the role the church plays as a safe space for the Mexican migrant community in southwest Montana.

Chapter 6

1. I found that Women Infants and Children (WIC) was one of the few social programs that migrant women utilized. It seems that the hospitals are doing a good job informing women following childbirth of their children's eligibility for this program. Yoshikawa (2011) reports a similar finding.

2. Elena was one of many Medicaid recipients who aged out of the program when she turned nineteen. At age nineteen most teenagers become ineligible for CHIP and face more stringent eligibility requirements for Medicaid. For more details see the Kaiser Family Foundation (2010) policy brief: *Aging Out of Medicaid: What Is the Risk of Becoming Uninsured?*

3. Rural crime is understudied. From the research that has been done, we know that there is tremendous variation in crime rates across rural communities (Rotolo and Tittle 2006).

4. See Dreby (2012) for a similar finding.

5. Important exceptions are those who live in the neighborhood around the state university. The elementary school there has an international focus inspired by the high number of foreign graduate students and visiting faculty whose children attend the school.

6. I have changed the name of Samantha's song in order to protect her identity.

7. We know from sociologists Annette Lareau (2003) and Julie Bettie (2003) that extracurricular activities are critical in terms of building social capital, which in turn expands opportunities for social mobility among poor and working-class youth. The connections children make on sport teams and in musical and theater groups can lead to connections that increase their future educational and professional opportunities. Most young Mexican children in Montana, while gleaning benefits from their time in school, are cut off from network-expanding opportunities that are available after the school day has ended.

Chapter 7

1. See also Hayashi (2007) for description of racial ruptures in Idaho and the Mountain West.

2. Geographer Emily Skop (2012) details the important role of what she terms "transitory" and "permanent spaces" to the well-being of the emerging Indian community in Phoenix. When the Indian migrants in her study were finally able to establish a permanent community center, the center became the backbone of Indian heritage in the area. Whereas Mexicans in Montana have yet to establish this type of "permanent space," "transitory spaces" such as churches, the food bank and community clinics serve as havens and gathering places.

3. See Sociologists Hagan (2008) and Levitt (2007) for detail about the importance of religion in the migrant experience.

4. The first was in 2008, when the Bozeman Community Clinic offered to distribute health materials in Spanish following a *misa*. The church snubbed the Community Clinic because the clinics offer birth control counseling and services. Soon thereafter, I was working with Latinos y Salud and the Montana Human Rights Network to organize a know your rights forum at the church. Here the complexity of Catholic social justice identity was laid bare. The church, while exerting passionate leadership in the struggle for migrant rights and workers' rights, excludes, and even admonishes, citizens and noncitizens alike who are struggling for social justice on the basis of gender and sexuality. I fear that the church's strong stance against homosexuality and alternative sexual orientations has intensified the social isolation of some Mexican migrants who are oppressed by the framework of compulsory heterosexuality. It has also discouraged other community members who have alternative gender identities from participating in church-based functions that paradoxically tout the celebration of tolerance and diversity.

5. Buck Taylor was well positioned to begin CORO. He moved to Bozeman from Chicago, where he directed a migrant health clinic. He has a lot of experience working with unauthorized populations.

6. In the winter of 2013, Hunt even found himself helping Ernesto find a way to get his brother's body to Jalisco after his brother was killed in a farm accident in Wisconsin. Ernesto considers Hunt "one of the family."

Chapter 8

1. See Wilkinson (2013).

2. The Manhattan Institute for Policy Research, as cited in Wilkinson (2013), touts the Inter-Mountain West as the region with the highest rate of job growth over the past ten years, at 14.7 percent. The population of the Inter-Mountain West has grown by 20 percent.

References

Abrego, Leisy. 2014. *Sacrificing Family: Navigating Laws, Labor and Love Across Borders*. Stanford: Stanford University Press.

Abrego, Leisy. 2006. "'I Can't Go to College Because I Don't Have Papers': Incorporation Patterns of Latino Undocumented Youth." *Latino Studies* 4(3): 212–31.

Abrego, Leisy and Cecilia Menjívar. 2011. "Immigrant Latina Mothers as Victims of Legal Violence." *International Journal of Sociology of the Family* 37(1): 9–26.

Aguilar, Arturo, Georgia Hartman, David Keyes, Lisa Markman and Max Matus. 2010. "Coping with La Crisis." In *Mexican Migration and the U.S. Economic Crisis: A Transnational Perspective*, edited by Wayne A. Cornelius, David Fitzgerald, Pedro Lewin Fisher and Leah Muse-Orlinoff, pp. 15–46. San Diego, CA: Center for Comparative Immigration Studies, University of California, San Diego.

Anastario, Michael and Leah Schmalzbauer. 2008. "Piloting the Time Diary Method among Honduran Immigrants: Gendered Time Use." *Journal of Immigrant and Minority Health* 10(5): 437–43.

Anderson, Elijah. 2011. *The Cosmopolitan Canopy: Race and Civility in Everyday Life*. New York: W. W. Norton Company.

Anrig, Greg and Tova Andrea Wang. 2006. "Introduction." In *Immigration's New Frontiers: Experiences from the Emerging Gateway States*, edited by Greg Anrig and Tova Andrea Wang, pp. 1–6. New York: Century Foundation Press.

Aysa, María and Douglas Massey. 2004. "Wives Left Behind: The Labor Market Behavior of Women in Migrant Communities." In *Crossing the Border*, edited by Jorge Duran and Douglas Massey, pp. 131–46. New York: Russell Sage Foundation.

Barnett, Cynthia and F. Carson Mencken. 2002. "Social Disorganization Theory and the Contextual Nature of Crime in Nonmetropolitan Counties." *Rural Sociology* 67(3): 372–93.

Beneria, Lourdes. 2010. "Globalization, Women's Work, and Care Needs: The Urgency of Reconciliation Policies." *North Carolina Law Review* 88(5): 1502–25.

Bettie, Julie. 2003. *Women without Class: Girls, Race and Identity*. Berkeley: University of California Press.

Blunt, Judy. 2002. *Breaking Clean*. New York: Knopf.

Boehm, Deborah. 2012. *Intimate Migrations: Gender, Family, and Illegality among Transnational Mexicans*. New York: New York University Press.

Bohon, Stephanie. 2006. "Georgia's Response to New Immigration." In *Immigration's New Frontiers: Experiences from the Emerging Gateway States*, edited by Greg Anrig and Tova Andrea Wang, pp. 67–100. New York: Century Foundation Press.

Boodman, Sandra G. 2006. "In Harm's Way: Guns and Kids." *Washington Post*, May 29. Retrieved at www.washingtonpost.com/wp.dyn/content/article/2006/05/29/AR2006052900755.html.

Bourdieu, Pierre. 1984. *Distinction: A Social Critique of the Judgement of Taste*. Cambridge, MA: Harvard University Press.

Bourdieu, Pierre. 1977. *Outline of a Theory of Practice*. Cambridge, UK: Cambridge University Press.

Boushey, Heather. 2009. *Infographic: The Importance of Women Breadwinners*. Washington, DC: Center for American Progress.

Brown, David and Louis Swanson. 2003. "Introduction: Rural America Enters the New Millennium." In *Challenges for Rural America in the Twenty-First Century*, edited by David L. Brown and Louis E. Swanson, pp. 1–15. University Park: Pennsylvania State University Press.

Bunce, Michael. 2003. "Reproducing Rural Idylls." In *Country Visions*, edited by Paul Cloke and Jo Little, pp. 14–30. London: Pearson.

Bunce, Michael. 1994. *The Countryside Ideal: Anglo-American Images of Landscape*. London: Routledge.

Burstein, John. 2007. *U.S.-Mexico Agricultural Trade and Rural Poverty in Mexico*. Woodrow Wilson International Center for Scholars. Washington, DC. Retrieved at http://www.wilsoncenter.org/topics/pubs/Mexico_Agriculture_rpt_English1.pdf.

Carling, Jorgen, Cecilia Menjívar and Leah Schmalzbauer. 2012. "Central Themes in the Study of Transnational Parenthood." *Journal of Ethnic and Migration Studies* 38: 191–217.

Ceballo, Rosario. 2004. "From Barrios to Yale: The Role of Parenting Strategies in Latino Families." *Hispanic Journal of Behavioral Sciences* 26(2): 171–86.

Cerutti, Marcela and Douglas Massey. 2001. "On the Auspices of Female Migration from Mexico to the United States." *Demography* 38(2): 187–200.

Chavez, Leo. 2008. *The Latino Threat: Constructing Citizens, Immigrants and the Nation State*. Stanford: Stanford University Press.

Chavez, Leo. 1998. *Shadowed Lives: Undocumented Immigrants in American Society*. New York: Harcourt Brace.

Cloke, Paul. 2006. "Conceptualizing Rurality." In *Handbook of Rural Studies*, edited by Paul Cloke, Terry Marsden and Patrick Mooney, pp. 18–28. London: Sage.

Deeb-Sossa, Natalia and Jennifer Bickham Mendez. 2008. "Enforcing Borders in the Nuevo South: Shifting Identities and Imagined Communities." *Gender and Society* 22(5): 613–38.

De Genova, Nicholas. 2010. "The Deportation Regime: Sovereignty, Space and the Freedom of Movement." In *The Deportation Regime: Sovereignty, Space, and the Freedom of Movement*, edited by Nicholas De Genova and Nathalie Peutz, pp. 33–65. Durham, NC: Duke University Press.

De Genova, Nicholas. 2005. *Working the Boundaries: Race, Space, and "Illegality" in Mexican Chicago*. Durham, NC: Duke University Press.

Diggs, Nancy Brown. 2011. *Hidden in the Heartland: The New Wave of Immigrants and the Challenge to America*. East Lansing: Michigan State University Press.

Doig, Ivan. 1979. *This House of Sky: Landscapes of a Western Mind*. Orlando, FL: Harcourt.

Donato, Katharine, Charles Tolbert, Alfred Nucci and Yukio Kawano. 2008. "Changing Faces/Changing Places: The Emergence of Non-metropolitan Immigrant Gateways." In *New Faces in New Places: The Changing Geography of American Immigration*, edited by Douglas Massey, pp. 75–98. New York: Russell Sage Foundation.

Dreby, Joanna. 2012. "The Burden of Deportation on Children in Mexican Immigrant Families." *Journal of Marriage and Family* 74(4): 829–45.

Dreby, Joanna. 2010. *Divided by Borders: Mexican Migrants and Their Children*. Berkeley: University of California Press.

Dreby, Joanna. 2007. "Children and Power in Mexican Transnational Families." *Journal of Marriage and Family* 69(4): 1050–64.

Dreby, Joanna and Leah Schmalzbauer. 2013. "The Relational Contexts of Migration: Mexican Women in New Destination Sites." *Sociological Forum* 28(1): 1–26.

Ehrenreich, Barbara and Arlie Hochschild. 2002. *Global Woman: Nannies, Maids, and Sex Workers in the New Economy*. New York: Basic Books.

Falicou, Celia Jaes. 2002. "Ambiguous Loss: Risk and Resilience in Latino Immigrant Families." In *Latinos Remaking America*, edited by Marcelo Suarez-Orozco and Mariela Paez, pp. 274–88. Berkeley: University of California Press.

Fennelly, Katherine. 2008. "Prejudice towards Immigrants in the Midwest." In *New Faces in New Places: The Changing Geography of American Immigration*, edited by Douglas Massey, pp. 151–78. New York: Russell Sage Foundation.

Flores, Dan. 1999. "In Montana: The View from the Ranchette." *High Country News*. May 10. Paonia, CO.

George, Sheba. 2005. *When Women Come First: Gender and Class in Transnational Migration*. Berkeley: University of California Press.

Ghose, Rina. 2004. "Big Sky or Big Sprawl? Rural Gentrification and the Changing Cultural Landscape of Missoula, Montana." *Urban Geography* 25(6): 528–49.

Golash-Boza, Tanya. 2014. "Forced Transnationalism: Transnational Coping Strategies and Gendered Stigma among Jamaican Deportees." *Global Networks* 14: 63–79.

Golash-Boza, Tanya. 2012. *Immigration Nation: Raids, Detentions, and Deportations in Post 9/11 America*. Boulder, CO: Paradigm.

Golash-Boza, Tanya and Pierrette Hondagneu-Sotelo. 2013. "Latino Immigrant Men and the Deportation Crisis: A Gendered Racial Removal Program?" *Latino Studies* 11: 271–92.

Gonzalez, Roberto. 2011. "Learning to Be Illegal: Undocumented Youth and Shifting Legal Contexts in the Transition to Adulthood." *American Sociological Review* 74(4): 602–19.

Gonzalez, Roberto and Leo Chavez. 2012. "'Awakening to a Nightmare': Abjectivity and Illegality in the Lives of the Undocumented 1.5-Generation Latino Immigrants in the United States." *Current Anthropology* 55(3): 255–81.

Gonzalez-López, Gloria. 2005. *Erotic Journeys: Mexican Immigrants and Their Sex Lives*. Berkeley: University of California Press.

Gozdziak, Elzbieta M. and Susan R. Martin. 2005. "Challenges for the Future." In *Beyond the Gateway: Immigrants in a Changing America*, edited by Elzbieta M. Gozdziak and Susan F. Martin, pp. 277–83. Lanham, MD: Lexington Books.

Grasmuck, Sherri and Patricia Pessar. 1991. *Between Two Islands: Dominican International Migration*. Berkeley: University of California Press.

Greenblatt, Alan. 2013. "The Survivor: Sheriff Joe Arpaio Outlasts Political, Legal Trouble." *It's All Politics: National Public Radio News Hour*, May 30, 2013.

Guendelman, Sylvia, Christina Malin, Barbara Herr-Harthorn, and Patricia Noemi Vargas. 2001. "Orientations to Motherhood and Male Partner Support among Women in Mexico and Mexican-origin Women in the United States." *Social Science and Medicine* 52(12): 1805–13.

Gutmann, Matthew. 1996. *The Meanings of Macho: Being a Man in Mexico City*. Berkeley: University of California Press.

Hagan, Jacqueline. 2008. *Migration Miracle*. Cambridge, MA: Harvard University Press.

Hagan, Jacqueline. 1998. "Social Networks, Gender, and Immigrant Incorporation: Resources and Constraints." *American Sociological Review* 63 (February): 55–67.

Hagan, Jacqueline. 1994. *Deciding to Be Legal: A Maya Community in Houston.* Philadelphia: Temple University Press.

Hahamovitch, Cindy. 2003. "Creating the Perfect Immigrants: Guestworkers of the World in Historical Perspective." *Labor History* 44(1): 69–94.

Hammer, R. B. and R. L. Winkler. 2006. "Housing Affordability and Population Change in the Upper Midwestern North Woods." In *Population Change and Rural Society*, edited by William Kandel and D. L. Brown, pp. 277–92. Dordrecht, The Netherlands: Springer.

Hancock, Tina. 2007. "Sin Papeles: Undocumented Mexicanas in the Rural United States." *Affilia* 22(2): 175–84.

Hayashi, Robert. 2007. *Haunted by Waters: A Journey through Race and Place in the American West.* Iowa City: University of Iowa Press.

Hays, Sharon. 1996. *The Cultural Contradictions of Motherhood.* New Haven: Yale University Press.

Hernandez León, Rubén and Victor Zuñiga. 2005. "Appalachia Meets Aztlán: Mexican Immigration and Inter-Group Relations in Dalton, Georgia." In *New Destinations: Mexican Immigration in the United States*, edited by Victor Zuñiga and Rubén Hernández-León, pp. 244–73. New York: Russell Sage Foundation.

Hernández-León, Rubén and Victor Zuñiga. 2003. "Mexican Immigrant Communities in the South and Social Capital: The Case of Dalton, Georgia." *Southern Rural Sociology* 19(1): 20–45.

Hernández-León, Rubén and Victor Zuñiga. 2000. "'Making Carpet by the Mile': The Emergence of a Mexican Immigrant Community in an Industrial Region of the U.S. Historic South." *Social Science Quarterly* 81(1): 49–65.

Heymann, Jody. 2000. *The Widening Gap.* New York: Basic Books.

Hines, Dwight. 2010. "In Pursuit of Experience: The Postindustrial Gentrification of the Rural American West." *Ethnography* 11(2): 285–308.

Hirsch, Jennifer. 2003. *A Courtship after Marriage: Sexuality and Love in Mexican Transnational Families.* Berkeley: University of California Press.

Hirschman, Charles and Douglas S. Massey. 2008. "Places and Peoples: The New American Mosaic." In *New Faces in New Places: The Changing Geography of American Immigration*, edited by Douglas S. Massey, pp. 1–21. New York: Russell Sage.

Hochschild, Arlie. 1989. *The Time Bind.* New York: Henry Holt.

Hondagneu-Sotelo, Pierette. 2001. *Doméstica: Immigrant Workers Cleaning and Caring in the Shadows of Affluence.* Berkeley: University of California Press.

Hondagneu-Sotelo, Pierette. 1994. *Gendered Transitions: Mexican Experiences of Immigration.* Berkeley: University of California Press.

Hout, Michael, Asaf Levanon and Erin Cumberworth. 2011. "Job Loss and Unemployment." In *The Great Recession*, edited by David B. Grusky, Bruce Western and Christopher Wimer, pp. 59–81. New York: Russell Sage Foundation.

Immigration Policy Institute. 2011. *2011 American Community Survey and Census Data on Foreign Born by State*. Retrieved at www.migrationinformation.org/datahub/acscensus.cfm.

Jacobs, Jerry and Kathleen Gerson. 2004. *The Time Divide: Work, Family, and Gender Inequality*. Cambridge, MA: Harvard University Press.

Jensen, Leif. 2006. *New Immigrant Settlements in Rural America*. Durham, NH: Carsey Institute, University of New Hampshire.

Jiménez, Tomás. 2010. *Replenished Ethnicity: Mexican Americans, Immigration, and Identity*. Berkeley: University of California Press.

Kaiser Family Foundation. 2010. "Aging out of Medicaid: What Is the Risk of Becoming Uninsured?" Retrieved at kff_org/Medicaid/issue-brief/aging-out-of-medicaid-what-is=the/.

Kandel, William and John Cromartie. 2004. "New Patterns of Hispanic Settlement in Rural America." *Rural Development Research Report* 99. Washington, DC: U.S. Department of Agriculture, Economic Research Service.

Kanstroom, Daniel. 2007. *Deportation Nation: Outsiders in American History*. Cambridge, MA: Harvard University Press.

Keller, Julie C., Sarah E. Loyd and Michael M. Bell. 2012. "Creating and Consuming the Heartland: Representing the Feminine in the Rural and the Rural in the Feminine." Presented at the Rural Sociological Society 75th Annual Meeting. Chicago, IL.

Kevane, Bridget. 2008. "Montana." In *Latino America State-by-State*, edited by Mark Overmyer-Velazquez, pp. 476–88. Westport, CT: Greenwood.

Kibria, Nazli. 1993. *Family Tightrope: The Changing Lives of Vietnamese Americans*. Princeton: Princeton University Press.

Kil, Sang H., Cecilia Menjívar and Roxanne L. Doty. 2009. "Patriotism, Vigilantism, and the Brutalization of the US American Public." *Sociology of Crime, Law and Deviance* 13: 297–312.

Kittredge, William and Annick Smith. 1988. *The Last Best Place: A Montana Anthology*. Seattle: University of Washington Press.

Kollin, Susan. 2000. "Dead Man, Dead West." *Arizona Quarterly: A Journal of American Literature, Culture, and Theory* 56: 125–59.

Krannich, Richard S., A. E. Luloff and Donald R. Field. 2011. *People, Places and Landscapes: Social Change in High Amenity Rural Areas*. Dordrecht, The Netherlands: Springer.

Lareau, Annette. 2003. *Unequal Childhoods: Race, Class, and Family Life*. Berkeley: University of California Press.

Leach, Mark and Frank Bean. 2008. "The Structure and Dynamics of Mexican Migration to New Destinations in the United States." In *New Faces in New Places: The Changing Geography of American Immigration*, edited by Douglas S. Massey, pp. 51–74. New York: Russell Sage Foundation.

Lee, Elizabeth M. and Rory Kramer. 2013. "Out with the Old, In with the New:

Habitus and Social Mobility at Selective Colleges. *Sociology of Education* 86(1): 18–35.

Levitt, Peggy. 2007. *God Has No Passport: Immigrants and the Changing Religious Landscape*. New York: New Press.

Levitt, Peggy. 2001. *The Transnational Villagers*. Berkeley: University of California Press.

Light, Ivan. 2006. *Deflecting Immigration: Networks, Markets, and Regulation in Los Angeles*. New York: Russell Sage Foundation.

Little, Jo and Patricia Austin. 1996. "Women and the Rural Idyll." *Journal of Rural Studies* 12(2): 101–11.

Maguire, K. and A. L. Pastore. 1995. *Sourcebook of Criminal Justice Statistics 1994*. U.S. Department of Justice Programs, Bureau of Justice Statistics. Washington, DC.

Mahler, Sarah. 1996. *Salvadorans in Suburbia: Symbiosis and Conflict*. Boston, MA: Allyn and Bacon.

Mahler, Sarah. 1995. *American Dreaming: Immigrant Life on the Margins*. Princeton: Princeton University Press.

Malone, Michael P., Richard B. Roeder and William L. Lang. 1991. *Montana: A History of Two Centuries*. Seattle: University of Washington Press.

Marrow, Helen B. 2011. *New Destination Dreaming: Immigration, Race, and Legal Status in the Rural American South*. Stanford: Stanford University Press.

Marrow, Helen B. 2009. "Immigrant Bureaucratic Incorporation: The Dual Roles of Professional Missions and Government Policies." *American Sociological Review* 74: 756–76.

Massey, Doreen. 1993. *Space, Place, Gender*. Minneapolis: University of Minnesota Press.

Massey, Douglas S. 2010. "Interview with Douglas Massey: Measuring Effects of US Policy on Latin American Migration Patterns. American Academy of Political and Social Sciences." Retrieved January 10, 2011, at http://www.aapss. org/news/2010/07/06/douglas-massey-measuring -the-effects-of-us-policy-on-latin-american-migration-patterns.

Massey, Douglas S. 2008. "Assimilation in a New Geography." In *New Faces in New Places: The Changing Geography of American Immigration*, edited by Douglas S. Massey, pp. 343–53. New York: Russell Sage Foundation.

Massey, Douglas S. and Chiara Capoferro. 2008. "The Geographic Diversification of American Immigration." In *New Faces in New Places: The Changing Geography of American Immigration*, edited by Douglas Massey, pp. 25–50. New York: Russell Sage Foundation.

Massey, Doug S., Jorge Durand and Nolan J. Malone. 2002. *Beyond Smoke and Mirrors: Mexican Immigration in an Era of Economic Integration*. New York: Russell Sage Foundation.

Massey, Douglas S. and Rene Zenteno. 1999. "The Dynamics of Mass Migration." *Proceedings of the National Academy of Sciences* 96(9): 5328–35.

McCarthy, James. 2008. "Rural Geography: Globalizing the Countryside." *Progress in Human Geography* 32(1): 129–37.

Menjívar, Cecilia. 2011. *Enduring Violence: Ladina Women's Lives in Guatemala.* Berkeley: University of California Press.

Menjívar, Cecilia. 2000. *Fragmented Ties: Salvadoran Immigrant Networks in America.* Berkeley: University of California Press.

Menjívar, Cecilia. 1999. "The Intersection of Work and Gender: Central American Immigrant Women and Employment in California." In *Gender and U.S. Immigration: Contemporary Trends,* edited by Pierette Hondagneu-Sotelo. Berkeley: University of California Press.

Menjívar, Cecilia and Leisy Abrego. 2012. "Legal Violence: Immigration Law and the Lives of Central American Immigrants." *American Journal of Sociology* 117(5): 1380–1421.

Menjívar, Cecilia and Olivia Salcido. 2002. "Immigrant Women and Domestic Violence." *Gender and Society* 16(6): 898–920.

Migration Information Source. 2008. *Return Migration: Changing Directions?* Retrieved January 2010 at http://www.migrationinformation.org/USfocus/display.cfm?ID=707.

Millard, Ann and Jorge Chapa, eds. 2004. *Apple Pie and Enchiladas: Latino Newcomers in the Rural Midwest.* Austin: University of Texas Press.

Mirandé, Alfredo. 1997. *Hombres y Machos.* Boulder, CO: Westview Press.

Mummert, Gail. 1994. "From Metate to Despate." In *Women of the Mexican Countryside 1850–1990,* edited by Heather Fowler-Salamini and Mary Kay Vaughan, pp. 192–209. Tucson: University of Arizona Press.

Naples, Nancy. 2007. "The Social Regulation of Citizenship: An Intersectional Analysis of Migration and Incorporation in the Heartland." *Journal of Latino/a—Latin American Studies* 2(3): 16–23.

National Public Radio. 2007. "Documentary Highlights Montana's Meth Problem." *Morning Edition,* March 13, 2007. Retrieved at www.npr.org/templates/story/story.php?storyId=7867364.

Nelson, Lise and Nancy Hiemstra. 2008. "Latino Immigrants and the Renegotiation of Place and Belonging in Small Town America." *Social and Cultural Geography* 9(3): 319–42.

Nelson, Lise and Peter Nelson. 2011. "The Global Rural: Gentrification and Linked Migration in the Rural USA." *Progress in Human Geography* 35: 441–59.

Nelson, Peter and John Cromartie. 2009. *Baby Boom Migration and Its Impact on Rural America.* USDA, Economic Research Report No. 79.

Nelson, Peter, Alexander Oberg and Lise Nelson. 2010. "Rural Gentrification and Linked Migration in the United States." *Journal of Rural Studies* 26: 343–52.

Odem, Mary. 2008. "Unsettled in the Suburbs: Latino Immigration and Ethnic

Diversity in Metro Atlanta." In *Twenty-first Century Gateways: Immigrant Incorporation in Suburban American*, edited by Audrey Singer, Susan W. Hardwick and Caroline B. Brettell, pp. 105–36. Washington, DC: Brookings Institute Press.

Odem, Mary and Elaine Lacy. 2009. "Popular Attitudes and Public Policies: Southern Responses to Latino Immigration." In *Latino Immigrants and the Transformation of the U.S. South*, edited by Mary E. Odem and Elaine Lacy, pp. 143–63. Athens: University of Georgia Press.

Park, Lisa Sun-Hee and David Naguib Pellow. 2011. *The Slums of Aspen: Immigrants vs. the Environment in America's Eden*. New York: New York University Press.

Parrado, Emilio and Chenoa Flippen. 2005. "Migration and Gender among Mexican Women." *American Sociological Review* 70(4): 606–32.

Parrado, Emilio A. and William A. Kandel. 2008. "New Hispanic Migrant Destinations: A Tale of Two Industries." In *New Faces in New Places: The Changing Geography of American Immigration*, edited by Douglas S. Massey, pp. 99–123. New York: Russell Sage Foundation.

Parreñas, Rhacel. 2001. *Servants of Globalization: Women, Migration, and Domestic Work*. Palo Alto, CA: Stanford University Press.

Pastor, Manuel and Susan Alva. 2004. "Guest Workers and the New Transnationalism: Possibilities and Realities in an Age of Repression." *Social Justice* 31(1–2): 92–112.

Patel, Raj. 2008. *Stuffed and Starved: The Hidden Battle for the World Food System*. Brooklyn, NY: Melville House Publishing.

Perlmutter, Philip. 2002. "Minority Group Prejudice." *Society* (March/April): 59–65.

Pessar, Patricia. 1999. "The Role of Gender, Households, and Social Networks in the Migration Process." In *The Handbook of International Migration*, edited by Charles Hirschman, Philip Kasinitz and Josh DeWind, pp. 53–70. New York: Russell Sage Foundation.

Portes, Alejandro and Patricia Fernandez-Kelly. 2008. "No Margin for Error: Educational and Occupational Achievement among Disadvantaged Children of Immigrants." *ANNALS of the American Academy of Political and Social Science* 620: 12–36.

Portes, Alejandro and Ruben Rumbaut. 2001. *Legacies: The Story of the Second Immigrant Generation*. Berkeley: University of California Press.

Portes, Alejandro and Ruben Rumbaut. 1996. *Immigrant America: A Portrait*. Berkeley: University of California Press.

Power, Thomas Michael. 1996. *Lost Landscapes and Failed Economies*. New York: Island Press.

Raj, Anita and Jay Silverman. 2002. "Violence against Immigrant Women: The Roles of Culture, Context, and Legal Immigrant Status on Intimate Partner Violence." *Violence Against Women* 8(3): 367–98.

Rios, Victor M. 2011. *Punished: Policing the Lives of Black and Latino Boys*. New York: New York University Press.

Rasker, Ray and Dennis Glick. 1994. "Footloose Entrepreneurs: Pioneers of the New West?" *Illahee* 10(1): 34–43.

Rotolo, Thomas and Charles Tittle. 2006. "Population Size, Change and Crime in U.S. Cities." *Journal of Quantitative Criminology* 22(4): 341–67.

Rumbaut, Ruben and Walter Ewing. 2007. *The Myth of Immigrant Criminality and the Paradox of Assimilation: Incarceration Rates among Native and Foreign-Born Men*. Washington, DC: Immigration Policy Center.

Salcido, Olivia and Madelaine Adelman. 2004. "He Has Me Tied with the Blessed and Damned Papers: Undocumented Immigrant Battered Women in Phoenix, Arizona." *Human Organization* 63(2): 162–72.

Sampson, Robert. 2008. "Rethinking Crime and Immigration." *Contexts* 7: 28–33.

Santos, Carlos, Cecilia Menjívar and Erin Godfrey. 2013. "Effects of SB 1070 on Children." In *Latino Policies and Arizona's Immigration Law SB 1070*, edited by Lisa Magaña and Erik Lee, pp. 79–92. New York: Springer.

Sassen, Saskia. 1998. *Globalization and Its Discontents*. New York: New Press.

Schmalzbauer, Leah. Forthcoming. "Temporary and Transnational: Gender and Emotion in the Lives of Mexican Guestworker Father." *Ethnic and Racial Studies*.

Schmalzbauer, Leah. 2013. "Motherhood and Transformation in the Field: Reflections on Positionality, Meaning and Trust." In *Family and Work in Everyday Ethnography*, edited by Tamara Brown and Joanna Dreby. Philadelphia, PA: Temple University Press.

Schmalzbauer, Leah. 2011. "'Doing Gender,' Ensuring Survival: Mexican Migration and Economic Crisis in the Rural Mountain West." *Rural Sociology* 76(4): 441–60.

Schmalzbauer, Leah. 2009. "Gender on a New Frontier: Mexican Migration in the Rural Mountain West." *Gender and Society* 23(6): 747–67.

Schmalzbauer, Leah. 2005. "Transamerican Dreamers: The Relationship of Honduran Transmigrants to the American Dream and Consumer Society." *Berkeley Journal of Sociology* 39: 3–31.

Schmalzbauer, Leah. 2004. "Searching for Wages and Mothering from Afar: The Case of Honduran Transnational Families." *Journal of Marriage and Family* 66(5): 1317–31.

Schontzler, Gail. 2010. "Gallatin County Has Lost Thousands of Jobs, but Census Is Still at Record High." *Bozeman Daily Chronicle*, April 18, 2010.

Schor, Juliet. 1992. *The Overworked American: The Unexpected Decline of Leisure*. New York: Basic Books.

Seeley, Andrew, Cynthia J. Arnson and Eric L. Olson. 2013. *Crime and Violence in Mexico and Central America: An Evolving but Incomplete US Policy Response*. Migration Policy Institute. Woodrow Wilson Center. Washington, DC.

Sherman, Jennifer. 2013. "Surviving the Great Recession: Growing Need and the Stigmatized Safety Net." *Social Problems* 60: 1–24.

Silver, Alexis. 2012. "Aging into Exclusion and Social Transparency: Undocumented Immigrant Youth and the Transition to Adulthood." *Latino Studies* 10(4): 499–522.

Silvey, Rachel. 2006. "Geographies of Gender and Migration: Spatializing Social Difference." *International Migration Review* 40(1): 64–81.

Singer, Audrey. 2008. "Twenty-first Century Gateways: An Introduction." In *Twenty-first Century Gateways: Immigrant Integration in Suburban America,* edited by Audrey Singer, Susan W. Hardwick and Caroline B. Brettell, pp. 3–30. Washington, DC: Brookings Institution Press.

Singer, Audrey. 2004. "The Rise of New Immigrant Gateways." Washington, DC: Brookings Institution, Living Cities Census Series (February).

Singer, Audrey, Susan W. Hardwick and Caroline B. Brettell, eds. 2008. *Twenty-first Century Gateways: Immigrant Incorporation in Suburban America.* Washington, DC: Brookings Institution Press.

Skop, Emily. 2012. *The Immigration and Settlement of Asian Indians in Phoenix, Arizona 1965–2011: Ethnic Pride v. Racial Discrimination in the Suburbs.* Lampeter, UK: Edwin Mellen Press.

Slater, Tom. 2011. "Gentrification of the City." In *The New Blackwell Companion to the City*, edited by Gary Bridge and Sophie Watson, pp. 571–85. Oxford, UK: Blackwell Publishing.

Smith, Michael and Richard S. Krannich. 2000. "Culture Clash Revisited: Newcomer and Longer-term Residents' Attitudes toward Land Use, Development, and Environmental Issues in Rural Communities of the Rocky Mountain West." *Rural Sociology* 65(3): 396–421.

Smith, Robert. 2006. *Mexican New York: Transnational Lives of New Immigrants.* Berkeley: University of California Press.

Steinback, John. 1962. *Travels with Charley: In Search of America.* New York: Penguin Books.

Striffler, Steve. 2007. *Chicken: The Dangerous Transformation of America's Favorite Food.* New Haven: Yale University Press.

Suárez-Orozco, Carola and Marcelo Suárez-Orozco. 1995. *Transformations: Immigration, Family Life and Achievement Motivation among Latino Adolescents.* Stanford: Stanford University Press.

Thai, Hung Cam. 2008. *For Better or for Worse: Vietnamese International Marriages in the New Global Economy.* New Brunswick, NJ: Rutgers University Press.

Tickamyer, Ann R. and Debra A. Henderson. 2003. "Rural Women: New Roles for the New Century." In *Challenges for Rural America in the Twenty-First Century*, edited by David L. Brown and Louis E. Swanson, pp. 109–17. University Park: Pennsylvania State University.

Uken, Cindy. 2012. "High Country Crisis: Montana's Suicide Rate Leads the Nation." *Billings Gazette*, November 25, 2012.

U.S. Census Bureau. 2013. *State and County Quick Facts: Gallatin County, Montana.* Retrieved at http://quickfacts.census.gov/qfd/states/30/30031.html.

U.S. Census Bureau. 2011. *American Community Survey 1-Year Estimates.* Selected Characteristics of the Native and Foreign-Born Populations. Retrieved at http://factfinder2.census.gov/faces/nav/jsf/pages/searchresults.xhtml?refresh=t.

U.S. Census Bureau. 2010. *State and County Quick Facts: Montana.* Retrieved at http://quickfacts.census.gov/qfd/states/30000.html.

U.S. Department of Homeland Security. 2011. *FY 2011: ICE Announces Year-end Removal Numbers, Highlights Focus on Key Priorities Including Threats to Public Safety and National Security.* Retrieved at http://www.ice.gov/news/releases/1110/111018washingtondc.htm.

U.S. Department of Homeland Security, Office of Immigration Statistics. 2010. *Immigration Enforcement Actions: 2010.* Retrieved at http://www.dhs.gov/xlibrary/assets/statistics/publications/enforcement-ar-2010.pdf.

USA.com. 2013. U.S. Crime Index State Rank. Retrieved at www.usa.com/rank/us—crime—index—state-rank.htm?hl=MT?hlst=MT.

Valenzuela, Angela. 1999. *Subtractive Schooling: U.S.-Mexican Youth and the Politics of Caring.* Albany: State University of New York Press.

Vasquez, Jessica. 2011. *Mexican Americans across Generations: Immigrant Families, Racial Realities.* New York: New York University Press.

Villalón, Roberta. 2010. *Violence against Latina Immigrants: Citizenship, Inequality, and Community.* New York: New York University Press.

Werwath Associates. 2012. *Affordable Housing Needs Assessment for the City of Bozeman, MT.* Retrieved at www.bozeman.net/Smarty/files/09/09afba32-2f5d-4b33-8d33-69b1189d0c12.pdf.

Wessler, Seth Freed. 2011. "U.S. Deports 46K Parents with Citizen Children in Just Six Months," *Colorlines.* Retrieved at http://colorlines.com/archives/2011/11/shocking_data_on_parents_deported_with_citizen_children.html.

West, Candace and Don Zimmerman. 1987. "Doing Gender." *Gender and Society* 1(2): 125–51.

Wilkinson, Todd. 2013. "Return of the Rocky Mountain High." *Christian Science Monitor*, June 9.

Wilkinson, Todd. 2013. *Last Stand: Ted Turner's Quest to Save a Troubled Planet.* Guilford, CT: Lyon's Press.

Woods, Michael. 2007. "Engaging the Global Countryside: Globalization, Hybridity and the Reconstitution of Rural Place." *Progress in Human Geography* 31(4): 485–507.

Wycoff, William. 2006. *On the Road Again: Montana's Changing Landscape.* Seattle: University of Washington Press.

Yoshikawa, Hirokazu. 2011. *Immigrants Raising Citizens: Undocumented Parents and Their Young Children.* New York: Russell Sage Foundation.

Zelizer, Viviana. 1985. *Pricing the Priceless Child: The Changing Social Value of Children*. Princeton: Princeton University Press.

Zuñiga, Victor and Rubén Hernández-León. 2009. "The Dalton Story: Mexican Immigrant and Social Transformation in the Carpet Capital of the World." In *Latino Immigrants and the Transformation of the U.S. South*, edited by Mary E. Odem and Elaine Lacy, pp. 34–50. Athens: University of Georgia Press.

Zuñiga, Victor and Rubén Hernández-León, eds. 2005. *New Destinations: Mexican Immigration to the United States*. New York: Russell Sage Foundation.

Index

The authorized representative in the EU for product safety and compliance is:
Mare Nostrum Group
B.V Doelen 72
4831 GR Breda
The Netherlands

www.ingramcontent.com/pod-product-compliance
Lightning Source LLC
Chambersburg PA
CBHW030819270326
41928CB00007B/800